NO ONE IS KEEPING SECRET ABOUT
SPY DUST

"Fascinating. . . . Avoiding the noir clichés of the spy genre, the Mendezes offer an eye-opening look at the complex business of gathering intelligence and spreading a few lies to disrupt the opposition. . . . Solid storytelling brought to bear on engaging material."

—*Kirkus Reviews*

"It's amazing the CIA has allowed these two former officers to say so much. . . . So if you want to know what real spying is like, here's a firsthand, exciting account."

—Admiral Stansfield Turner, former head of the CIA

"[*Spy Dust*], which passed the CIA's publication review board, makes a post–September 11th case for spooks—reminding us that the most successful operations are the ones we never hear about."

—*The New Yorker*

"If the United States of America is to lead and thrive throughout the 21st century, the people of our land must understand and participate in safeguarding our security. *Spy Dust* is a recruiting poster for service in intelligence as part of that work. Antonio and Jonna Mendez write as dazzling experts in an exotic tale documenting their espionage role in the ringing down of the Cold War."

—A. Denis Clift, President of the Joint Military Intelligence College

OTHER NONFICTION BOOKS BY ANTONIO J. MENDEZ

The Master of Disguise

OTHER NONFICTION BOOKS BY BRUCE HENDERSON

Fatal North

Trace Evidence

And the Sea Will Tell

SPY DUST

Two Masters of Disguise Reveal the

Tools and Operations That

Helped Win the Cold War

ANTONIO AND JONNA MENDEZ

with BRUCE HENDERSON

ATRIA BOOKS

NEW YORK LONDON TORONTO SYDNEY SINGAPORE

The CIA's Publications Review Board has reviewed the manuscript for this book to assist the authors in eliminating classified information, and poses no security objection to its publication. This review, however, should not be construed as an official release of information, confirmation of its accuracy, or endorsement of the authors' views.

ATRIA BOOKS
1230 Avenue of the Americas
New York, NY 10020

ISBN: 0-7434-2852-8
0-7434-2853-6 (Pbk)

First Atria Books trade paperback edition October 2003

10 9 8 7 6 5 4 3 2 1

ATRIA BOOKS is a trademark of Simon & Schuster, Inc.

Illustration credits:
Renaissance Mayflower Hotel, Washington, D.C.: 4
H. Keith Melton at www.spyimages.net: 1, 2, 3, 5, 8, 9, 11, 12, 13, 14, 15, 16, 17, 18, 19, 20, 21, 22, 23, 24, 25, 26, 27, 28, 33
Authors' private collection: 6, 7, 10, 29, 30, 31, 32, 34

Manufactured in the United States of America

For information regarding special discounts for bulk purchases,
please contact Simon & Schuster Special Sales at 1-800-456-6798 or
business@simonandschuster.com

This book is for Jesse,
Our Heart of Hearts,
So he can know how it all began

The story you are about to read is true. Or at least it is as true as we can write it. When one is trying to commit to paper the secret history of history, things take odd twists and turns. Nonfiction espionage must be written with foremost regard for any continuing intelligence equities that might still be involved. To that end this book has been reviewed by the CIA's Publication Review Board. Years ago, when we began employment with the CIA, we both signed secrecy agreements stipulating that the Agency would be allowed to review any writings we might ever do and remove any information considered harmful to ongoing operations, techniques, or personnel. We still have many friends and colleagues who continue their work with the CIA, and we know that many of the foreign agents and sources with whom we worked are continuing to provide invaluable intelligence to the U.S. government. We would never jeopardize their lives or otherwise threaten their security.

In that spirit our reader will need to know that some details of our story have been blurred. Geographic details have been generalized, so that "Subcontinent" and "South Asian capital" are as specific as it can get in several instances. Nearly all names except our own have been changed. Some dates have been slightly shifted, although the time line in the book does represent the broad dates of the operations described. Several characters are composite characters, and this was done in order to obscure their identities. All of the above was done not for stylistic reasons, but to expedite the telling of this story, set during the last five years of the Cold War.

Following the events of September 11, 2001, we hope that the American reader will find some reassurance in this story that U.S. intelligence services are alive and well and have been for many years. The Cold War battleground has segued into the war against terrorism, but shadowy targets and unseen threats are nothing new—the CIA has been engaged in this battle for years.

The code of the spy has always been, "Never celebrate your successes or explain your failures." While this always made sense from the point of view of security, it has nevertheless deprived the American people of the information they need to properly evaluate the work that their intelligence agencies are doing. With a few exceptions, it will always be this way. But we hope the story we are about to tell will offer a measure of courage, a sense that the right things are being done for the right reasons, and that honorable men do prevail. George Tenet, Director of Central Intelligence (DCI), said himself that the American public must know about the CIA's history in order "to judge for itself the contribution made by the intelligence community to the successful conduct of the Cold War."

Espionage is not a career to be undertaken lightly, and along the way there have been and will be human losses, both American and foreign. For reasons of national security many of those who have been lost cannot be named even in death, neither the Americans nor the foreigners who worked and died so bravely for the cause of freedom. But we can honor each and every one of them for a job well done. We hope that this book will further that process.

ANTONIO AND JONNA MENDEZ

SPY DUST

THE YEAR OF THE SPY

Washington, D.C.
April 16, 1985

The lobby of the Mayflower Hotel in downtown Washington was one cavernous hallway with medallions of oriental carpet at carefully measured intervals. A row of crystal chandeliers was strung down the city-block-long corridor, and their reflections danced in the multitude of gold-framed mirrors lining the walls. The hotel had many entrances, sitting as it did at a strategic intersection of Connecticut Avenue and De Sales Street, four blocks from the White House. A prestigious location for more than half a century, the Mayflower had served as a site for numerous presidential inaugural balls.

On this date, a new footnote was to be added to the hotel's colorful history.

In the bar just off the lobby, a man was sitting at a corner table so that he could observe the foot traffic on both Connecticut and De Sales. He had been waiting for more than thirty minutes and, nervous by nature, had already downed a couple of double vodka martinis. This waiting game went against his grain. He got up and walked into the lobby, where he stood looking down the great length of the hotel promenade, which was filling with small groups of people gathering for lunch or drinks, or just chatting.

The person he was expecting was not among the crowd.

He seemed slightly out of place in these plush surroundings. It wasn't just the Montgomery Ward polyester sports coat or the dirty Hush Puppies he wore or even his bad teeth. It was the accumulation of all these details that suggested a man who didn't belong.

He went back to the bar and lit another cigarette; he had been smoking continuously since his arrival. Pulling a letter-sized envelope out of his coat pocket, he placed it on the table, squaring its long side with the table's edge. He tapped his fingers softly on the envelope, hesitated, then picked it up and put it back into his pocket. The bar was beginning to fill up with the lunch crowd.

He checked his watch again and looked around the bar. The rich, English club atmosphere—the dark leather and mahogany—that was designed to cosset and relax gave him no feeling of ease or belonging.

He began to fume. This meeting had been scheduled and rescheduled three times, and now here he was being stood up like some unimportant peon.

The more he thought about the slight, the angrier he got.

The envelope in his pocket was blank; inside it, a smaller envelope had the name *Stanislav Androsov* written on it. Androsov was the KGB rezident in Washington—the highest-ranking Soviet spy in America's capital. The name on the letter inside the smaller envelope was not Androsov's, however, but rather his KGB working name: KRONIN. Using this name would make it clear to the Soviet that another professional intelligence officer had written this letter, which itself was short and to the point, offering to exchange dollars for pounds of flesh: $50,000 cash for the names of three Soviet citizens working for the CIA in Washington.

Out of patience, the man drained his drink and stormed from the bar. He crossed the busy street and headed quickly to the Soviet Embassy two blocks away. When he arrived, he walked through the spiked metal gate of the ornate mansion without hesitation, even though he knew that the FBI maintained a routine observation post to note and photograph all embassy visitors. Once inside, he slipped the envelope through a glass partition to the guard on duty.

The guard opened the blank outer envelope, read the name on the inner envelope, and looked up. Without uttering a word, the guard nodded his understanding of what to do with the letter.

The deed was done.

CIA Operations Officer Aldrich Ames left the imposing structure housing the Soviet ambassador and his staff, and retired to yet another bar on Sixteenth Street.

Sante Fe, New Mexico
September 21, 1985

The thirtyish couple in a faded Olds drove in the dark, which had fallen suddenly, as it does in the high desert when the sun finishes its pyrotechnic display. The air was already crisp with fall, which at this altitude came early.

The woman, an attractive brunette with short, curly hair and blue eyes, was driving. She appeared to have been crying. In the passenger seat sat her husband—a slender, mustached man. Cut from an Ivy League mold, he appeared unflappable.

On the floorboard by his feet sat the form of a makeshift dummy. Looking down, he mentally rehearsed how to move the form, smoothly and quickly, up off the floor, onto the seat between them, and open the latch on the car door, all in one motion—as he had been shown by the CIA officers who had trained him three years earlier.

The car made a left off Canyon Road, approaching the escape site.

The man saw no trailing car through the right side mirror, which he had adjusted for himself, not the driver. The lack of visible surveillance always made a case officer nervous. When surveillance couldn't be seen, a well-trained operative had to wonder: *Have I lost them, or are they clever enough to keep tabs on me without being seen?*

The woman made another left, and they were now heading downhill, nearing the bailout point at the house with shrubbery in front.

The man had disabled the brake lights at a restaurant up the road—standard procedure on an operational run—so that there would be no telltale red flash when the driver slowed the car briefly for the passenger to roll out. He had also removed the bulb in the dome light of the car in their garage before leaving for dinner.

Leaning over slightly, the man moved his coat aside and brought the dummy up onto the seat. He jammed the edge of the rubber end of the plumber's plunger into the crack between the seat back and bottom cushion so the dummy would not bob and sway as the car continued on. This telltale head waggle was dubbed "the chicken effect" by the CIA's technical services people and, to a trailing surveillance car, could be a dead giveaway that the silhouette was not that of a real person.

He had taken delight in the fact that he was using, as part of the dummy, the same wig he had been given at "the Camp," an isolated compound of several hundred acres south of Washington, D.C., along the Atlantic seaboard. This was where the CIA trained all its case officers, as part of their disguise orientation, before deploying them overseas.

Resting on its head-shaped Styrofoam block, the wig completed the dummy's head. The torso was formed by a wire coat hanger attached to the handle of the plunger with duct tape. Over the hanger was draped a designer-label khaki field jacket the man had bought at a large mall in the Washington area, before they had moved to Santa Fe.

"Okay, this is it," she said, turning sharply onto the side street.

They looked into each other's eyes for a split second; then, he was gone.

In the parlance of the FBI, he was "in the wind." The Bureau had been surveilling him round-the-clock ever since a KGB defector had led them to him a month before. He had been fired from the CIA two years earlier for petty theft and lying. Since then, as a measure of revenge, he had volunteered his services to the Soviets.

The ruse he had just pulled off, with the assistance of his very capable wife, Mary—who had been trained in such matters by the CIA so she could join her husband on assignment—had given him a twenty-four-hour head start.

Edward Lee Howard would already be out of the country by the time the FBI realized he had defected to the Soviet Union.

Westchester County, New York
September 31, 1985

The mole sat in his windowless, soundproofed basement sanctuary, its door locked.

He unlocked the two-drawer file cabinet next to his computer and removed a small black notebook. He thumbed through it to a particular page and then placed it on his desktop, open and weighted down with a Diet Coke.

The room was his refuge and his haven—the one place in the world where he felt totally in charge. He was the master of this space, both the twelve-by-sixteen-foot room and the window to the world that his computer opened up to him. He was a senior counterintelligence agent for the Federal Bureau of Investigation, so there were few places he couldn't go—in cyberspace or otherwise—and not many files he couldn't access.

The guys at the office had no idea, simply no clue about his ability to manipulate them and the information that they all depended on. They were so busy kissing up and having their long, beer-filled lunches that they spent little time observing what actually went on around them. *Fools!* So busy getting their tickets punched that they were oblivious of the real danger in their midst. He had watched them get promoted ahead of schedule, ahead of him, moving up through the echelons of the bureaucracy, while he plodded on in place. The new boss especially got under his skin. The man had seemed nice enough when he first arrived at the New York Field Office. But then there had been the little barbs, the smirking and the quietness when he entered the room, and he knew that this guy, too, was part of the clique—that group that had excluded him almost from day one.

Well, wouldn't they be surprised if they knew what he was about to do? Wouldn't they sit up and pay attention?

There was a crucifix on his desk, an ornate icon given to him by his wife on his last birthday. He had taken it into work, intending to keep it there as a symbol of all that he held dear and of the faith that he embraced along with his family. But after he had hung it on the wall behind his desk, there had been several comments—one a clumsy reference to the separation between church and state—and so he had brought it here, giving it a place of honor in his private sanctuary.

He returned to the business at hand. Opening a drawer in the computer desk, he pulled out a pair of white cotton gloves—the kind used in photographic laboratories and darkrooms to handle delicate negatives. Putting them on, he picked up a stack of ink-jet computer paper and positioned it in the printer. He paused for a moment, mentally composing the first line, removing the gloves, then began his first note—the one that would set the stage for all to follow. It would be a Valentine. He wanted them to appreciate the brilliance of the plan, yet he wanted it to be personal. He hoped they would show his signature—they would receive it only once—to one of their graphologists, who would be quick to point out that they were dealing with an individual of consequence and intelligence, a romantic, a man with vision, a man worth knowing. Certainly they would be able to come up with the $100,000 he needed, and quickly.

> Dear Mr. Cherkashin:
>
> Soon, I will send a box of documents to Mr. Degtyar. They are from certain of the most sensitive and highly compartmented projects of the U.S. intelligence community. . . .
>
> I must warn of certain risks to my security of which you may not be aware. Your service has recently suffered some setbacks. I warn that Mr. Boris Yuzhin, Mr. Sergey Motorin, and Mr. Valeriy Martynov have been recruited by our "special services."

Satisfied that he had just sealed the fate of three top spies for America, he put the gloves back on, signed the letter with a pseudonym, put it into an envelope, and sealed the flap. Clearly and carefully, he printed a name and address on the envelope, adding his own fictitious return address. He knew with whom he was dealing. He had written to Viktor Cherkashin, the KGB's chief of counterintelligence at the Soviet Embassy in Washington, and was proposing to pass his information to Viktor M. Degtyar, the press secretary at the embassy and, more important, a KGB counterintelligence officer.

He affixed the proper postage to the letter and then set it aside. He would mail it tomorrow in Prince George's County, in Maryland, on his drive down to FBI headquarters.

If his information impressed them, as he knew it would, he was certain that the Soviets would not try to find out his identity. He would prove too valuable for them to take the chance of spooking him or inadvertently doing anything to finger him.

FBI Special Agent Robert Hanssen left his private world and stepped into the brighter light of early evening. He collected his wife and two of their six children for their drive to attend early evening mass and confession. He went daily with his wife and any of the children who were available. He found comfort in that.

During a span of five months and fourteen days in 1985, three Americans went over to the other side in the heat of the Cold War. Only one was known about; it would be years before the identity of the other two highly placed spies, one in the CIA and the other in the FBI, would surface.

The damage done by the three traitors to U.S. intelligence operations, specifically in Moscow, was unprecedented. The story of what happened to the men and women working in the field against this wave of treachery has never been told.

Until now.

ONE

INDOCHINA

Winter 1973

Tony Mendez
CIA Technical Operations Officer
Specialties: Disguise and false documentation

I was being buffeted around in the backseat of a dilapidated gray Austin as Jack Maxwell drove quickly through the pitch black night. He spun the steering wheel back and forth with one beefy hand, and with the other deftly shifted gears like a race car driver as we sped down the narrow, winding streets of this moldering tropical city.

I knew that even though we couldn't see them in the dark, every structure we passed was mildewed and slowly crumbling back into the black loam and teeming vegetation from where it had come long before the British carved out their colonial outpost here more than a century ago.

Maxwell, a large man with sloping shoulders, was slouched against the right-hand door, on the driver's side of the old car. He had borrowed this wreck from one of the office secretaries for his nighttime forays. He was wearing a pair of tortoiseshell glasses, a Band-Aid mustache, and a floppy hat, one of the many quick-change disguises that I had devised for him and his intelligence sources to use for their meetings after dark. Such subterfuge was the only way CIA officers could meet their assets—locals recruited by U.S. intelligence—in this hostile environment.

Maxwell would sometimes have eight or nine operational meetings a night, which pushed the bounds of good security practices. Most meetings took place in the old car while he drove his asset around on the back streets, debriefing them while continuing to run surveillance-detection runs—SDRs, as they are known in the spy trade—to ensure they weren't being followed.

Tonight was a special trip. We would be breaking new ground on this case, and thanks to my disguises, Maxwell would be bringing his best agent home for a sit-down meeting in the civilized surroundings of his house, an almost unheard of luxury.

We were approaching a double corner as we passed the swimming club where Maxwell would execute a rolling car pickup. He slowed down, pressed on the brake pedal long enough for the forward motion of the car to be interrupted for half a heartbeat. He timed this stop to occur just as he passed behind the hedge on our left, next to the corner of the club building.

A dark figure moved out from behind the hedge at the same instant and entered the left front passenger door as I opened and closed it in one motion. The dome light had not come on.

The figure crouched safely on the floorboard of the car as Maxwell released his pressure on the brake pedal and our momentum carried us forward again. He pressed smoothly on the accelerator, and we continued on a circuitous route to the residential district out by the lake to our first destination.

The top-secret GAMBIT disguise was positioned on my lap. I had created it for the man at an earlier meeting, and I hoped to conduct a final fitting tonight. I planned to do this in the dark car as we moved along, in case we passed someone who knew him.

We started down a deserted stretch, and the man code-named

SAPPHIRE had crawled up off the floor and was now sitting up directly in front of me. He knew what to expect as I reached over to show him how to put on the disguise. By the time Maxwell arrived at his cover stop, I had made final adjustments to SAPPHIRE's new persona and was handing him a small leather-bound credential, which he reviewed, then slipped into his pocket.

The houseboy and gate man at the cover stop didn't give us a second look as we waited in the car chatting while Maxwell made his phantom delivery to a friend, the cover reason for this trip.

Shortly, we were headed back to Maxwell's house, where I had been staying since my arrival from Washington, D.C. We had rounded a corner and were proceeding down a side street behind an enormous golden stupa, a Buddhist shrine, that marked the center of town.

Suddenly we were caught in the high beams of a vehicle blocking the center of the road. There were two uniformed and armed soldiers standing in front of the headlights of a camouflaged scout car. They signaled us to halt.

Maxwell stood on the brakes, and the ancient car lurched to a stop.

One of the military men approached the car on the passenger side and rapped on the glass with his swagger stick. SAPPHIRE rolled down the window, and the officer leaned his head so far into the car I was sure they would touch noses.

But he was not looking at SAPPHIRE at all. Instead, his gaze was focused on Maxwell.

"Evening, sir. May I see your papers?"

Maxwell presented his credential, handing it over in front of SAPPHIRE.

The officer shined his light on it, and then returned it. "Very good, sir. And what about these two gentlemen?"

Both SAPPHIRE and I were ready with our documents as well. His were in the credential case that I had given him minutes earlier.

After a quick look, the officer handed both of them back to SAPPHIRE and snapped to attention. "Thank you, Excellency," he said.

SAPPHIRE saluted back, and we were soon on our way.

A little later, we were relaxing over drinks at Maxwell's place, reliving the events of the evening. Maxwell suddenly turned to me. "By the way," he said, "that officer was awfully impressed with SAPPHIRE. What was that all about?"

"I knew the disguise would make him look older and distinguished," I said, "so I made him an attaché from an Eastern European country—with the rank of general."

SAPPHIRE smiled, enjoying the promotion that he had carried off perfectly.

The young Russian KGB officer already had a distinct military bearing.

TWO

ASIAN SUBCONTINENT

Spring 1987

Jonna Goeser
CIA Technical Operations Officer
Specialties: Disguise, false documentation, and clandestine photography

I came awake all at once. Something had moved in the darkness of my hotel room. The sheer curtains covering the wooden shutters had shifted slightly; a thin sliver of light pierced the room.

I tensed and, lying still, opened my eyes narrowly.

There was movement at the door, where a beam of light appeared, then was broken momentarily as something crossed in front of it.

In the shadows, someone was gliding across the room, silently but with purpose.

Another noise now: the soft metallic clink of silver on china and the gush of liquid being poured. The scent of chai filled the room; an invisible cloud of cinnamon, cardamom, and cloves.

Breakfast had arrived in the style of the Raj, served discreetly, I could now discern, by a small dark man wearing a white uniform and matching gloves and a turban. As the server backed quietly across the room, angling perfectly toward the barely open door, I offered silent thanks to the British Empire. In a region where most things did not work and almost nothing worked well, when it came to creature comforts, the British had left a legacy that still endured. While the local women were neither valued nor pampered, a western woman, particularly one traveling alone, was better cared for in this culture than back home.

The door closed with a solid click, and the elegantly appointed room, with its vaulted ceiling, was once again cast into darkness. A slow roar began making its way into my consciousness; the traffic noise and bustle of the street below were increasing, the voices from the market beginning to rise, the horns of impatient drivers sounding more frequently, and the wail of a mosque's call to prayer echoed in the far distance.

I parted the mosquito net shrouding the bed and slipped into my robe, then went to the window, drew the curtains aside, and unlatched the heavy shutters. Morning light poured into the room, harsh and bright, as jolting as the cacophony from the street.

On the table sat a silver tray of morning tea, part of the signature service of any Spencer Company hotel on the subcontinent. I poured a cup, lacing it heavily with hot milk and sugar, the way the locals drank it.

Following an old habit of using early morning for correspondence, I went to the desk centered in front of the window, placed a sheet of hotel stationery from another city and another visit on its surface, and began a note to my older sister.

Dear Jennifer,

I will spend today feeling bad about not getting a birthday card off to you, but I thought if you knew I was traveling, you might forgive me. I miss you, not just the normal kind of missing, but I don't really have anybody close here whom I can talk to.

It's wonderful weather in this part of the world. The mornings start off misty and cool; then the afternoons are very warm, with intense sun but a really mild breeze. Roses bloom in the winter, the climate is so mild! Perfect, as far as I am concerned.

Things with John are no better. We continue to drift apart, very amicably but very steadily. We are both traveling enormously and in fact spend little time at home together. But even when that does happen, it is not worth the wait. Our interests are so different and our ideas so divergent. I don't know what to do about it, but I do know nothing can be done out here. Maybe when we return to the States, we can figure something out.

Hoping your birthday is (was) fun.
Love, Jonna

I headed into the porcelain and gold-plated turn-of-the-century bath. As always when entering the shower here, I hesitated before moving under the stream of rusty water. I had never been entirely convinced that this murky water could be cleansing, but a quick shower always worked wonders clearing the fuzzy corners of my mind. The hot water washed away not only the dust of the day but also the blur of the night before, remnants of the late hours spent in the hotel casino watching my boss, Tom "Woody" Smallwood, winning a lot of money.

Perversely, the more he drank the more he won at roulette. Before we entered the casino, Woody had told me that if I wanted to win some money, I should stick with him. "I usually win a lot, at least during the first ten to twenty minutes," he said nonchalantly. The trick, he added, was to quit at that point. "If you want to bet along with me, be my guest." And so I had. After fifteen minutes he swept together a pile of chips and cashed them in. I did the same, albeit a much smaller pile. He counted his out slowly, and announced that he had won almost $1,500. *Why do the jerks of the world have so much luck?* I wondered. I had about $400. The only problem was that it was in the local currency—and it could not be taken out of the country.

"Knock me up in the morning," Woody had slurred later that night as I left him fumbling with the key to his room down the hall. He favored British phrasing because he thought it sounded risqué and intelligent.

Smallwood was a short, heavyset man with a potbelly that protruded unnaturally from his frame. His dark hair did not exhibit any gray at all, a detail that made me wonder if he was vain enough to color it. His face was dominated by a pair of unruly eyebrows that were his most expressive feature. His eyes, on the other hand, always seemed to be under complete control; they never gave him away.

On a Sunday afternoon two days earlier, he had called and asked me to meet him at the office right away. I had been on assignment on the subcontinent for several months, along with my husband, John Goeser, who was also a CIA officer. Smallwood had been called in by the communications officer to read a night-action cable—an NIACT, as they were designated—which could not wait for normal business hours. No matter what time of the day or night, when an NIACT came in, you dropped everything. "Pack your bag; we're leaving tonight," Woody added brusquely before I heard the click on the other end of the line.

The cable, parts of which he read to me an hour later, was of the highest security classification. It was obvious he did not want to hand it to me. By now, I was accustomed to his control issues, but they still rankled. My security clearance was as high as his, and I had every right to learn for myself the full extent of the operational requirements that were being levied on us. In fact, for me not to do so could endanger the mission as well as my own safety and that of those I was working with. From what I had gleaned, we had received an urgent request for photo surveillance, which meant a concealed-camera operation of some kind would be necessary.

"What else do they need from us?" I had asked, wanting to go prepared for any contingency.

"Don't worry about it now," Woody said, brusquely waving my concerns aside.

This was my fourth overseas tour with the CIA—my second as a technical operations officer—and I had dealt with all kinds.

I first joined the Agency at the age of twenty-one as a clerk-secretary and had come up through the ranks. This, finally, was my dream overseas assignment—with the notable exception of the man I now found myself working for. Since first glimpsing this exotic country two years earlier on a temporary tour of duty, I had gone to extraordinary lengths to be assigned here. This had included changing career disciplines—moving from the CIA's photography division into disguise work. I had been among a class of ten technical service officers handpicked for a year's training in all disciplines. Invitations to join the course were exclusive and highly coveted; the opportunity was hard won and consequently prized. Graduates of the course could usually name their next tour of duty.

"No one sells asshole insurance," I had heard Tony Mendez, head of the Disguise and Documents Division of the Office of Technical Service (OTS), say more than once back at headquarters in Washington, D.C., while counseling someone who had complained about having to deal with a difficult personality within the Agency. "You have to learn to operate inside the organization the same way you have to learn how to operate against the enemy." Now working under Tony's auspices in OTS, I was confident in his ability to represent my best interests at headquarters, no matter how difficult my relationship with my direct supervisor in the field had become. I had come to trust Tony and relied on him as I did few others.

In fact, it had been Tony who had taught me most of the lessons that had allowed me to succeed in this business. The idea of being on someone's team had been foreign to me, and Tony had spent some time actively trying to recruit me to join his group. Like a fool, I had initially turned him down, not understanding the opportunity he was offering me to advance in the largely male milieu of covert intelligence operations. Eventually, I wised up and went for it. Now, Tony was nothing less than a life-line stretching halfway around the world, providing me with my main support and always watching my back.

Over time, Tony had become not only a professional colleague but also a friend. There was nobody better equipped to be my mentor and protector. A discerning senior manager who always put the personal touch into his negotiations, he had assured me that he could nail down this overseas assignment for me and then had done so in spite of opposition from Tom Smallwood. When things began to get really nasty, with Smallwood sending uncomplimentary cables—back-channel cables that only higher-ups saw—Tony deftly began deflecting them, pointing out their inaccuracies and untruths. Tony was simply the most effective manager I had ever had.

Before I had won this assignment, Smallwood had told me in Washington that he did not have much use for my particular skills, which were disguise and documentation. He would have preferred to fill my slot with another audio officer—someone who dealt in electronics. I countered that I would also bring to his group a strong photo capability, but he was unimpressed. Unofficially, I believed that Smallwood did not want a professional woman in *any* capacity assigned to his unit. In truth, I had never met a man I could not work with, but then came Tom Smallwood, and my lucky streak ran out. Even if he wasn't damaging my career—thanks to Tony—Smallwood was, at the very least, making life miserable for me.

My husband John and I—receiving dual assignments in the field thanks in large measure to Tony's bureaucratic wrangling—had set-tled into the heat and tropical pace of a world not much different than a century before. Many of the things that had drawn me back to this region I still found riveting. The culture was rich and thickly layered: the local history was full of pashas and rajas, all ele-phant-borne; oriental carpets were woven on almost every street corner; and the local cuisine was spicy and delicious. The climate was hot and dry, with just enough of a monsoon season every year to enable a true gardener to have some success. The photographer part of me was drawn to the desert over and over again, trying to capture the exotic colors and faces that lived out there in small, exquisite houses shaped out of dried cow dung. Their interiors were constructed almost like the adobe work of New Mexico—fireplaces and shelves were simply modeled into the walls—and the shelves were full of hand-hammered copper dishes and brilliant textiles. Physically small and handsome, the people themselves were fascinating. It was amazing to my western eye that the deeper you penetrated into the desert, the more outrageously colorful their clothing and accessories became. Chartreuse, fuchsia, magenta, and jolting yellows were the most common hues. The natives conveyed an elegance that belied their simple and impoverished condition.

Back in the teeming capital city where we were based, a full ensemble of servants took care of us: a talented cook, gardeners, gate guards, a driver, a housekeeper, and a laundry boy tended our palatial pink rococo mansion. Inside, a three-story circular staircase was crowned with a cupola, and the marble floors were covered with hand-knotted silk rugs. In the end, I could put up with Smallwood as long as I could stay on the road half the time and not have to work with him too often. This trip, however, was too important to worry about another round of in-my-face harassment.

Smallwood was the technical officer-in-charge, the boss of our forward-deployed tech unit, a group of officers who, together, could respond to almost any operational requirement. Need to break into an office? steal a code book? disguise an agent? photo-graph a document? rescue an informant? communicate with your asset? We could do all of that and much more. I had always thought of the Office of Technical Service and its techs as "Q," from the James Bond movies, and was not too wide of the mark. There were a few differences though: we seldom simply issued our equipment to a case officer and let him run with it in the field; instead we usually accompanied the officer and the gear around the world, wherever it was needed, and made sure it worked. And second, unlike in all those Bond movies, intelligence officers seldom carried guns, except in a war zone, although we were all trained in weapons. I had qualified as a marksman with a Smith & Wesson .38 revolver and a Colt .45 automatic, and from a hundred paces could hit just about anything I cared to shoot at.

Our tech field unit was one of several such units positioned around the world, consisting of technical officers and their equipment. We supported all sorts of operations from these units, and the officers likely to be assigned to a unit were either exceptional in their field of expertise or broadly based in their skills, and sometimes both. As someone who could do both disguise and documents, with a second skill of photography, I was considered to be highly flexible. Our group's traveling area covered the Asian subcontinent—all the way from Pakistan to Burma, and from Sri Lanka to the Himalayas—but we would occasionally respond to special requests for our skills from outside our geographic area, places such as Hong Kong and Singapore. In general, I found this part of the world very agreeable, and my job never boring.

The other officers in our unit were men, except for the secretary. I stood out as the only woman field operative and had to put up with mostly good-natured teasing and ribbing from the guys. Occasionally, the harassment level would get cranked up a bit— for instance, when one of our big bosses came visiting and the evening's entertainment would become "guys only." Still no big deal for me; I saw them daily and considered them friends. But I was never Tom Smallwood's friend, not even at the beginning, and he wasted no time in letting me know it. I had been advised by various peers and managers at headquarters not to expend too much energy going to war with Smallwood, and I had to remind myself constantly of this very sound piece of advice.

That's what it was like at home—a wonderful residence, a reasonable office filled mostly with capable and amicable colleagues, an exotic setting, and a job full of high adventure and worldwide travel. *So what's wrong with this picture?* I regularly asked myself, basking at the pool of a four-star hotel like the Mandarin in Hong Kong or, my favorite, the Oriental in Bangkok, while awaiting contact instructions. We were working for the world's most effective intelligence agency, doing honorable work, and getting a look behind the scenes. Occasionally, we were also allowed to stir up the dust and attempt to change those events.

Of course, we were not the only intelligence service out there. Working toward similar goals were the Israelis (Mossad) and the British (MI6), who had always been top-notch. Our old enemies the Soviets (KGB), the East Germans (HVA), and the Cubans (DGI) were just about as good as we were, occasionally better, and they certainly kept us very watchful and concerned about their intentions.

Sunday's hurried flight with Woody had had its moments. After his initial briefing, I had packed equipment bags with the cameras and accessories I thought would be needed, and met my chief at our local airport in the early evening. It was hot and humid again, and inside the airport terminal the crowds were so large that it was almost unbearable. I had made this flight many times before and thought I would amuse Woody with a little routine I had perfected.

"I don't know why," I said, "but this airline seems to think I am someone of consequence. Stick with me and you'll see how they treat a western woman."

At that moment, the chief of operations for the airline appeared behind the counter, walked around the baggage loading station, and came over. "Good to see you, good to see you!" he exclaimed, pumping my hand furiously.

The man's grooming was almost as perplexing as his behavior. He had no beard but a face full of hair thanks to peculiar sideburns that ended with a horizontal band that extended almost across each cheek to his nose.

I smiled gleefully at Woody as we were taken to the head of the long check-in line and presented to the ticket clerk as if we were visiting royalty. We checked our luggage but would hand carry our equipment bags onto the plane. Our airline friend saw to it that we skirted the X-ray machines, too, and he personally escorted us to the plane, even coming on board with us. "Memsahib seat," I whispered to Woody. "They always put me there." He responded with a quizzical look. We were taken to the front row, left side, and the operations chief stowed our bags overhead, shook my hand again, then departed.

"What the hell was that?" Woody asked.

"I'm still not sure," I admitted.

When I first started using this airport, the operations chief had asked me if I was a Pan Am flight attendant in such a way that I assumed an affirmative answer would have entitled me to certain professional courtesies. Even though I told him I was not with an airline, the royal treatment ensued, and had been repeated every time he saw me. I had come to call it the Memsahib Syndrome. When the British were here, they ruled the whole area with an iron glove. Trains were on time; records were in order; streets were paralleled and all of the corners squared. But while the men—the *sahibs*—have faded into history, it seems that the memory of those British women—*memsahibs*—remains vividly intact. They must have been something. I had learned that whenever I traveled in the subcontinent, all I had to do was wear a western dress and stockings and I would command enormous respect from the locals. I ended up in VIP lounges, at the head of any line, and my bags were first off the plane. Whatever it was, it made it hard to move around quietly and unnoticed. To do that, I had to turn myself into one of those Lonely Planet types and get out my backpack and Birkenstocks.

Smallwood ordered a beer before the plane had even taxied out to the runway, and though it was against the rules, they brought it to him because he was a westerner. As soon as we were airborne and had leveled off at our cruising altitude, he reclined his seat as far back as it would go, sipped his beer, and began briefing me on our mission.

"This is what we call a 'smoking-bolt' operation," he said quietly.

The term was new to me. I'd been involved in many different kinds of espionage operations, but had never heard of a "smoking bolt."

"You're in for the ride of your life, if you're up to it," Woody continued, raising a bushy eyebrow at me. "We're going to break into a Soviet stronghold, find the KGB's Sanctum, and steal one of their KAPELLE devices. Lock, stock, and barrel."

The revelation hit me like a bombshell, and I caught my breath, trying not to give any outward sign of surprise. I was amazed that he was going into such detail in such a public place.

"We'll be meeting up with and supporting a unique, compartmented Agency team. These guys are an elite group of specialists, a bunch of cat burglars, second-story men, and safecrackers, trained to steal anything not nailed down. They specialize in really high-end security materials. The way they go about it is not so much about stealth as it is big brass balls. Rumor is that they are professional wise guys recruited and trained for this one purpose, but not fit for headquarters duty. We'll be providing any technical support they need and probably be doing things we have never done before, so be ready for some surprises. And, by the way, we have to be out on the street first thing in the morning for a car pickup with the team leader."

Smallwood told me that the KAPELLE, a top-secret communication device, had been at the top of the Agency's shopping list for several years. The stakes would be huge in this operation; it was a big risk with a high profile, and an amazing prize dangling before us.

"This will be one for the record book," he offered, "if anyone is keeping score. Just don't screw up. No mistakes. Headquarters is watching."

With his unruly eyebrows raised, he looked hard at me. Woody didn't get worked up too often, and when he did, it was worth noting. "No mistakes" was his mantra, his way of doing business. Of course, what it normally did was discourage his officers from taking chances and risking failure in order to succeed. His adrenaline was flowing now, though, and given the important and challenging nature of our assignment, so was mine.

Over his second beer, Woody related some of the long and colorful history of this type of operation. There had been a wholesale rash of these "snatch-and-grab" operations during World War II. OSS (the Office of Strategic Services, the forerunner of the CIA) and British commandos were well versed in techniques for the surgical penetration of an enemy's strongholds to capture a vital piece of hardware such as an advanced weapon component or high-security communications gear. But that was during wartime.

I knew that during the Cold War the KGB, FBI, and other counterintelligence organizations had found it expedient to breach the security of foreign legations when a case could be made for such a blatant action. In fact, there was a recently signed executive order issued by President Reagan that gave the attorney general the authority to approve an FBI "black bag job" against an "official foreign" installation for counterintelligence purposes. But I was only aware of our own surreptitious-entry unit in OTS, whose job was to assist our audio operations officers in gaining access to a target. I had had no idea that another CIA team existed for the purpose of purloining an enemy's hardware, leaving nothing behind but the "smoking bolts" where it had been fastened down.

Historically, most of our operations were designed to penetrate an enemy's stronghold and steal their secrets but to do it with such stealth that we could go back and steal new secrets the following week. We took great care to keep our agents in place and alive for this purpose.

This entry, on the other hand, would be a conspicuous act that could precipitate an international incident if the perpetrators were known to be sponsored by the U.S. It was also the type of event that could provoke retaliation against American targets elsewhere in the world. It was our job, as OTS technical officers, to provide the appropriate cover and technical tradecraft to the team so that their true identity and affiliation were not known, even though the Soviets were sure to suspect it was the work of a sophisticated, western intelligence service.

Deniability. That's what we would be expected to provide.

I sat back in my seat and wrestled with the concept. We were informed of only a small portion of any given operation. I struggled to put together the available pieces of this one. It seemed to me that if we flagrantly stole the KAPELLE device, their reaction would be to make immediate changes to equipment, codes, and other tradecraft that would limit the usefulness of the device to whoever stole it. *We must have some old score to settle,* I thought, *something major.*

Woody had further explained that these smoking-bolt operations were like a throwback to the days when the Native American tribes would use the technique of warfare known as "making a coup on the enemy." If a member of a rival tribe could breach the security of another tribe's stronghold and grab something or strike a blow and then run away before anyone could react, it was as good as a battle won. A smoking-bolt operation had to be kind of like that, but with deniability.

I looked at him blankly. He was not going to hand me the cable detailing the operational plan, but was fully prepared to give me this history lesson over his beer at 35,000 feet! What a piece of work he was. I had a sneaking hunch there was more to this operation than met the eye, but I didn't share that with Woody. What good would it do? He had certainly given no sign of intending to deal me in as an equal anytime soon.

Even as I finished my morning tea, the memory of the briefing I had received on KAPELLE and the smoking-bolt operation was exhilarating, and I could barely wait to get going. Checking my watch, I saw it was almost time to go and collect Woody for our planned rendezvous with the entry-team leader.

Out of habit, I made sure that my room was neatly organized and my suitcase closed and locked. Inside the case, I had constructed a little trap—a small arrangement of film canisters, always in a special order, that would be softly toppled if the case was opened. It would be good to know if someone was looking that closely at my belongings.

I stepped over to the window and took one more look at the mountainous landscape looming in the distance. Some of the world's highest peaks were thrusting up from the mist-filled valley. Snowcaps were glowing with the warm hues of the sunrise.

It was time to go.

I slipped on a pair of freshly pressed khaki pants. The matching jacket went on over a black silk tank top, the suntan made makeup almost superfluous, and my hair was short and easy to deal with. I couldn't find the needlepoint pouch that contained the small bottle of my perfume and spent several minutes looking before finally locating it on the floor behind the bureau. I had discovered this intoxicating mixture of sandalwood and patchouli scents in the local bazaar. I had to be careful when and where I wore it, though; the perfume lingered and friends claimed they could tell if I had passed through a room even after I was gone. It had become my signature.

A few minutes later, I rapped on the dark hardwood door of Smallwood's room.

No answer. I knocked again, this time harder and longer.

I heard a chair screech as if someone had bumped into it. Fumbling with the latch, Woody opened the door just wide enough for one reddened eye to peer out. I could see enough of him to realize he was not dressed.

"Woody, we've got a meeting," I said urgently.

"You go, I'll catch up with you later," he said, closing the door in my face.

We had gone over the details of the car pickup time and site before going out the night before, so I knew how to make it to the meeting on my own. I set out on foot, aware that it was a lengthy walk to the planned rendezvous on the outskirts of town.

I strolled through the ancient bazaar, which had probably not changed in appearance since the fifteenth century. In the coolness of the early morning, the smoke and soot of the dung fires rolled out of low, dark doorways leading to dank hovels as the local citizens began brewing their morning tea. I maneuvered carefully, avoiding the heaps of garbage and dog feces that made the narrow curving streets hard to navigate in full daylight, let alone in the low-lying morning mist. I was a dedicated runner and always packed my running shoes and some sweats whenever I traveled. But I would not use them here—the streets were always so filthy and the terrain so uneven that a runner would be risking serious injury.

When I traveled, my cover varied—I had multiple identities ranging from tourist and photographer to diplomat. I could, in a real sense, be anybody I wanted. Right now, I was simply a western tourist with a camera and had alias credentials to back it up. This allowed me to move around the region like an ordinary sightseer without calling special attention to myself, and also to meet up from time to time with other Americans.

Within twenty minutes, I had made my way past the bazaar and through the winding lanes on the outskirts of town. High stone walls lined the streets, with the occasional gateway leading to some now defunct minor palace, once home to one of the all-powerful families who had ruled in these mountains, not unlike the maharajahs of India. The twists and turns of the narrow roadway made it easy to see whether anyone was following.

Chilly, high-altitude air spilled down from glaciers nestled precariously around the steeply angled surrounding peaks. As I moved beyond the pollution, I felt more vigorous and began to set a brisk pace up the steep incline. There were brief glimpses of the valley floor spreading out below me as the buildings became more widely spaced.

A small local shrine containing a deity appeared ahead, the goddess covered in a brilliant red powder of some sort; the wooden platform on which she sat was gilded on the edges and painted in a saffron hue. Long necklaces of frangipani and marigolds decorated the shrine, spilling over the edges and hanging almost to the ground. Several small candles were burning, and I could smell the sandalwood incense and the musky frangipani as I drew closer.

I heard the engine of the vehicle coming up behind me before I saw it. As it coasted up beside me on the far side of the road, I recognized it as a Land Rover. At that moment, the gaze of the driver riveted me. He possessed the coldest, bluest eyes I had ever seen. He had close-cropped hair and a full beard; his straight white teeth were exposed in a smile. While he was handsome in a conventional way, he looked vaguely menacing. As he rolled down the window, I found myself curious to hear his voice.

"Good morning," he said. "Is this the way to the Oberoi Hotel?"

That was the parole I had been given as a recognition signal. The chances of someone else asking for that particular hotel were slim, since it was on another side of town some ten miles away. He spoke with a slight accent, and slowly, the way they do in America's Deep South. *Georgia, perhaps. Just like Mom.*

"No, it's not," I answered. "But I can show you the way if you like."

The back door of the silver gray auto swung open, and I made out the silhouette of another man in the backseat. I moved quickly in through the open door, and the Land Rover drove away briskly. As we cruised silently back down toward town, I realized there were three men in the car.

Swallowing hard, I noticed that my heart was beating faster than normal, and it wasn't because of the brisk walk. *Deep breaths, slow down.*

A minute later, I ventured to break the silence. "Where are we headed?"

"We're driving by the jailhouse," said the driver.

"What's there?" I asked.

"We want to know where it is in case they take us there. We'll know which way to run if we can escape."

Nobody smiled.

KGB Major Sergey M. Motorin (CIA code name GTGAUZE) is returning on foot from a meeting with his CIA case officer. He turns off Arbat and heads west across the city to stop by his apartment.

Suddenly, two black Volgas screech to a halt. Men bounce out of the cars, run across the sidewalk, and push him up against a building.

Motorin knows what is coming, but there is nothing he can do about it.

He is arrested on the spot, and executed as a U.S. spy following lengthy interrogation and torture.

THREE

WASHINGTON, D.C.

Spring 1987

Tony Mendez
CIA Division Chief, Graphics and Authentication Division

Cobblestone streets lined with mature trees wound through a neighborhood of mansions and town houses perched on undulating terrain. Georgetown had a charm and elegance that had begun to be recognized during the Kennedy administration, when many high-level officials relocated here. Even "Wild Bill" Donovan, the original head of the OSS, had his house here back during World War II. The hallmarks of the charming area were power, position, money, trendy boutiques, embassies representing sovereigns worldwide, ethnic and cultural diversity, and restaurants among the finest in the nation's capital. It was also famous for some of the best music to be heard on the East Coast. It was an easy place in which to get lost, purposefully or not.

I was concealed from the street traffic by a corner of the Georgetown Market as I waited in the dimming light of dusk. They had been pursuing the targets for forty-five minutes by now, and I knew they should come sweeping into Georgetown at any minute.

The foot soldiers were already in the vicinity; I could hear their radio chatter on the earpiece I was wearing. The "feet" would have been dropped off as soon as it was anticipated that Georgetown was the final destination and that the operation was going down here. As soon as that had been determined, they would all come rolling in across Key Bridge, down M Street, Canal Road, and Wisconsin Avenue. They knew this part of the city like their own backyards—every alley, dead end, and footbridge across the C&O Canal.

The corner where I was standing was an area where they would normally deploy. Armed with only Motorola radios and a handful of quarters for pay phones, they would try their best to keep track of their quarry as they entered and moved through the vibrant quarter.

I recognized a pair of them across the street. A tall bearded man and a skinny blonde, each in a denim jacket and jeans, were strolling down the street, hand in hand. As I watched, the young woman stopped abruptly in front of a garish display and made a purchase from a street vendor. Stepping away from the pushcart, she opened the paper bag and brought out a new baseball hat with the Washington Redskins logo that she had just purchased. She pulled her hair into a ponytail, twisted up the ends, and stuffed it all under the hat. No longer holding hands, they now looked more like two guys than a couple.

Changing her looks on the fly, I thought. *Good for you, Katie.*

The pair stopped at a telephone booth, and the man entered to make a call. I wondered if they were performing a small drama that would allow them to scan the streetscape. Or were they calling "control" to report their position?

I had made sure that they wouldn't be able to spot me. As chief of operations involving disguise and documentation, I had access to all of the identity-alteration materials and techniques that the CIA had at its disposal. It was always fun to slip upstairs to the disguise labs in Central Building after hours and build a new look for myself that I could use on the street. After years of doing this for a living, I could compose a new face and a new demeanor in only a few minutes. Tonight I was wearing the look of an older citizen; I thought he was probably about sixty-five. His graying hair and mustache were closely cut, and his glasses were gold-rimmed and elegant, softly understated. He wore casual clothes, but they were expensive, allowing him to blend in. He carried a pipe and fiddled with it incessantly, although he never actually lit the thing. In fact, I had stopped smoking years ago and was not about to start again for any reason.

The corner where I was standing was designated Alpha. Located in the heart of Georgetown, it was the entrance to a challenging configuration of stairways and alleys that the surveillance team would have to deal with when they found the targets coming this way. While they knew the area well, it was almost impossible to defend. The "rabbits" had plenty of burrows in which to disappear.

I now spotted another of the foot soldiers on the opposite corner, moving toward me and looking directly at me, then passing me as he scanned the street. Knowing that I had not been "made" gave me the familiar sensation of relief mixed with satisfaction. The operative who passed me, Jim Blake from my graphics shop, was himself cleverly turned out as a homeless guy, complete with an empty paper cup, which he thrust at passersby as he walked unsteadily down the street. The crowd moved away from him in unison like a school of fish, not only avoiding him physically, but also refusing to make eye contact with a man so sadly down on his luck.

Way to go, Blake.

I was distracted by a fast-moving gold Volvo that made a right turn off M Street and headed down an alleyway—right into the heart of Alpha. The car passed so close to me that my coat blew open in its draft. I noticed that both the driver and the passenger were wearing khaki jackets, and the driver was a woman. I stepped farther back into the shadows while watching everything intently. The Volvo slowed down once it was off M Street, a main thoroughfare, and headed toward the next turn, a hard left.

I looked over my right shoulder, down M toward Key Bridge, and saw a Ford van moving in my direction, going just a little too fast. I knew they'd never make it. They had given the Volvo too much room.

A Ford Taurus, a little the worse for wear, made the same right turn as the Volvo, but as soon as they had line of sight again, the Volvo was clearing the next turn, a sharp left.

I wondered if they had noticed the taillights, and made a mental note to ask.

By the time the Taurus had made the same left, the Volvo had disappeared into the gloom, entering the enormous underground parking garage for Georgetown Park Mall. There was one small detail during the maneuver, however, that had gone unnoticed—a small motion hidden inside the larger motion, the key to successful evasion.

Two members of the surveillance team went dashing by me into the alley, playing catch-up, but I knew it was too late.

One of their quarries was gone; he was in the wind. He had escaped surveillance.

Two hours later, I was sitting with two members of an elite cadre code-named ZEPHYR. We were in the One Step Down bar on M Street, just outside of Georgetown. The surveillance exercise had lasted four hours, and we were all exhausted.

The ZEPHYRs had both my admiration and sympathy. They were by far more physically spent than the SST (Special Surveillance Team), who did this every night and were accustomed to the physical demands. Too, the ZEPHYRs were coming off a long, exhausting training program and had, on top of that, been packing their household effects, as they were leaving early tomorrow for their Moscow assignments. They had ordered beers and had discarded their matching jackets on a chair at the next table.

I had worked with the man, Les Williams, years ago, when he first came into the Agency. He had struck me then as an unusually capable officer with a bright future ahead of him. Tall, slim, and blond, with dark-rimmed glasses and the conservative style of Washington's government bureaucrats, he looked more the part of a student than a spy in training. The only telltale clue was his muscled physique and athletic gait, which did not quite fit the rest of his look. However, at this moment, he was visibly flushed and he drained his glass a little too fast.

The young female ZEPHYR, Gina Tolbert, sipped her drink and waited quietly.

I ordered a second round.

"So how'd it go?" I asked. "Were you able to spot any surveillance? Anyone make you suspicious?"

The two exchanged glances, and Gina spoke first. I wasn't surprised that management within the CIA's Soviet and East European Division (SE Division) considered her the star of this particular team. I had learned in previous exercises with ZEPHYRs that the quieter, less flashy members often performed as well as or better than their more flamboyant colleagues. Gina had been one such woman—belying her art history major at a Five Sisters college, seemingly born to the hardscrabble world of espionage. Many women were naturally more observant on the street than their male counterparts—maybe they had been required to learn this as a kind of urban survival tool.

In any case, Gina did not let me down.

"I saw a couple in Georgetown Park Mall who looked like they didn't belong," she said, tossing her long, straight hair over her shoulder. Her voice was husky and soft, and I had to lean forward to hear her. "A tall guy with a beard, and a shorter woman, both wearing denim. Then there was another couple, a guy and a girl, who seemed to linger too long outside of Clyde's. I thought maybe we had seen them before."

She looked at Les and he nodded in agreement.

During their training, I had drilled into them—and all ZEPHYRs—a mantra that could guide them in determining whether they were the subject of hostile surveillance:

Once is an accident.
Twice, a coincidence.
Three times, an enemy action.

I called it one of our "Moscow rules." Although no one had written them down, they were the precepts we all understood for conducting our operations in the most difficult of operating environments: the Soviet capital. By the time they got to Moscow, everyone knew these rules. They were dead simple, and full of common sense: Never make surveillance mad or embarrassed—they will shut you down. Never look over your shoulder or steal free looks in store windows when on the street. Make them think it was their fault that they had lost you, not vice versa, because KGB officers knew better than to report their own mistakes.

A handsome, suntanned, athletic couple, these two ZEPHYRs had just endured a six-month training course given to all case officers prior to assigning them to a "denied area"—Moscow, Havana, or Beijing, the most hostile places in the world for U.S. intelligence officers to operate. A large chunk of those six months had been spent training in detecting surveillance. Les Williams and Gina Tolbert had acquitted themselves well in the course and were considered ready to go. This evening had been a sort of postgraduate course in advanced surveillance detection, and they had experienced their share of real-world problems.

Most of the ZEPHYRs would come to this last exercise with a full head of steam and confidence in their ability to spot surveil-

lance—two traits that could make them dangerous to themselves
and others. One of the outcomes of such an evening with my
handpicked Special Surveillance Team was to bring them back to
earth, and put some fear in them. At the same time, we had
shown them that they could execute an escape from close surveillance without being detected.

If a case officer in a hostile area thought that he either did not
have surveillance or had managed to lose it, he might try to contact an agent working in place for the CIA, or try to make a dead
drop, mail a letter, or put up a signal. If the case officer was
wrong, if he *did* have surveillance while performing one of those
acts, he might as well take out a loaded gun and put it to the head
of his agent—the Soviets certainly would. This was a life-and-
death business, and there was no room for error.

I watched the door, knowing that the SST team, volunteers I
had assembled from different departments within the CIA, would
begin trickling in.

"Great job on the bailout."

I started with the highlights and conclusions of the evening
before picking apart their every move. I knew I had probably
been the only one in a position to observe it when Les had left
the car. It would be interesting to learn at what point the SST
team realized that they were no longer with him.

The door to the bar was constantly opening and closing, and
we had positioned ourselves so that we could watch the crowd
flow in and out. It opened now, and a small group of women
stepped through the door. Lorraine Collins, a thirty-something
triathlete, was in pedal pushers and loafers without socks, carrying
nine-month-old Allen on her hip. Following closely was Victoria
Sanderson, a vivacious blonde engineer dressed in a bright pink
running suit with a pink headband and a backpack. Bringing up
the rear was Ellen Bonelli, one of our graphic artists, wearing the
black spandex outfit of a bicycle messenger and carrying her

helmet and backpack in her left hand. Her two-way radio hung bandoleer-like across her chest. They waved and took a table near us, then ordered from the waitress.

Les looked at Gina. "I think I saw the messenger earlier," he said. "When we were coming out of Georgetown Park Mall on Wisconsin Street, she was going in."

Gina nodded in agreement, her dark hair falling over her face.

The next time the door opened, a blustery wind held it there long enough for a group of young people to enter the bar. One couple, hand in hand, looked at us and waved. The tall bearded fellow, Jim Smith, and his sidekick, Katie Monroe, still wearing the Redskins hat, nodded to us, and then they began moving tables together to make a long row with enough room for a couple of dozen people.

The ZEPHYR couple looked at each other in amazement, just beginning to understand the dimensions of the surveillance exercise they had gone through, and the scope of the assembled team.

Fifteen minutes later, the full team of twenty-six men and women sat around our two "rabbits" at our newly constructed communal table. We were rehashing the evening's events and weighing the outcome. We were talking much too loud, but the other inhabitants of the bar paid no attention to us; they were engaged in their own discussions. The music on the jukebox was blaring—the reason we liked this place—and Duke Ellington was holding forth louder than any of us with the melodic "Night Train."

"You were moving a little too fast on M Street," I told Deanna Williams and Renee Halpern, the two women who manned Control, the Ford van. It bristled with state-of-the-art electronics and served as a moveable wardrobe room that contained many of the props used by the team—the bicycles, the pram, even Renee's tiny dog, Lulu, who loved to go along for the ride. The magnetic signs for the van were organized behind the driver's seat. My favorite sign was the "Tony's Pizza" with a jazzy logo and a local phone number; if someone called it, they would be informed of "trouble on the line." The foot surveillance was controlled from the van, whose occupants reported, via radio, the direction and location of the targets to the rest of the team, and deployed the coverage to the most strategic areas.

"Did anybody notice the taillights on the Volvo?" I asked the group.

Only the car that had been nearest the Volvo as it turned the last two corners had noticed that the taillights were disconnected. They would not have noticed, nor should they, that the interior dome light had also been turned off. Trailing surveillance would have no visual alerts that the car had stopped or slowed or that the door had opened briefly. When Les and Gina had made that second turn and Gina had briefly hit the brakes, Les had bailed out of the car and vaulted over the waist-high concrete wall. It had been a picture-perfect escape; that part of the exercise had gone extremely well.

The rest of the evening had been the best lesson that the ZEPHYRs would receive on surveillance detection. They now knew that a team of twenty-six people had followed them for hours as they traversed, on foot and by vehicle, the forty-square-mile operational site. With the use of simple disguise techniques, many of their "tails" had remained invisible even to this well-trained and vigilant couple.

They could make no such errors in judgment on the mean streets of a place like Moscow.

After the group dispersed at around 10 PM, I decided to head home. Before leaving, however, I called the Directorate of Operations duty officer to check in.

Over the past few days, I had noticed a flurry of high-priority cable traffic from somewhere along the South Asian frontier. Even though the cable action indicators were for a compartmented activity, there was one cryptonym—an operational code word—in the subject line indicating a possible exfiltration of a local agent, which could require my division's involvement. I was aware that Jonna Goeser, one of my best technical operations officers, had traveled to the same location a few days before for what must have looked like a routine photo-surveillance job. If she had subsequently become involved in an operation where an important agent and his family had to be moved out of harm's way, I knew there should be the beginnings of an exfiltration plan showing up in the operational cable traffic.

"Duty officer," a young male voice answered sleepily.

"Hi, this is Tony Mendez checking in before I head up the road."

"Yeah, Tony. There's another NIACT here. We called your duty guy a while ago to come in and take a look. He thought it could keep until morning. It's from one of your people looking for some operational advice. Looks like she's in a bit of a jam."

Jonna? "I'll come and take a peek, since I'm in the neighborhood."

"We'll keep the lights on."

I left Georgetown via Key Bridge and turned north onto the George Washington Parkway. This drive was one of my favorites, even though I made it every day. The scenery regularly awed me, no matter what the season was. Once across the Potomac the GW Parkway paralleled the river all the way to the CIA grounds. Initially, the spires of Georgetown University lined the palisades on the opposite side, towering above the old shops and residences. Down at the river's edge were the boathouses, wonderful old Victorian edifices that housed the crewing shells and pennants of several winning crew clubs. I passed the Three Sisters, a rock formation in the river where the D.C. government was perpetually threatening to put in a new bridge in spite of loud protests from the residents of Georgetown. I took the exit at Route 123 and braked at the first red light. Six years later, this same intersection would be the scene of a murderous ambush by Mir Aimal Kansi, a radical Pakistani Muslim with a demented grudge against the United States. Packing automatic weapons, Kansi would take out his hatred on unsuspecting CIA employees—killing three—as they sat in their cars waiting for the light to change. Kansi fled back to Pakistan, and it took almost five years before the CIA and FBI were able to track him down and capture him.

I pulled into the CIA compound, and a Security Protective Officer (SPO) waved me through the security gate as I flashed my laminated blue badge. The massive white marble-and-granite building loomed among the trees of the forested campus like a vigilant beast that never slept. At this hour the only way in was the south entrance of the original headquarters building. Once inside, instead of merely inserting my badge into the turnstile and passing through the gate, as I would during working hours, I had to sign in at the guard desk, indicating my destination and badge number.

The cavernous "D" corridor was now dimly lit and evolved through the gloom into the "E" corridor as I moved straight ahead, past the darkened lobby on my right. My footsteps echoed off the spotless marble walls and anonymous steel doors, painted in pastel colors, with black combination locks. The elevator made a quick trip to the seventh floor. When I stepped off it, I took a hard left and headed down the darkened, seventh-floor "F" corridor.

The duty officer's door was standing open, and a shaft of light streamed out into the hall. I strode in and went up to the familiar duty desk. I was struck, as usual, by the sense of electricity in the air of the brightly lit suite and the never-failing rush of adrenaline that came with being inside the worldwide operations center of the CIA's Clandestine Service.

There was the obligatory clatter of cipher machines filling the air; the round, boldfaced, government-issue wall clocks reflecting plus or minus Zulu (Greenwich Mean Time) for London, Washington, Tokyo, and Moscow; and the demeanor of intense concentration of the half-dozen staffers either sitting at desks shuffling through mounds of paper or making more copies and putting these into the row of mail slots. In the morning, these would be picked up by each of the various area divisions and staff components. The duty officer glanced at me and reached into a pile of folios of flimsy paper. Without a word, he handed me a stack stamped TOP SECRET above the code RYBAT, meaning restricted handling on a need-to-know basis only.

I sat down at a nearby empty desk, rubbed my tired eyes, and began reading.

The message was long and couched in guarded terms, yet it had all the earmarks of the mounting of an exfiltration for an agent code-named TUGBOAT. By their very nature, clandestine operations could compromise a foreign national working for the CIA in place in his or her country. It was vital to know when it was time to remove such local agents—or "local assets"—or you risked seeing them and their families picked up, and later gone missing. Besides being a personal and professional loss, such an occurrence would not bode well for future recruiting in the region. It was the task of my officers worldwide to recognize the need for such plans before it was too late. Exfiltration readiness was one of our major responsibilities, and it couldn't be done well without early involvement and planning.

The good news was that Jonna was on the scene, and I knew her to be a skilled field officer with good operational sense and right-on instincts. But relatively new to her current position, she had never been in such a precarious situation before, and she might not recognize some of the dangers or be able to envision their solutions. I thought about ways I might help her sort things out—from afar. But first, I had to figure out exactly what the hell was going on out on the subcontinent.

I began to type out my reply, pausing between sentences to

compose my thoughts. After I finished the message, I printed it out and walked it over to the duty officer.

"It's an 'IMMEDIATE,'" I said. "Want me to give it to commo?"

"Go home, Tony," the duty officer said. "That's what they pay me for."

I made a mental note to find out more about this top-secret, highly compartmented operation as I climbed into my new sports car and drove out of the main gate, onto Route 123, heading for home.

Thirty minutes later I woke up in a ditch, my lap covered with broken glass.

The engine of my car was racing at a high-pitched scream and the rear wheels were churning, trying to get a purchase on the loose soil and tangled brush in the ditch.

When I grasped my predicament, I reached down and turned off the ignition. I released my seat belt and crawled out of the broken window on the driver's side of my black Nissan 300ZX. This was the third time in recent months I had dozed off and left the road on my way back home late at night. My insurance agent would not be pleased.

Since the death of my wife, Karen, from cancer ten months earlier, I had been driving the sixty miles into Washington, D.C., instead of commuting by train. There was no longer anyone to rush home to, since the kids were grown and gone off to college or to their own lives elsewhere; the house was too big and too empty for just me. I would find myself wandering through her flower beds, which now, unlike when Karen had tended them, always seemed out of peak bloom. The huge house we had built with our own hands on forty wooded acres—while living in a one-room log cabin for two years with three children—was beginning to show some neglect. I had bought this sleek car recently so that the drive back and forth to work, at least, would be enjoyable. But I had been working more than the standard ten-hour days at my CIA job in the months since I had headed up the Graphics and Authentication Division of OTS. Bone-deep exhaustion had become a constant, along with the late-hour debriefings over pitchers of beer, so common among Agency employees seeking some cushion between work and home.

I scrambled to my feet and crunched through the frost-covered vines and brambles, up and out of the ditch and onto the hard surface of the two-lane country road.

After catching a ride most of the way home, I walked the final two miles. My black wing tips had not been made for this snow-covered trek, and it was a bit of a hike. Following a short rest and troubled dreams, I fired up my four-wheel-drive truck the next morning, and drove down the road to pull the Nissan from the ditch. I left the wrecked vehicle in a farmer's cornfield—out of the way of the county sheriff patrol—to be collected by a tow truck, and headed to work, down the George Washington Parkway, past CIA headquarters, to my in-town office.

My office at Foggy Bottom overlooked a courtyard from the second floor of Central Building. The red brick turn-of-the-century structure was one of three buildings occupied by OTS. The OSS, which began operations in 1942, used this compound at 2430 E Street, NW, during World War II. The CIA had its headquarters here from its formation in 1947 until 1962, when it moved to its new and more secure digs at Langley. Parts of OTS had remained behind, and it seemed that we had been in these historic buildings forever.

Dropping my things on a chair, I went back down the stairs. I liked walking through the cherry tree lined courtyard past East Building, where Allen Dulles had once had his office. The ghost of "Wild Bill" Donovan lingered here, as vividly as it did in Georgetown. The daffodils were beginning to bud early, as they often did in this protected garden.

I entered the front door of the gray limestone South Building, flashing my badge to a muscular black SPO, who smiled and nodded me through. Officer Anderson was the minister of a small local Washington, D.C., church in his other life, and his red Cadillac convertible was always proudly parked to the side of East Building.

I gave him my usual greeting, "Morning, Preacher!"

I continued down the corridor to the left and took the stairs to the second floor. Entering the OTS Registry, I picked up my morning cables sent in from around the globe during the night. A substantial part of foreign intelligence work involves reading and answering scores of staff communications on a daily basis. Only through the flow of these cables does the pulse of CIA field operations stay constant and steady.

I was on the lookout this morning for any clarification of the operation going down in Jonna's area. After several cups of coffee and a string of interruptions from my division staff and the telephone, I had worked my way through the morning stack. Other than the message I had read the night before, there was nothing new from the Hindu Kush mountains. Upon reading the NIACT message again, I noticed one of the code words indicating a Soviet and East European Division (SE) tie-in to the operation.

Of course. This was the connection I needed.

In typical SE fashion, they were compartmenting another one of their operations in order to limit the number of CIA staffers who knew about it. The need-to-know principle was a fine security procedure, but since Edward Lee Howard's defection to the Soviet Union a year earlier, I had noticed that SE Division's usual stringent need-to-know practices had increased tenfold and were bordering on paranoia. That's why shortly after I took over my current post I had wrangled an assignment for one of my most experienced and trusted officers as a resident member of SE Division at Langley. Jacob Jordan was a senior technical operations officer and an exfiltration expert. I had worked with him for six years in the Far East and South Asia during the Vietnam era, inventing new disguise technology and running some harrowing exfiltration operations with important defectors in situations involving hostile pursuit. I trusted him implicitly.

Now ensconced at headquarters, Jordan was the ideal officer to represent some of OTS's interests at SE Division. He could help open up lines of communication when something was brewing so that OTS could avoid being blindsided after something was well underway. Even when he did not hear of an operation from SE, he could get wind of it from some other source. Then he would track it down to the working-level desk officer who, while trying to get the job done, would be doing his best to limit lateral knowledge to only peers within the organization on a need-to-know basis. Once Jordan identified this desk officer, he could point out that it made sense to get the corresponding OTS specialists involved. Hopefully, the desk officer would see the light and open up the files ever so slightly. But sometimes, even the desk officer would not know the complete nature of the operation. His knowledge might be restricted by means of a vertical compartment, used when information should not be shared completely with a subordinate or a supervisor, being imposed by his senior managers to protect the true nature of the operation from one of their own.

I picked up my green phone, the secure line to headquarters, and dialed a familiar number. A short while later, Jacob Jordan stood in my office, holding an enlightening message.

"I got a copy through Mary Peters," he explained. "She had to twist some tails, but she knows how to do that and make them like it."

"Yeah, Mary's great."

Mary Peters was a case officer in charge of the small technical branch in SE Division. Jordan and I had worked with her in Moscow in the 1970s. She had been ambushed by the KGB while putting down a dead drop for a Russian agent on a railroad bridge

over the Moscow River. The way that Mary had comported herself with the KGB while undergoing hostile interrogation had
made her a living legend in the CIA.

I watched Jordan mop his brow with a perfectly pressed linen
handkerchief. He was one of those American intelligence officers
who had adopted many British affectations. During the early
days, when Jordan was a young officer and the Agency was
newly created, members of the British service had acted as big
brothers to the CIA. Everything about his manner and dress
belied his midwestern roots. His extended duty in British protec-
torates like Hong Kong over the years had served as his finishing
school.

Jordan was a wiry, tanned six-footer with thinning blond hair
parted to one side and combed neatly. In training for the Boston
Marathon, he was still perspiring lightly from his daily seven-mile
run from Langley to Foggy Bottom.

"I got to the appropriate desk officer in SE External," said Jordan, "and he seemed a bit at sea on this as well. But from what I
can decipher, TUGBOAT is apparently a local Near East Division
agent who is helping with something going down against an SE
target. The operation is being run by a specialized team who get
their command and control from a special intelligence channel
originating out of the Citadel."

The Citadel was the headquarters of a supersecret U.S. intelli-
gence department that specialized in the technical collection of
electronic intelligence (ELINT), communications intelligence
(COMINT), and signal intelligence (SIGINT), in contrast to
HUMINT, or human intelligence, the type of operations that
OTS normally supported.

"I smell another vertical SE compartment here," Jordan said
thoughtfully. "It'll take me a few days to penetrate."

As I said, Jacob Jordan was a good source for me. He knew the
intelligence game involved not only learning what you could

about the enemy, but also running fact-finding operations against our own people.

I hoped Jonna could somehow make sense of things from her end, and stay safe and productive. I knew that the slightest slip on her part would result in more negative communiques to headquarters from her field boss, who was not a big fan of hers. It would be good not to give him extra ammo in his effort to discredit Jonna.

As Jordan departed, my chief of disguise, Doris Neams, was waiting in the outer office. I waved her in. She was a small, stylish blonde with a no-nonsense attitude. I had recognized that she was well suited to working in our predominantly male environment when she started as an apprentice in my disguise section a decade earlier. She had since developed a working style of cutting through the preliminaries, laying out the problem, suggesting a solution, and leaving with a plan in place. We could have used more like her.

"Hey, boss, thought you'd like to see this unusual memorandum we just got though a special channel. I am not sure what to make of it."

Neams and I sat down while I read through the classified memo.

The request had come in from a collateral agency, veiled in the jargon of the business, but I assumed it was from the Citadel. They wanted a kind of quick ethnic change disguise for a special team to use in a sensitive target area. I had a strong hunch it was Jonna's operation.

"Any idea where this is going to take place and what the team is doing?" I asked.

"Not yet," she said. "But I'll keep you posted."

Neams stood and began to leave. "Oh, by the way," she said, stopping in her tracks, "I heard the most amazing piece of news at today's staff meeting. Seems that some senator is getting ready to read into the *Congressional Record* a recounting of Howard's escape." She looked at me closely. "I mean, the *whole* thing. How he used the training we gave him to elude surveillance. Can you believe that one of our old Moscow silver bullets is going to become public?"

"Silver bullets" were highly compartmented techniques reserved for operations in Moscow, the most challenging theater of operations. We thought of them as highly proprietary.

I knew that Edward Lee Howard, the fired and disgruntled CIA officer who had defected to the Soviet Union two years earlier, had used some crude form of one silver-bullet technique to throw off the FBI tails. Still, I didn't think that public dissemination of bits and pieces of his method of escaping detection would limit our use of our more sophisticated devices for throwing off KGB surveillance in Moscow.

"Knowing what we use is one thing," I said. "Detecting it is another."

On my way out of Central Building to my parking spot that evening, I caught sight of Maria Santori exiting South Building. She was a technical operations officer in Jonna's old Clandestine Imaging Division (CID) and a good friend, not only to me but to Jonna. Maria had recently returned from an extended trip to the South Asian subcontinent.

"Maria, hello. Got a few minutes?"

"Sure," she said, flashing her winning smile.

She was a slim, tall brunette who, like Jonna, had climbed up through the ranks. At one point they had both been assigned to the front office of the director of OTS. Jonna had been the executive secretary to the director, and Maria was the deputy's secretary. When Jonna moved into operations, Maria took over her job. I had encouraged Maria to move into the operational ranks when I was the OTS career management officer. She had made the transition effortlessly.

When my wife took ill, Maria had become a sympathetic listener. After Karen's death, Maria had gone through a tough divorce, so she and I had taken turns counseling each other through hard times.

"We haven't talked since you got back from the subcontinent. Can I buy you a drink at the Westpark?"

I was as eager for an old friend's company as I was for operational information.

"I'll meet you there," she said. "Six o'clock?"

As we relaxed over drinks at the rooftop bar of the Westpark Hotel and gazed out across the Potomac River toward Georgetown, now glittering in the early evening light, Maria told me her firsthand impressions of the tension building between Jonna and her boss.

Ten floors below, commuter traffic poured across Key Bridge, the headlights and taillights forming long yellow and red ribbons in the dusk. But the atmosphere in the leather-and-mahogany bar was quiet and comfortable. This was a favorite location of mine for a private chat with my close associates. The Westpark was also the launching point for many of the SST field exercises with the ZEPHYRs, since neither CIA personnel nor those of any of the other intelligence services in the area frequented it.

"I knew about her boss, and Jonna did, too, before she left," I said. "I just hope she's keeping her head down and not being set up for a fall."

"She's doing a great job," Maria said. "Like every self-respecting operations officer, she doesn't want to come back to headquarters and push paperwork."

CIA field chiefs enjoyed great autonomy, much like the captain of a ship. If a CIA officer didn't get along with the field unit chief, help could seem a long way off.

"I saw her keeping out of his way as much as possible," Maria said. "She can handle a lot, but she's got a lot to handle, Tony. Not just her boss."

Maria went on to tell me about Jonna's marital troubles.

Jonna certainly did have a full plate.

"But she has a great reputation everywhere I went in her area," Maria said.

Early the next morning, I was checking the morning cable traffic when my secure phone rang. It was Jacob Jordan at headquarters.

"We have an audience with Mr. Rhenquist. Can you make nine o'clock?"

Jordan and I joined Mary Peters and Martin Tucker, the chief of SE Division's internal U.S.S.R. operations, in the fifth-floor corner office of Miles Rhenquist, chief of Soviet and East European Division.

Rhenquist, a short, haughty man in his sixties with a shock of white hair and a perpetually red face, was standing behind his large walnut desk with his back to the room, peering out the window at the canopy of trees. This bucolic setting gave the CIA's secluded grounds the reputation around Washington of being a "campus" for spooks. Those present were passing around a flimsy, yellow, multipage cable, which had urgent citations:

IMMEDIATE TO: DIRECTOR

CITE: MOSCOW

SECRET–RESTRICTED HANDLING–EYES ONLY

Rhenquist turned and spoke in his precise manner. "You can all see that another one of our case officers has been ambushed and declared persona non grata in Moscow. And on top of that, we have lost another valuable Soviet asset, no doubt already dead. I am very worried we don't know how to run operations in Moscow anymore. If we're not careful, we will end up in the same fix we were in in 1977."

Tucker, a chunky, dark man with black curly hair and horn-rimmed glasses, shifted uncomfortably in his chair. Mary Peters was an attractive long-haired blonde who was prone to smiling in spite of what she was thinking. She gave Rhenquist an uncharacteristically hard stare.

I well remembered those dark days in July 1977 when Peters had been ambushed on a Moscow bridge, and I could see, from her pained expression, that Rhenquist had hit a nerve. But nobody could possibly blame her for being set up by the KGB after her agent, code-named TRINITY, had been interrogated by the KGB. TRINITY had been one of the most valuable CIA assets in history; he had given us strategic missile intelligence that helped during the SALT I negotiations in 1976–1977. Nobody could withstand the brutal KGB interrogation tactics for long. This was why some agents asked for an "L" pill, a lethal back door, a way out if they were captured. A cyanide capsule, concealed in the barrel of TRINITY's Mont Blanc pen by OTS engineers, had been there when he needed it. He had asked his KGB captors for his favorite pen so he could write his confession, bit off the tip of the pen, and was dead before he hit the floor. The KGB had no idea as to the identity of the CIA case officer making drops to TRINITY, so they lay in wait, hanging from the bottom of the bridge scaffolding, expecting someone to arrive at the scheduled time in the dark. They sprang up from a makeshift hatch in the bridge and surrounded a stunned Peters, who had no place to hide. There were more than thirty of them in sight when they hauled her off to Lubyanka Prison. She was released later that night and sent home the next day. Her photograph was splashed across newspapers worldwide, effectively ending her days as a deep-cover case officer in the field.

In 1977, after losing TRINITY and suffering the ordeal of Mary Peters's public exposure, Director of Central Intelligence Stansfield Turner had openly threatened to shut down Moscow Station, so frustrated was he at our inability to operate effectively there.

Rhenquist's reference to the decade-old case was unfair. The operational problems in Moscow since Howard's defection were far more difficult to fathom. I was beginning to think, as were some of my colleagues, that the KGB had some other way of predicting our every move in Moscow. One possibility was a mysterious substance used by the KGB that we came to call spy dust. Since the 1970s this material had been showing up in odd places; a whitish powder sprinkled on doormats, steering wheels, documents, shoes, and many other things that our officers in Moscow might touch. Since then, we had received consistent reports from the field on the KGB's ability to track its targets without having to keep them in sight, a very scary thought, indeed.

I had already tasked my SST team to come up with ways to track the ZEPHYRs, while they were in training, using methods similar to those used by the KGB. OTS engineers were doing scientific studies to augment these scenarios and assemble a matrix of the various possible threats.

These ideas had been brought up in meetings with Rhenquist before, and he usually just went ballistic and attacked the messenger. The messenger these days tended to be his U.S.S.R. operations chief.

"I hold you responsible for fixing this problem," Rhenquist told Tucker. "You are the line manager in charge, and either you fix it or we will find someone who can."

Rhenquist was literally spitting these words at his Soviet ops chief.

Tucker took this abuse in silence. I wondered if he was remembering how preferable it was to be in the field, where the action was. No case officer relished a headquarters assignment, with its never-ending meetings and the mountains of paper, but worst of all was having to attend the throne of the chief of SE Division when he was seriously pissed. It appeared that the very future of the CIA's Moscow operations hung in the balance.

Tucker held his head down and studied the floor as he rose with the rest of us to escape the lion's den.

Peters spoke up. "Miles, we need another moment of your time."

When Tucker saw that she was referring to herself, plus me and Jordan, he gratefully beat a retreat.

As the other two sat back down, I stepped forward and handed Rhenquist another RESTRICTED HANDLING message, which, in accordance with security procedures, I had carried double-wrapped and secured in a specially made locked portfolio.

Deflating slightly, Rhenquist slumped down in his chair, put his chin on his chest, and pulled his glasses down to the tip of his nose as he read the message.

When he finished, he peered over his glasses at me.

"What's your question?"

Although I was somewhat junior to Rhenquist, I was not in his chain of command. He was my customer—and a powerful one at that. It was my job, as chief of an OTS division, to protect my precious and limited disguise and documentation personnel and resources from misuse on operations. All technical officers are specially trained to take on their more senior customers and hold their feet to the fire on compartmented information if they were misusing technical officers or their capabilities. This would include the White House, if necessary. I was certainly not intimidated by the SE chief.

"I have an OTS officer on the ground out there, and I am not sure she is getting the straight story," I said. "I need to make sure she has everything she needs before we commit any more resources or find ourselves in a jam. We have talked to the desk officer in charge in your external operations branch, but he doesn't have all the answers either."

I stopped speaking because Rhenquist's face looked as if a black cloud had moved across it.

"You tried to get information on SE external operations without my approval?"

The room filled with a long moment of heavy, awkward silence.

"This time, Mendez," Rhenquist growled, "you've gone too far."

Mary Peters caught my eye from across the room. She knew what I knew—it was Rhenquist who had gone too far, and possibly let the cat out of the bag. It seemed we had stumbled across another SE spoofing operation in which all was not as it appeared to be.

Nobody said a word as we filed out of the room.

KGB Lieutenant Colonel Valeriy F. Martynov, CIA code-named GTGENTILE, is executed by a single shot to the head.

His wife and son were allowed to visit him briefly in his cell before his execution.

FOUR

ASIAN SUBCONTINENT

Spring 1987

Jonna

The driver of the Land Rover that had picked me up was Eric Cooper, the entry-team leader. After locating the local jail and generally getting our bearings in the city, we had dropped off the other two members of the team in the center of town, and Cooper and I proceeded to a hotel where we rented a room with a view of the Soviet compound that was our target, which would function as an observation post (OP).

As we completed the preliminary photographic casing of the Soviet stronghold from the window of the hotel room—I would develop the film later that day—Cooper went over the details of the operation.

His team was a unique group of individuals with unusual and dangerous skills. Locksmiths who would dangle from mountain-climbing pitons in an urban environment, ninjalike shadows armed with the latest in electronics, computer geeks who work out at the gym. Very good at their jobs, the team was pretty much a desperate and dangerous tool-of-last-resort—they were called in only when less high-risk options wouldn't work. Most of them didn't have a long career doing this type of work, so it was usually a group of younger rather than older guys.

The team would be more or less left to their own devices, since their operational expertise was something no one else could help them with. Also, their forged identity papers, issued by our documents section at headquarters, were quite in order, and their cover as tourists—the same as mine—was more than sufficient in this remote mountain town where more than two hundred thousand tourists flocked each year.

Cooper said this particular Soviet legation had been targeted because of the short staff here in this small, relatively insignificant country. With less than half the manpower available at most other Soviet installations, this staff was stretched thin. Adding to our advantage was the fact that their annual vacation was pulling people away from these mountains back to Mother Russia. The Agency, and the team's chain of command at the Citadel, were betting that when all of these factors came to bear on their compound, the KGB's security here would not be as stringent as it would be in a major capital.

The more Cooper talked, the more I wondered, *Has he been there before?*

As high-level KGB defector Victor Sheymov, who came over to our side in 1980, had confirmed to U.S. Intelligence—and later in his own published memoirs*—most Soviet garrisons around the world had special secure rooms, to include: the KGB's rezidentura, or station; the GRU (the Soviet military intelligence organization and sister service to the KGB) rezidentura; and the Sanctum, where the KAPELLE device was kept in a special enclosure.

Cooper shot me a glance with those steely blue eyes and smiled. He was handsome, and had an aura of danger and excitement. I found my mind drifting.

---

*Victor Sheymov, *Tower of Secrets* (Annapolis, MD: Naval Institute Press, 1993).

"I'm not losing you here, am I?" he asked a bit too patroniz-
ingly.

"Keep going," I said, my cheeks reddening despite my effort to
appear cool.

The rezidenturas were places set aside for classified work free
from the threat of technical intercept, he went on, but they were
not considered secure enough for the storage of classified materials, which were brought in during the workday and always
returned at night to the Sanctum for secure storage. Usually, all
classified materials used in the KGB's operations and sent in the
diplomatic pouch were on undeveloped thirty-five-millimeter
film, and only direct contact paper copies were made of classified
documents or cipher traffic for use in the Sanctum. The paper
could not be easily copied, and it could be quickly destroyed if the
stronghold were to be overrun.

"This adds another measure of security," Cooper sighed, "in a
landscape littered with measures of security."

"You wouldn't be making the big bucks if it was easy," I
chided, knowing that he was on the same pay scale as the rest
of us government employees, and none of us were here because
of the salary. *Or was it possible that second-story guys got paid
more?*

Because of my photo work at the Agency, I knew we had been
developing a "film loop" concealment for our small cameras. This
device would allow a KGB agent working for us to make copies
of the images on the filmstrips while pretending to be simply
viewing the film in the rezidentura, even in front of other KGB
officers in the same room.

We had every reason to believe that the physical security of the
Sanctum would be formidable. And why wouldn't it be, considering the Soviet state secrets it held? They were built like a bank
vault, with thick walls and huge metal doors that protected the
single entrance. The vault would be hidden by an innocuous

doorway, much like the other doorways in the compound buildings. Usually, neither of these doors had a key lock. The heavy
metal security door had redundant dead bolts and combination
locks.

Cooper paused for a moment in his narration. I could see that
he was mentally placing himself inside the space he was describing. I was now certain he had been inside one of these innermost
KGB sanctuaries before; he knew exactly where everything was
located and what each next step should be. I had worked with
many professional and capable colleagues in the course of my CIA
career, but I was truly astounded with this man's knowledge, pre-
paredness, and obvious courage.

As I finished packing up the photo gear, room service arrived
with the fresh lime and sodas we had ordered. Cooper opened the
door and tipped the waiter, and as he did so, I ducked out of
sight. We sat down on the outside balcony and sipped our drinks
in view of the mountains.

"How long have you been doing this, Eric?" I asked.

"Just about forever," he said, sucking on a lime. "But each new
job is basically starting from scratch. The adrenaline rush is addictive."

I knew what he meant. Although it was impossible to mention
it on a CIA recruiting poster, most field operatives were adrenaline junkies. If we weren't, no amount of money would be able
to get us to do some of the things we did. I would always remember the almost physical thrill that had shot through me the first
time I had met with a Russian asset.

"As my division chief, Tony Mendez, always says, 'If we weren't
doing this, we'd all be robbing banks.' "

Eric grinned, his eyes flashing in recognition.

After a moment of silence, I resumed our discussion.

"Aren't there guards in the Sanctum?"

In most strongholds, he explained, a sentry was on duty all the time with a secret viewing aperture inside the vaulted area where he could monitor the anteroom.

"He can open the outer door with a switch," Cooper stated matter-of-factly. "The outer door has a concealed button which signals the sentry. When the bell is pressed, the sentry pushes his own button, opening the cover-door lock and admitting the visitor. Once the cover door is locked behind the visitor, and the sentry verifies the identity of the visitor by looking through the peephole, he opens the vault door."

"You *have* been there before," I said, lowering my eyes to my glass.

Cooper pretended not to have heard me.

The security didn't stop there, he continued.

His demeanor, as he waltzed me thorough the secret rooms, suddenly reminded me of an expert military briefer. *That's it*, I thought, *he's ex-military.* Without a conscious effort, I guessed Navy SEAL.

He explained that the Sanctum was divided by a barrier isolating the inner and outer chambers. The KAPELLE operator, also known as a "pianist," worked in the inner part. He was always escorted by a security guard when leaving the stronghold alone and, as a hedge against defection, if he was married, his spouse could not accompany him, even for a stroll to the marketplace.

"Some marriage," I offered.

Cooper looked at me and smiled devilishly. "Who in the world would want to defect with his own wife?"

That was as lighthearted as it got.

The Sanctum afforded secure compartments for the most secret discussions. In the inner part, the classified materials were stored in safes. Also in the inner part would be "the Hole," our final destination. "It's where KAPELLE is kept."

"How big is this Hole?" I asked.

"Two meters high, wide, and long."

I shivered, remembering several hours I had spent as a child playing a lengthy game of hide-and-seek with my sister, Jennifer. Somewhere in the middle of the game she had managed to lock me inside the cabinet under the sink while I was hiding there. Then she had gone outside and begun another game with friends who came by, forgetting my imprisonment. I had spent what seemed like hours locked in that dark space that reeked of Clorox, Drano, and harsh cleansers.

The door to the Hole, secured by a hydraulic dead bolt, was designed to provide electromagnetic and acoustical shielding of the KAPELLE device, he explained. As a result, the inside of the Hole was flooded with electromagnetic "noise." There was no air-conditioning in this cramped space, and the only physical connection between the enclosure and the outer vaulted room was through legs that the cubicle sat atop, thereby cushioning its physical contact with the building and limiting accoustical noise.

I set my glass down on the balcony table. "This sounds like working on a submarine," I said. "One of my recurring night-mares."

"I'll have to remember that," he replied with more than casual interest.

That fear of small places had transferred to a real claustrophobia; any tight passage or small closet gave me the creeps. My one visit aboard a submarine had been short. I had run the last twenty yards down the passageway when I saw a crack of daylight at the end. Periodically, I still dreamed about the experience, always awaking in a sweat.

"This is where it gets fun," Eric continued. His briefing had gone way beyond my end of the operation. Obviously, he trusted me as a colleague. This was such a difference in attitude from that of Smallwood, my nemesis, that I felt touched—even honored.

Once the entry team got inside the enclosure, they would find the KAPELLE bolted down to the floor. The term *smoking-bolt operation,* I had already learned, was Agency slang for describing the swiftness of a snatch, as in, "There was nothing left but the smoking bolts on the floor."

Downsized like many of our smaller CIA contingents in the Third World, the entire KGB staff here was probably only two people: the KGB rezident, or chief, and the KAPELLE operator. The KAPELLE device at this backwater outpost would be the same as those elsewhere, only not subject to an around-the-clock guard. The KGB no doubt believed, however, that the physical security measures in place could be relied on to keep its top-secret device safe in this quiet corner of the world.

Slowly and with no wasted motion, I raised my camera so that the viewfinder was filled with the scene. One false move and the moment would be lost.

Two young Buddhist monks, in saffron and cinnamon robes and with shaved heads, were flying a red kite off the side of the mountain.

I depressed the shutter button and moved quietly away.

The boys were so engrossed that they had not even noticed me.

As the afternoon sun began its decline, I was climbing what seemed an endless set of stone stairs leading up through a mist to the top of an almost vertical emerald green mountain. In the distance was a twelve-mile-wide fertile valley formed from an extinct lake bottom. Forty miles to the north and dwarfing other nearby mountaintops, sawtooth peaks rose more than four miles high. The late sun colored them in pastels; they resembled a veil connecting the earth to the clouds.

This long-forgotten outpost on the old Silk Route lay nestled in the center of the valley like an encrusted jewel in the palm of a giant hand. The surrounding chestnut forest and giant rhododendrons were teeming with monkeys; many of them scampered alongside me up the moldering stairs or stood in my way, challenging me with screeching hisses.

I stopped and turned for a moment, framing and shooting several more pictures with my well-traveled Nikon F3. Then I continued a seemingly casual conversation with my colleague, Joe Muldoon, a local resident CIA case officer, as we continued up the steps. I was bringing him up to date on my activities that afternoon with the snatch team. He would never meet the members of the elite team—if there was a problem down the road, he would be able to deny everything. But in reality, any serious probe into the Soviet compound would require the services of the local CIA contingent.

Muldoon was an elf of a man. A shock of gray hair just a bit too long and a magnificent mustache that swept up at its ends accentuated his Irish blue eyes. They were very kind eyes. He was dressed in the casual bush clothes common to foreign residents hereabouts. Although we were alone except for the horde of chattering blue-bellied rhesus monkeys, we spoke softly. This required us to pay close attention to each other's words, while the noises from the monkey-sentries provided a good measure of security from inquiring ears.

"The hotel room has a good line of sight to the Soviet compound," I explained. "We cased the place and were able to chart the staff's routine. I got some good long-lens shots of the buildings, the commo antennas, and the antenna leads running into the building."

I told Muldoon that the power lines and the heavy-duty air handlers on the roof made our team think that the Sanctum was on the second floor of the center compound building and that the device they were after would be secured inside it. The overhead imagery from CIA satellites should help us confirm that, although I had learned the KGB took every precaution to disguise the exact location of such sensitive equipment. The entry team was conducting an electromagnetic-emanations survey this afternoon, hoping to zero in on the electronic noise of their target area. The team still needed a ground-level reconnaissance of the target compound courtyard, and I'd be helping handle the technical end of that.

Muldoon told me that the local CIA chief planned to ask the head of the U.S. Mission to send an official invitation to the Soviet head of mission, which would be good cover for the messenger—the chief—to enter the Soviet compound and take the close-in photographic images needed to finalize the plan for entry.

Our long walk that morning to the high precipice, far away from town, afforded a measure of privacy and security for a meeting with a local agent, code-named TUGBOAT, who was going to help the team gain access to the center building of the Soviet stronghold. Such a face-to-face was the only way I could decide firsthand what I needed to do to disguise him for his part of the operation. TUGBOAT had already taken great risks working locally for the CIA, and by now he was readily identifiable in this small town. I quietly cursed my boss, who had assured me that this trip was to be a simple photo-surveillance operation. As a result, I had left behind my disguise materials and other tools I could have used to change TUGBOAT's look and identity.

TUGBOAT was a local security type whom Muldoon had recruited previously to help the Agency with local counter-narcotics activities, a dangerous item on the CIA's operational directive any place in the world. Here, the trail had led into the highest levels of local leadership, making the work that much more hazardous.

Espionage can be a deadly game, of course, but it is usually most life-threatening for a foreign or locally recruited agent. Counterterrorism and counternarcotics operations, however, are different animals. The rules of diplomacy do not come into play, and the targeted individuals are more inclined to shoot, randomly if need be, before asking questions. Diplomacy is out the window, and a criminal's code of survival is more the order of the day.

As a result of his counternarcotics operations, Muldoon had already been paid a visit by a couple of thugs who showed up at his door late one night making threats. Not wanting to take any chances, he had started taking extraordinary security measures, including carrying a nine-millimeter Browning automatic in his belt. He had his gun today, under his bush jacket, for our clandestine meeting with TUGBOAT, which was unusual behavior for a CIA case officer. Normally, we were armed only in a war zone. But given how high the stakes were now, Muldoon's every action had become more careful and thought out.

After a breather, we continued up the long flight of steps.

"I can't believe headquarters is approving such an outrageous plan," Muldoon said. "But I understand the risk is worth it. The chief says we are to serve up our best assets and efforts. And so, Jonna, I'm happy to be at your service. The fact is, we haven't had much excitement in this town in a long while. We run our operations against the local drug traffickers and have an occasional heated tennis match with a Russian or a Chinese."

I could see that Muldoon was one of those people who found humor in everything, including adversity. I liked this slight, gregarious man with a big heart. His "cover job" in the American community was looking after the affairs of errant U.S. citizens who traveled here hoping to dabble in the easy supply of exotic drugs—"chasing the dragon," as he called it. Most of these foreigners weren't accustomed to such pure substances, and when one of them fatally overdosed, he arranged for their remains to be shipped back to their next of kin. Because there were no local embalming practices, that meant fresh corpses in crude coffins made locally. The "storage problem," as he put it, was exacerbated by the scarcity of refrigeration, most of which was owned by Americans.

"On any given weekend," Muldoon went on, "you can count on finding one or two bodies stuffed in the back of the walk-in freezer at the American commissary, waiting for a Monday morning flight back home."

I learned that the official drug-related death rate in the country had declined in the past year, but only due to some significant changes in the way such deaths were reported. "If a corpse is found in bed in a hotel room with drug paraphernalia all over the room, and with a tourniquet tying off the arm, it only counts as a drug death if the needle is still in the arm," Muldoon explained. "If the needle has slipped out and fallen to the floor, as it usually does, the death is not listed as drug-related."

I listened, enthralled and amazed as always at how bureaucracies could blatantly manipulate and juggle numbers to achieve favorable results.

When we climbed the last step, we arrived at the grounds of a remote temple. My already shortened breath was taken away for a moment.

The huge, low dome of a blazing gold stupa stood in the center of a stone plaza. Affixed around the base—a glittering mound—were a thousand prayer wheels, the major focus of any Tibetan Buddhist temple. Fastened from the spire on top and all around the circumference of the dome were hundreds of small, brightly colored prayer flags and streamers fluttering in the wind. Saffron-robed monks moved slowly through the vast plaza, the smallest of them mere children.

The full effect of the scene took some time to absorb. Without hesitation, I went to work recording the exotic setting with my camera. As I did, Muldoon kept a watchful eye on the scene around us, looking for signs of hostile surveillance. My loosely devised cover as a typical western tourist provided a convincing reason for me to snap pictures.

After about a half hour of shooting, I had worked my way around to the other side of the plaza, where a secluded narrow corridor led into the shadows.

I felt him, rather than saw him, standing there.

TUGBOAT was a small man with a presence that overshadowed his size. He looked like most of the local population: slight, with dark hair and eyes, clean-shaven, coffee-colored skin. His eyes were the first thing you noticed about him. Narrow, observant, intelligent, they measured me with a steady gaze. I guessed him to be in his mid-thirties.

Muldoon was the first to speak, stepping forward and extending his hand. "Glad you could come. This is my colleague, Jane. She flew in yesterday from Washington and is ready to go to work. She brought all of the latest disguise materials."

I felt my stomach flip over, although not at the lie about my coming in from Washington. Case officers would use this line routinely to make their assets feel important and to make it seem as if CIA headquarters was following every twist and turn in their operation. Rather, I was uneasy because I hadn't yet told Muldoon that I had not brought anything with me for a disguise case.

As I started to extend my hand to TUGBOAT, I noticed that he was not reciprocating. I quickly ended up adjusting my camera strap instead.

"This is just an initial review," I explained. "I needed to see what you look like. I'm also familiarizing myself with the rest of the population. Somewhere in there, I'll design for you a new look that will blend in on the street while concealing your true identity."

TUGBOAT nodded thoughtfully, then turned to Muldoon to say something. It was only then that I saw the disfiguring birthmark that ran down the right side of his face, starting at the temple and spilling out onto his right cheek.

Oh, great! I'm screwed. There I was with absolutely nothing to work with, and this guy was wearing a neon sign on his face that could be seen a block away.

We continued chatting for a few minutes while I scrutinized TUGBOAT's mannerisms, and as we parted, I observed him as he moved down the path. As Muldoon and I headed back down the mountain, I explained the challenge of this particular piece of work, finally admitting to him that I had no disguise materials with me, nothing at all.

"Guess we're just gonna have to get creative," Muldoon said agreeably.

Rather than becoming upset, as other case officers might have done, he was accepting my difficult challenge as his own. I liked him even better for his generous attitude.

The thought gave me an idea. "Joe, when you get back to the office, ask each of the officers to bring in tomorrow morning any cosmetics that their wives have on hand. Foundation, powder, eyeliner, eyebrow pencils—anything will help."

I also asked him to have the staffers pool their disguise kits. I knew that each officer was issued one before leaving for a foreign assignment, and I wanted to see everything they had—glasses, mustaches, wigs. Out of these odds and ends, perhaps I could knit together something convincing.

"You got it," Muldoon said.

We arranged to meet in the morning at the safe house, and he promised to have all of the material there when I arrived. He asked whether I was okay on my own for the evening, or whether I needed anything. I said I was fine. I was planning a shopping trip to the local bazaar to see what I could find for our project. We shook hands and parted.

At ten o'clock the next morning, I proceeded to the safe

house in the city center. Taking the customary precautions to ensure that I was not being followed, I walked a circuitous route through the old part of town in the general direction of one of the many tourist attractions. I cut through an alley and came upon an open sewer slicing through the center of the road. Such an obstacle had not been covered in our surveillance training. I held my breath and stepped gingerly over the puddles of raw sewage, then made a hard left and emerged onto the adjoining street.

I turned into the third entrance on my right, and knocked lightly.

Joe Muldoon, wearing an ear-to-ear grin, opened the door immediately. "Good morning, Jonna. Come in and get a load of what I brought for you."

Moving through the entrance, I saw a dining room table piled high with plastic bags. Muldoon told me that the wives had really gotten into it, as they didn't often get to participate. It looked as if they had pulled out all the stops.

I sat down at the table, and began to go through the bags.

"This is good stuff, Joe."

As I began to assemble the necessary materials, Muldoon left to collect TUGBOAT in a car that bore local license plates—in contrast to his official vehicle: an American-made car with official plates. He said he'd be back in an hour, but I didn't answer or even look up. I was too busy examining a can of Dr. Scholl's foot powder, thinking about the wondrous possibilities it presented.

When Muldoon returned, he drove directly into the garage and closed the door before allowing his passenger, hidden from sight on the floorboard of the car, to get out. They entered the side door of the house. I was waiting for them in the dining room. The pile of plastic bags was gone, and on the dining room table was assembled an assortment of cosmetics and applicators, lined up in almost surgical precision. A pile of clean white towels, a brush and comb, and a hinged mirror were also in place.

I welcomed TUGBOAT and asked Muldoon to excuse us.

During my training days, Tony had told me repeatedly that a confident asset could successfully wear a less-than-perfect disguise, but even the best disguise on a hesitant subject would never hold up to close scrutiny. Though these disguise materials could be attributed to luck, TUGBOAT's final appearance would be a test of my skill. Passing scrutiny, however, would depend on TUG-BOAT's demeanor; he had to feel, from the inside out, that he looked different.

Forty-five minutes later, I summoned Muldoon from the adjacent room. He put down the newspaper he was reading, walked into the dining room, and stopped.

Sitting on a chair next to the table was an older man who appeared to be about sixty. He had close-cropped gray hair, combed straight back and revealing a widow's peak. His hair was whiter at the temples, and his mustache was large and gray. He wore dark-rimmed glasses, and when he removed them, deep wrinkles were noticeable around his eyes, a feature common among older citizens at this high altitude—prima facie evidence, I had decided, that the ozone layer really was burning away. He held a distinctive hat that I had picked up in the bazaar, one that many police officers wore along with their uniforms. Best of all: his complexion was clear, with no blemishes.

Muldoon let out a low whistle. "How in *hell* did you do that?"

"Trade secrets," I said, smiling.

I held up a small container of Dermablend, a cosmetic used to hide surgical scars, varicose veins, and even tattoos. I had remembered putting together a local officer's disguise kit and including the Dermablend to hide the distinctive tattoo of a cute little skunk on his forearm. Then I nodded toward the table, where the can of Dr. Scholl's foot powder was sitting. As far as I was concerned, it would forever be known as Dr. Scholl's Hair Whitening Powder.

When I asked TUGBOAT to address our visitor, a silver-capped front tooth became obvious. For the icing on the cake, when TUGBOAT got up and walked across the room, he had a discreet but discernible limp, the result of an Ace bandage wrapped around his right knee.

"Very nice job," Muldoon said appreciatively.

I explained that I had photographed TUGBOAT in disguise for black-and-white ID photos. I had tried to find photo paper and fixer the day before with no luck, but I hoped I still might find what I needed at the bazaar. I told Muldoon that I needed a darkroom to work in. We would photograph TUGBOAT's real government ID card with my thirty-five-millimeter camera and enlarge it to an eleven-by-fourteen print, change his name and title to make him a cop, photograph that, then print it at its regular billfold size and laminate it. I explained that I would still need an official-looking inked stamp with the national logo on it.

TUGBOAT looked up. "I can get that. I see those lying about at the Post and Telegraph office. It would be easy enough to walk off with one."

His voice was soft and his English was accented, but clear.

"That's a great idea, but let me have one of my guys get it," Muldoon said. "You, my friend, are too valuable to risk at this point."

The next morning, Muldoon and TUGBOAT returned to the safe house at the predetermined hour. I was waiting in the dining room with the newly forged police ID card. When I showed it to TUGBOAT and Muldoon, they looked at it in amazement. While the card appeared to be old, the photo of TUGBOAT was crisp and clear. The aged police officer stared out of the card at them, looking rather stern.

The ID card had to be just right. I knew that the initial use of his disguise would be at twilight, at the gates to the stronghold, and that it would be these credentials, not his face, that would undergo the most intense scrutiny.

The purple stamp of the country seal was slightly smudged, the lamination was scratched and chipped, and there was just the right amount of dirt on the card to make it believable.

"How'd you do this?" Muldoon wanted to know.

It had taken me most of the night to produce the smudged and abraded identity document. The real problem had been finding fresh photo chemicals in this little off-the-beaten-path wreck of a Third World city. I had purchased and tested four packages of photographic fixer before finding one fresh enough to make the photograph permanent.

I explained that the photo and language on the card were easy enough, and the authenticating stamp was just the right touch. "But it looked too precise, you know? So I poured some hot coffee on it, laid it on the garage floor, and rubbed it on the cement with my shoe."

The card had acquired the patina of almost everything in this country: aged, dirty, and smudged. In fact, it was perfect, well worth the long day and night I had turned in without Tom Smallwood's help.

Muldoon and TUGBOAT left the safe house, and I heard the sound of the car's motor fade into the morning.

I sat down on a hard-backed chair and let my back relax.

Fifteen minutes later, after I had reassembled the most-useable materials into a single disguise kit, the silence was broken with the noisy arrival of Smallwood, looking surprisingly chipper and ready to go, along with Eric Cooper, looking dashing as usual.

I hadn't seen my boss since he'd slammed his hotel room door in my face two mornings ago. "Get some sleep?" I asked him.

"Sleep will kill you. In fact, I've been making more money at the roulette tables, and Eric has been a great help."

I could see that the two bosses on the job were birds of a feather—the kind that got their energy from carousing. Part of the spy culture was the undeniable fact that operations officers are addicted to the action; they burn the candle at both ends in the field, then collapse immobile during their infrequent time off with their families. We were all guilty of this flaw.

The next item for the casing of the target had to be ready by the following morning, when the CIA chief would deliver the invitation from the U.S. head of mission to the Soviet head of mission. This would provide an opportunity for collecting imagery close in from the courtyard so the entry team would know which doors were the most likely candidates for accessing the main building and Sanctum.

Woody and I left the safe house together, and made a surveillance detection run—an hour-long drive through town and some of the surrounding countryside—to make certain we were not being followed. We ended up at the local CIA chief's house. As with the residences of most important foreigners in the city, it was located in a walled compound complete with a gate guard. Once inside, we were directed to a car parked out of sight at the back of the property. The car bore diplomatic license plates and would be the one used to deliver the invitation.

The job at hand was to modify the interior of the vehicle to accommodate a remotely triggered commercial video camera with a wide-angle twenty-eight-millimeter lens. We used this camera often for photo surveillance because it was small and lightweight.

Smallwood retrieved a bag of tools provided by the chief, and we set to work. First we took the seats out of the car and set

them on the lawn. Then, the passenger headrest was separated
from the seat. We removed the cover from the headrest and
took out some of the padding. We were carefully measuring the
size of the cavity needed for the camera when a loud bell rang
at the gate.

The chief's wife quickly came out of the house. "It's the
Swedish chargé, a friend of mine. I can't send her away! Come
inside. Quickly."

Smallwood and I swept up the tools, set the disassembled headrest and camera inside the car, and dashed into the house. We
heard the sound of two women talking.

A female chargé, I reflected with pride.

My appreciation for the progress of women in the arena of
world diplomacy ended abruptly when we heard the yapping of
more than one small dog. As we stood in the darkened bathroom at the back of the house, we heard the dogs running down
the hallway at full throttle, their little claws clicking on the hard
tile floors.

The chargé was in hot pursuit of her dogs, calling them back
and laughing.

As I saw the first dog rounding the corner, I quickly closed and
locked the bathroom door. Smallwood and I held our breath as
the yapping dogs assaulted the door with their tiny paws.

After the chargé and her pesky entourage finally departed,
Woody and I returned to our task. We removed more of the foam
padding from the headrest, creating a hollow space large enough
to insert the camera. Once it was in place, we covered the lens
with a polarizing material that concealed the lens but allowed the
camera to see through it. We then put the cover back on the
headrest, cutting a slit just long enough for the lens to shoot
through. Putting the headrest back onto the metal posts that con-
nected the unit to the seat, we ran the remote shutter cable down
through one of the posts. Then the cable was routed just under

the seat upholstery and exited near the center console, where it could easily be manipulated by the driver.

An hour later, the CIA chief returned home. He walked around his car, admiring our handiwork. After asking about the technical capabilities of the video camera, and assuring himself that it was not easily seen, he decided to take the cam-car for a test drive. We piled into the backseat with another bag of equipment, and he beeped the horn at his gate. The guard swung the gates open slowly and we headed off into the city.

Nearing the central bazaar, the chief began videotaping the scenery, slowing the car down as he did. We, in turn, pulled out our small, pocket-sized video monitor and made sure that the detail we needed was there at slow speeds. The chief pulled into and out of several parking areas, simulating the entry to and circling of the Soviet compound that he would be undertaking. Because of the position of the camera, he would have to be careful to circle in a counterclockwise direction.

Upon returning to his residence, we all reviewed the tape.

The images were sharp and crisp. Perfect.

The next morning, the plan was set in motion.

The modified vehicle, with the CIA chief again at its wheel, made a call on the Soviet compound. After he showed his identity papers to the guard at the gates on the street, the gates swung open, and the car pulled into the courtyard inside the compound.

Behind the high stone walls, hidden from casual scrutiny, stood a compound with three main buildings in it. The center building itself was by far the grandest and was conspicuous by its size. A second, smaller building appeared to be a security and motor-pool building. The third structure had a number of people moving in and out of it and was probably the logistical center, with a cafeteria and other support offices.

As the car moved into the compound and circled slowly left around the courtyard before parking, the video camera in the passenger side headrest recorded the scene outside—the doors, the locks, the antennas, the windows, the guards—all of the information that the entry team would want to study close-up.

The chief got out of the car, walked up the steps of the center building, and entered briefly. He left an envelope for the head of the mission with the receptionist. Inside was an invitation to an official function being given jointly by the host government and the U.S. Mission. Then he returned to his car and slowly drove away.

Step one had been a piece of cake.

Later that evening, I rendered TUGBOAT unrecognizable once again. Disguised as a local cop, he approached the guard at the gate of the Soviet compound. It was past normal business hours and the center building was presumed to be empty. After presenting his ID card to the guard, TUGBOAT explained politely that he was conducting an Internal Ministry security check of all foreign facilities in the city. He further explained to the guard that he would need access to the compound in order to inspect and check many of the exterior building locks.

When the guard hesitated, TUGBOAT reached into his pocket and handed the guard a considerable roll of money, wrapped in a rubber band. He knew that the guard would be more cooperative if encouraged with a bribe, and when he told him that there might even be a second inspection—that is, the opportunity for another roll of bills—the guard smiled and opened the gate enough to allow TUGBOAT to slip inside.

It took only forty-five minutes for TUGBOAT to make calibrations of all of the exterior locks our team would be facing in the next phase of the operation. This technique was a quick way to determine exactly how to cut a key to fit each particular lock.

The locks on these doors would have to be opened rapidly when the team went in to make the snatch.

When he was finished, TUGBOAT, with a nod to the guard, departed the compound, with the specifications we would need to make all the necessary keys.

I made sure that all of the blinds were closed, then walked through the living room of the safe house, down the hallway, and stood by the door to the garage.

The sound of a motor out on the narrow street and then on the other side of the mildewed plaster wall had alerted me that a vehicle was pulling in. I was sure they had arrived, but waited until the garage door slammed shut before opening the door slightly and peering through into the half-light.

I could just see the dark figures emerge as they slowly exited the Land Rover. Five of them filed past me into the dimly lit room. It was an eerie scene; five strangers unrecognizable as Americans stood before me wearing the facial features, skin tones, and ethnic clothing of the local population. There was an uneasy moment while I scrutinized their appearance.

"Excellent," I murmured, exhaling with relief. The team had just completed their first trial outing and had come back none the worse for wear. Before deploying for this operation, they had visited our disguise labs at headquarters to be measured and fitted. As the OTS officer on the ground here, I would be responsible, if necessary, for any fine-tuning of the materials. Sometimes, even major revisions were called for in the field. The work done by my colleagues at headquarters, though, had been excellent. I required each team member to do a slow 360-degree turn before my eyes, and saw no flaws in their transformations.

The team had made several dry run exercises at one of our remote training sites south of Washington, D.C. Disguise officers had attended as well, performing final fittings and training. After loading into the ops van with all of their equipment, they had rehearsed making their way to a mock-up of the target. Once inside that courtyard, they had exited the van and practiced breaching the locks into the target building.

While the summer heat and humidity on the southeast coast of the United States could be oppressive at times, the high humidity here was causing us some concern, and so, tonight, we had decided to test the disguise systems under local conditions. We drove and walked around for an hour, during which the disguises held up well. But I was still concerned whether the team could stand to wear them for as long as required.

"Can we take off these getups?" one of the team members asked as soon as we returned to the safe house.

I knew the disguises were uncomfortable and a little strange-feeling. One has a certain paranoia when wearing disguises in public for the first time. These guys were obviously not used to wearing them and would need more practice. I would send them out in public a few more times so they could develop not only their stamina, but also their confidence in how well the disguises worked. When the time arrived for them to go to work in the Soviet compound, I didn't want them distracted from the job because they were uncomfortable or worried about how they looked.

"Sure, you can take them off," I said. "Just be sure to keep track of your materials so you can quickly get back into character—your own character, not someone else's." They laughed, thinking that this was funny, although they knew I was serious.

I went into the kitchen and brought out a six-pack of cold Heineken, an import not available on the local market. Joe Muldoon, ever the helpful facilitator, had supplied the precious loot out of his operational stash.

From my world travels, I knew that each station and base had an area where the "goodies" were kept—usually under lock and key. The goodies varied from city to city and country to country, but they were always things unavailable locally that could be used to sweeten a relationship or grease a palm. In the Muslim world, it might be liquor and *Playboy* magazines; in Africa, American designer jeans. In this country, where there were few imports and scorching temperatures, it was imported beer. Each member picked up an ice-cold can, and we sat down together in the living room to review the plan.

"It was pretty hot with all that stuff on," Eric Cooper admitted as he downed a couple of gulps of beer. "Hope we don't have to wear them for long."

With most of the fragments for the operation in place, Eric's next job was to prepare a coherent minute-by-minute scenario that would lay out for each member of the team his particular job. This detailed blueprint would constitute the official operational plan and would be put on the wire to Langley and the Citadel for final approval

"Okay," said Cooper. "Let's get started."

He began with the reminder that this job had to be performed surreptitiously and quickly. The operational goal, of course, was to remove the KAPELLE device from the second floor of the Soviet stronghold. The machine would then be transported out of the country and put into the care of another set of U.S. intelligence officers. They would be responsible for moving it through official channels to the Citadel, its final destination.

On a designated Sunday evening in the near future, we knew the entire Soviet staff planned to be away at a hunting camp one hundred kilometers south, located on a tropical belt along the base of the mountain range. Our local CIA chief had arranged, through friendly government contacts, for the Soviets to be the honored guests of one of the local nabobs, a cousin to the major chieftain, for a weekend hunt. In addition, the country's top politicians would be attending the event. This was a great honor for the Soviets, and none of them could turn down the invitation without offending the local chieftain and central government. The tiger in these regions was an endangered species, so hunting of this type was rarely done anymore. The great *tarai* at the private hunting preserve was boggy, malarial, thickly overgrown, and remained one of the few sportsmen's paradises on this side of the border. Russians are avid hunters anyway, and as we had hoped, the whole contingent had jumped at the chance to do it in style like the minor princes, a century ago: aboard elephants following native "beaters," who would move around in the bush ahead of them on foot, scaring the tiger into the hunters' range.

The perimeter security at the Soviets' gated compound would be left to the *chokadar,* who by this time had been well taken care of by TUGBOAT. He continued to believe TUGBOAT was a member of the local constabulary concerned with maintaining good security discipline on the property. After the Soviets had departed, TUGBOAT would alert the gate man that he would be bringing a team of security experts in after hours to do a surprise inspection of the compound.

The second line of defense for the center building in the compound, and ultimately the KGB's Sanctum, was the various layers of carefully designed and constructed physical security. These included the sophisticated key-operated locks on the exterior doors, for which duplicate keys had already been made. Then there was the little problem of the hidden button for the electric lock that opened a particular interior door. This door was on the second floor and looked like any other of the locked doors. It led to the cramped anteroom and the eight-inch-thick steel door leading to the reinforced concrete vault.

Cooper stopped his narrative, allowing himself time to jot something down on the yellow lined pad in his lap.

I could see that he was calculating times for each step and had a stopwatch in his left hand. This guy was a pro.

The vault would have a combination tumbler lock securing two hardened-steel dead bolts, he explained. This was it—the entrance to the Sanctum, where the KAPELLE was bolted down inside the steel enclosure of the Hole, with yet another steel door secured by a special hydraulic lock.

He started and stopped his stopwatch one last time, then made a note.

The members of the crack entry team had been extensively cross-trained. By this time, they had made sure they were fully prepared to defeat all these security measures once inside the compound. They knew that no security device is impervious to unauthorized entry, if left unattended, and every physical security device is rated by the time it takes to defeat it. Generally, the time is measured in hours. This team, however, typically measured its "time on target" in minutes and seconds.

The team's expertise had been built through years of effort. It operated on an almost military concept of target analysis, first obtaining hard intelligence about the security devices it would face. This was augmented by the acquisition or replication of the devices themselves. Finally, it developed unique means and techniques to defeat the security devices, often spending millions of dollars on multiyear contracts to add new technical weapons to its arsenal. In the end, the team had nothing short of the technical capability to penetrate any security device that could be manufactured.

I had always wondered how the Agency deprogrammed these guys when they retired. In civilian life, what could they possibly do other than get into trouble?

Cooper continued with his detailed plan for the operation.

The team would enter the compound in a van that was being driven into the country by yet another CIA officer, using commercial cover. His only assignment was to drive the van into and then back out of the country, with the stolen device on board when the time came to leave. The trip was long and arduous, over a road built by the local tribes using primitive methods. It had been hacked out of the jungles and mountain passes by hand and paved in many places using crossed sections of trees like garden stepping stones. Even if everything went off without a hitch, the journey would take days.

Upon arrival here, in the next day or two, the CIA officer was to deliver the vehicle to a garage rented in town through a local contact. Then he would wait in a hotel until the operation was completed. Once he successfully delivered the van to the garage, it would be freshly painted with an easily removable paint, decorated with the logo of a local business, then scuffed and dirtied up and given local license plates. The supplies for the temporary paint job, the logos, and the license plates had all been sent in separately from home. I would assist another technical officer from our OTS base in their application. After the operation, the process would be reversed—the van returned to its original appearance, the phony license plates removed. It was not unlike putting a disguise on the van—it would accomplish the same thing. The U.S. government would have deniability, and in the end the van, like the six foreign faces, would vanish.

The van would contain a very special large wooden crate, custom-built by our lab to hold and cradle the delicate Soviet KAPELLE device. The crate would be stenciled with a fictitious commercial logo and would have the appropriate customs markings and tags, prepared by our documents and graphics experts. These would show that the contents, supposedly a piece of testing equipment, had been brought into the country legally and could be readily exported as well. The crate had been specifically sized to fit into an official-looking container once it was delivered into official U.S. intelligence channels in the neighboring country.

Cooper, who would be the driver in and out of the compound during the operation, would be in charge of safekeeping the disguises and entry equipment.

"Jonna and I will pick up the van at 1930 hours at the garage and ensure that the crate, the tools, and the disguise materials are on board," he said. "After we put on our disguises, we will head off to pick up each team member. Everyone should be in the van by 1940 hours. Then we will head back down the valley toward town to pick up TUGBOAT. He will be waiting at the edge of the bazaar wearing his disguise. I've shown each of you his photo so that you can help us recognize him. We will pick him up at 1950 hours. Then we'll head for the stronghold using an indirect route to ensure there is no surveillance. We have done two dry runs in our Land Rover, and the timing works out fine."

Cooper, a natural leader in his element, was outlining the plan as if he'd known it all his life. "Once we arrive at the stronghold, the *chokadar* will be expecting us and should open the gate without hesitation. TUGBOAT will ask the guard to depart immediately and will hand him more cash than he has ever seen in his life. He will never need to return, as he'll have enough money to take his family with him."

Cooper took a long pull from his beer. "Once we are inside the compound, our workday starts." He smiled that charming smile. "You assholes have all had plenty of practice to get ready for this day."

He swung his gaze around the room, scrutinizing the other four members with the pride of a patriarch inspecting his clan. "I expect you to go through those locks and doors like a hot knife through butter—only faster."

I understood the entire plan now and fully appreciated all the work that had been put into it. "Since you will be hidden in the back of the van, you won't need to put on the disguise materials until about five minutes out from the mission gates," I said. "Does the van have air-conditioning?"

Cooper looked at me as though I was a prima donna. "No, there wasn't anything with AC where we acquired this heap. For five minutes, I think we can tough it out."

In the cooler evening air, the disguises should not pose a problem. It was only in the crowded, stuffy van that they would be uncomfortable. Cooper and I would be in our disguises all through the operation, but in the van we would be up front by the windows, where we could get some fresh air while it was moving. It was my job to handle any emergencies with the various disguises, and he was the lookout and wheelman if we had to get away quickly, so he would stick by the van while we were in the compound. TUGBOAT would be with him in case there was a need to deal with any concerned locals who might happen by. Once the entry team and I were through the main gate and in— past the first of the exterior locks—the team's disguises could come off. And after the KAPELLE device was in the van, the team members could either don their disguises again and leave in the van with Cooper, TUGBOAT, and me, or exit the compound any way they chose as long as the coast looked clear. If there was a flap and they couldn't reach the van, they would all go over the back wall, where there was easy access from the inside, and melt into the night.

And I'll be leading the charge, I thought. If for some reason the Soviets came home while we were still there, these guys were not going to believe how fast a woman could move, even one who looked like a local guy!

The team members would then leave the country incrementally over the next few days, making sure to adhere to their cover patterns.

The only member of the team potentially at risk then would be TUGBOAT, if the KGB discovered his connection to the theft. Our exfiltration planning for TUGBOAT and his family was rapidly falling into place. TUGBOAT, however, hoped this would not be necessary, and so did I. Pro-western by nature, he was helping us for all the right reasons—not for money, but because he did not like the presence of representatives of the "Evil Empire" in his native land. He was risking a lot.

All the bases seemed to be covered for our final ops plan, so I left Cooper and the guys talking about the challenges presented by the various locks that had been calibrated or otherwise prepared for, and I went into the adjacent room to do a final check of the disguise materials. I found minor adjustments needed to be made, and worked on those.

As soon as I had arrived in-country, I had received a cable from headquarters asking me to round up the team's travel documents and photograph them. The film was sent immediately back to headquarters by courier to aid in the preparation of the TUGBOAT exfiltration plan. The border cachets and visas in the team's passports served as exemplars for TUGBOAT and his family's alias travel documents if they needed to escape. The turnaround time in getting the false papers back had been record-breaking.

I had recognized Tony's touch in a number of the communications coming out of headquarters that addressed the details of the operation. Usually a hands-off manager, he clearly recognized the critical stakes involved with this one. I was sure he was following it closely, as were his own superiors. I knew that Tony would be paying special attention to the parts that dealt with the security afforded by well-designed disguise-and-documentation packages and good planning. I could just imagine him, his hooded green-hazel eyes steadily scrutinizing the cable traffic, every now and then putting in a call to a subordinate or getting

1. A flask of spy dust, with a brush for its application.

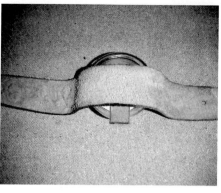

2. KGB counterintelligence officers carried flasks of spy dust in their belts.

3. A KGB artist's rendition of how spy dust was applied (the man painting the doormat). The man on the chair is photographing documents, and he is being surveilled by the man upstairs.

4. The lobby of the Renaissance Mayflower Hotel in Washington, D
It was here that Aldrich Ames wait
for his KGB contact ready to betray
CIA secrets in April 1985.

5. The logo of the OTS's
Special Surveillance Team.

6. Jonna on safari on the Subcontinent, 1987.

7. After the death of his first wife in 1986, Tony bought himself a fast car and threw himself even more deeply into his job at the CIA.

8 and 9. Two views of a tree-stump concealment with a high-tech sensor inside. This is an alleged CIA KAPELLE-type sensor deployed in the Soviet Union and subsequently discovered by the KGB Second Chief Directorate.

10. 2430 E St. NW, Washington, D.C., the original headquarters of the OSS, then the CIA, until 1961. Tony and Jonna were based in the building in the bottom left-hand corner of the complex when they were working together for the Graphics and Authentication Division of the OTS during the 1980s.

11. Lubyanka, also known as The Center, headquarters of the KGB on Dzerzhinsky Square, Moscow, in the 1980s.

12 and 13. Two KGB surveillance shots of the CIA spy Adolf Tolkachev, code-named SPHERE, being ambushed in June 1985.

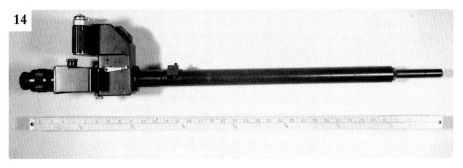

14, 15, and 16. A silent drill (14) used by the KGB to implant a wall camera and tubes from an adjoining room to the target's room, and (15 and 16) wall camera components.

17. A KGB illustration of their surveillance of Corporal Clayton J. Lonetree being compromised by a female Soviet agent, a "swallow," as filmed through a wall camera concealment.

18. Vitaly Yurchenko, former head of the KGB's foreign counterintelligence. He defected to the U.S. in August 1985, then defected back to the Soviet Union the following year, and is now a security guard for a Russian bank.

19. The KGB display of spy gear allegedly issued to TRINITY by the CIA. According to the KGB, these include: pens and Bic lighters that concealed small cameras; a pen with an ampoule of poison hidden in its barrel so TRINITY could take his own life if he was caught; a variety of shortwave radios for receiving OWVL broadcasts, and One Time Pads (OTPs) used to decipher those broadcasts; secret writing materials, instructions, and diagrams on microfilm showing dead drop and signal sites for use by TRINITY and his CIA handlers; a collection of dead drop concealment devices used to pass materials to TRINITY and for him to pass intelligence materials back—an old wooden block, a hollow cobblestone, a piece of used electrical cable; a selection of old car parts in which TRINITY could store his spy materials and hide them in his garage; a stereo headset in which miniature cameras could be hidden; a pen in which a long strip of microfilm could have been kept; a small-caliber semi-automatic pistol and a stun gun.

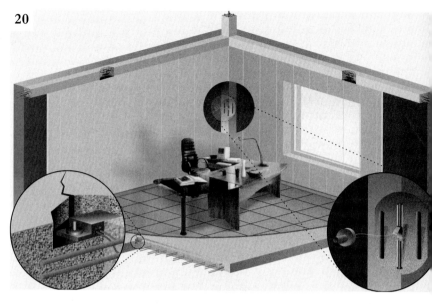

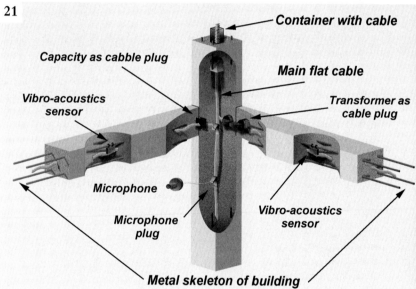

Container with cable

Capacity as cabble plug

Main flat cable

Vibro-acoustics sensor

Transformer as cable plug

Microphone

Microphone plug

Vibro-acoustics sensor

Metal skeleton of building

20, 21 and (opposite) 22. Three views of the KGB official bugging plans for the new U.S. Embassy in Moscow. 20 and 21 show the bugs in a typical office, and how they were integrated into the building structure itself. 22 illustrates how the tunnels were constructed several stories beneath the embassy, and that a KGB senior officer could actually walk upright through one of them. He is wearing his dress uniform and carrying a briefcase with the latest intercepted intelligence gleaned from the bugs. In one of the smaller tunnels above, a KGB technician is installing wires to activate more of the bugs.

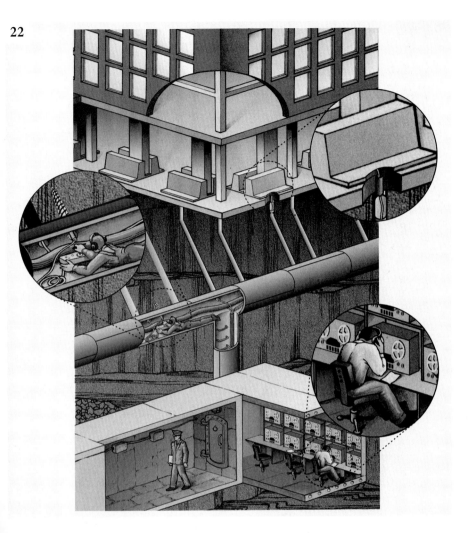

23. The crest of the SVR's "11 Institute" (note the symbol of the two-headed eagle, now used as the emblem for the Russian republic), the KGB unit that developed, implemented, and manned the audio penetration plans against the new U.S. Embassy in Moscow. They are still bugging the Americans today.

24. The emblem of the Technical Surveillance Group of the CIA's OTS, responsible for audio and visual bugs.

25, 26, and 27. The Vienna Procedure. As Tony and Gerald Swazie noted, many spies came to Vienna during the Cold War years to conduct their clandestine business. These three images relate to a meeting set up in the late seventies between the KGB and their agent John Walker. In order to ensure that he wasn't being surveilled by either the CIA or Austrian counterintelligence before their meeting, they devised complicated routes for him to walk (25), always under the watchful eye of the members of the KGB's First Chief Directorate. If any suspicious activity was spotted, the meeting would be postponed. Walker was instructed to make his way from his hotel (26) to the route's starting point at a kitchen cabinet store (27), and "for easy identification please carry your camera bag on your left and hold a small paper bag in your right hand."

28. This alleged CIA One Time Pad (OTP) was reportedly used by the CIA's clandestine agents working in Moscow to decipher One Way Voice Link (OWVL) shortwave broadcasts from the West. These broadcasts were supposed to have come on a preset schedule and on a variety of frequencies. They would have been impossible for the KGB to decipher because a different page in the OTP was used for each broadcast. In spite of their intercept capabilities, it would also have been extremely difficult for the KGB to determine who was receiving the broadcast in a given geographic area because the agent under suspicion would have been trained to record the broadcast as quickly as possible to avoid tracking by triangulation. The agent would decode the number groups later to obtain his new instructions, then hide the OTP and the microfilm containing the broadcast schedule in case he was stopped and searched.

29. Moscow, July 1988. A view through Tony's rearview mirror. The small car between the tip of his elbow and the bus carries a KGB surveillance team.

30. Jonna at the Great Wall of China, September 1988.

31. Jonna and Che Guevara in Havana, November 1988.

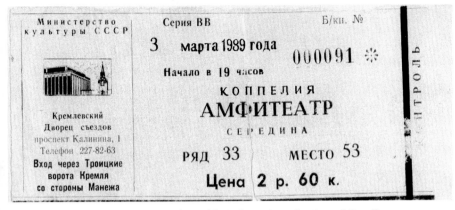

32. One of our tickets to the Bolshoi Theater's production of *Coppélia* at the Palace of Congresses.

33. Inside the Kremlin. On the left, the Palace of Congresses, the scene of the exfiltration of ORB and his wife. On the right, the Trinity Tower: the entrance, in conjunction with the footbridge behind it, was used as a KGB chokepoint, and it was here that the spy dust on Clint Bradley's and Rose Cohen's shoes set off the sensor.

34. The CIA Trailblazer in his studio, 1997.

on the secure line to a senior headquarters officer if he saw a flaw or wanted to make a suggestion. "It's in the details," he always counseled. "Take care of the details, and the rest will take care of itself."

Heading back into the living room, I heard loud laughter. I caught the punch line to a very risqué joke and tried to pretend that I hadn't heard it. Working with a bunch of guys, no matter how pleasant they tried to be, was always a bit of a dance. It was so tempting to try and be one of them, but that never really worked.

Anyway, it was an old joke. I'd already heard it.

The evening light had faded behind the looming mountaintops; one moment we had been bathed in liquid gold, then the darkness had fallen quickly and quietly, blanketing the small town in a blackish murk.

When we lost the light, the temperature and humidity usually fell quickly. We were counting on that to help keep all the disguises intact.

The van moved down the valley road at a slow but steady speed. There was some local traffic and the occasional oxcart or farm vehicle, but the real obstacle lay ahead in the valley: the low-lying smoke from the cook fires being stoked for the evening meals. Acrid and stinging, it caused eyes to tear and throats to burn.

We had already picked up the team members; they were gathered in the back of the van. They were putting on their disguises, helping each other as necessary, and getting their equipment ready.

I was satisfied with what I was seeing from my perch on the crate just behind the driver's seat. We all knew that the clock was ticking. Butterflies were beginning their dance in my stomach.

The van made a rolling stop, and TUGBOAT stepped in and sat down in the front passenger seat across from Eric Cooper.

"Five minutes," Cooper called out. His arm flashed skin much darker than his own as he handed TUGBOAT a small goatskin purse.

TUGBOAT opened it and counted the bills inside, then nodded and put the purse in his pocket. This was the *baksheesh* for the guard—the offer that the man would not be able to refuse.

Cooper drove carefully, knowing full well that we could not have an accident or be stopped for any reason. As the van rolled through the outskirts of the town and headed for the bazaar, we passed a group of western tourists assembled in front of one of the fabled temples. For a moment, I longed to be one of them, admiring the ancient landmarks and heading off to an evening of good food, drink, and pleasant conversation.

I watched TUGBOAT and Cooper sitting up front in their disguises and was satisfied with how convincing they both looked in this early evening light and under the occasional mercury-vapor lamp.

TUGBOAT's disguise materials were much improved from those I had improvised for the first part of the operation. Having had some additional supplies shipped in, I had also taught him how to put it on himself with the help of his wife so that we didn't have to meet clandestinely in advance.

"Somebody roll the windows up," a voice growled from the back of the van. "The smoke is killing our eyes."

Cooper complied, and gave the van some more gas. He knew that we couldn't keep those windows up for long; the temperature in the van was already climbing to an uncomfortable level.

The Soviet compound was on a quiet winding street on the outskirts of town. By the time we arrived at the gate, Cooper had been able to open the window, giving those of us in the back some relief.

The gate man was standing ready for our arrival, according to TUGBOAT's instructions. He swung open the large ornate iron gate just as we pulled up, and we coasted on through, coming to a gentle stop on the gravel courtyard.

The gate was already being swung closed.

Unfortunately, Cooper and the *chokadar* had misjudged their distances, and the heavy metal gate caught the van squarely just in front of the back right bumper. It bounced off with a mighty clang! We all froze for a second. I fought back an overwhelming urge to laugh at the absurdity of the situation. After all our planning, to be foiled by a metal gate!

Cooper coolly slipped the van into gear and moved it forward so the guard could finish his job. Once the gate was closed, the van swung around and began backing up to the main door of the center building. Before he'd come to a stop, the team members had the back doors open and were already jumping out with their tools and materials slung over their shoulders in black canvas tool bags. One of them carried a full load of ropes and winches, looking not unlike a Sherpa—the mountain guides western tourists like to hire—ready to begin a high-altitude mountain trek.

I quickly jumped out the back door too, and glanced around in time to see that TUGBOAT already had the guard to the side, over by the gate. He was softly and slowly giving the gate man instructions as he handed him the wad of money. The man nodded his head vigorously but could not take his eyes off the largesse he was holding. It must have been more money than he could have earned in a lifetime and would set him up with a herd of goats in some remote spot in the mountains where no one would ever find him. He could surround himself with his extended family, live out his days in comfort and leisure, and never have to come to this town again.

I witnessed this in an instant, and before I could look back to

see what the team members were doing, they were already
through the locks on the front door. The keys that had been prepared in advance fit perfectly, and the men had unlocked the
doors as though they did it every day. Two of them moved into
the foyer of the building, the other two returned to the back of
the van, where they unloaded the empty wooden crate gently
onto the ground. Then they brought the crate in and positioned it
on the floor in the center of the main foyer, readying it to receive
the KAPELLE machine.

As I moved up the steps, following them into the building, I
could see them in the unlit foyer removing their disguises and
putting the pieces down with great care. We had agreed in
advance on the positions of each team member's materials. They
had found a convenient place at the base of a marble pedestal
holding a white bust of Lenin and placed their stuff at twelve,
three, six, and nine o'clock around the base. No detail had been
overlooked in this plan—if the wrong man picked up the wrong
materials, it could take precious minutes to sort it out. Looking
at the arrangement around the bust, I longed for my camera—the
image was comical.

I positioned myself near the disguises so I could assist anyone
on the way out, or be ready to gather up the materials quickly
if needed. My own disguise would remain on throughout
the operation—it could prove useful if there was a need for
another "local" on the grounds or at the gate. I wanted to
focus on only the team and their needs, not worry about my
own stuff.

As I took my position, the four-man team was already on their
way up the flight of stairs, running to the second floor. They
were wearing special footwear: dark shoes with moleskin soles
that allowed them great flexibility but left no prints. They also
wore gloves, but these were more like the gloves that surgeons
use—powdered inside, but colored outside so that they looked

like human skin. Again, no fingerprints, and just as important, no sweating skin. It was a narrow, winding stairway, and I wondered how hard it would be to haul the KAPELLE back down. I knew from our planning sessions that they already had a good idea of the exact location of the Sanctum, thanks to the casings we had done earlier and the added advantage of a set of plans of the building provided by TUGBOAT. They also had the benefit of prior experience in regard to the typical location of the hidden button that opened the electric latch on the next door. Still, all of this information was just collateral when you were approaching the real thing.

One notable thing about the Soviets: when they established a procedure, they tended to use it without deviation. KGB defectors like Victor Sheymov had confirmed that the cipher locks on some of the KGB's most sensitive secured areas were all set on the same combination that never changed. This was both for convenience's sake and because most Sanctums had round-the-clock guards. The entry team thought they might even know the numbers, but if that combination didn't work, the team was prepared to force entry.

In the interests of speed, and if all else failed, the team could use a special device they had brought along to breach the vault door. They were already planning to use it against the hydraulic lock on the steel cipher enclosure. Much as a safecracker has to know just where to drill a combination lock on a safe, one had to know just where to pierce the vault door and the hydraulic lock on the cipher enclosure to open them rapidly.

Safecrackers in the movies sometimes use nitroglycerin to crack a safe quickly. The KGB and the CIA had many more sophisticated techniques at their disposal. The entry team had a device with them that OTS had encrypted PLASMA. It could fire a tiny shaped charge of explosive through a steel door and sever the exact part of the lock mechanism that would allow it to be opened immediately.

I heard two muffled thuds in the minutes the team was upstairs. PLASMA.

I looked out through the door into the graveled courtyard. There, taking in the evening air, squatted Cooper and TUG-BOAT, down on their haunches, smoking cigarettes, and looking to all the world like two of the local gentry passing gossip. They were actually being watchful lookouts, but they didn't see a need to acknowledge the noises. Our van was carefully parked out of sight from the street. Through the metal gates to the compound, I could see local traffic moving slowly down it, lights on, a smoky haze covering everything. Nothing unusual.

Suddenly, a pedestrian stopped outside the gates and called to our two sentries, motioning them over to the gate. Cooper gave TUGBOAT a long, slow look, and the local got up and walked over to the gate in an unhurried, casual manner. There was a brief conversation through the steel bars, and I saw TUGBOAT remove his credential and show it to the man; then there was a handshake. The pedestrian stepped back several feet and gave TUGBOAT a slight bow, then moved off into the darkness of the street. TUG-BOAT strolled back over to Cooper and squatted back down, lighting another cigarette. Things looked to be under control.

But sweat was now pouring down my back, trickling past my waistband and down past the small of my back.

I looked up toward the landing on the second floor and saw two team members rigging a tripod device on the rail of the open balcony above the foyer. The tripod had been carried in a sort of black quiver with a strap that was slung across the shoulder of the biggest guy. They pulled short pieces out of the quiver and screwed them together, forming the three legs. A jointed mechanism united these pieces at the head of the tripod. Clamps were pulled out of another bag and locked onto the legs, then attached to the railing. The one who I had thought looked like a Sherpa, with all of those ropes, began attaching them to the tripod rigging. Then they began attaching the bulky KAPELLE machine to the tripod with a lanyard so they could use the rigging like a miniature crane to lower the device down to the floor of the foyer.

Suddenly, one of the legs of the tripod wrenched away from the railing, and the whole apparatus began to reverberate. The big guy reached out and grabbed the collapsing leg, reattached the clamp, tightened it again, and shot the "Sherpa" a look. They hesitated for a moment, testing the problematic leg, then proceeded with their work.

I looked at my watch and realized that it had not been ten minutes since the van had stopped moving and the team had gone to work. The sweat was puddling in my gloves and my shoes. I felt as if I were in an undersea diving suit.

The machine dangled almost at eye level in front of me now, swinging gently on the rope harness that they had passed around it. Just then the entire team flew down the stairs, still moving noiselessly like cats, gently cradling the machine into the crate and bolting it down.

I was amazed that the infamous and sophisticated top-secret device looked like two decrepit old manual typewriters wired and bolted together with a large basket of rotor wheels mounted to the top.

As the team moved past me with the crate, gently sliding it back into the van, I took a quick turn around the base of Lenin to ensure that no souvenirs had been left behind. By the time I got back out into the courtyard, I saw TUGBOAT opening the gate for two of the team, while the "Sherpa" and the big guy headed to the back of the compound, where they would be going over the wall.

Cooper and I drove through the gate and headed toward the outskirts of the city to the garage, where the van would be repainted and the crate stenciled and documented. It would be driven across the border in less than twenty-four hours.

I found myself feeling sorry for TUGBOAT. The casual pedestrian had turned out to be an acquaintance of TUGBOAT's, and had been looking for another friend of his, the security guard. The coincidence would forever alter the lives of TUGBOAT and his family. Although the pedestrian had apparently not recognized TUGBOAT, we could not risk him later piecing together the voice and general profile of the man he had talked to at the gate that night. As a friend of the missing security guard's, the pedestrian might well be visited by KGB officers to find out what he knew. The U.S. government could not afford to deal with any blowback from this operation.

A week later, we exfiltrated TUGBOAT and his family out of the country to a place they had never seen and to a culture they would spend years trying to understand.

To the best of my knowledge, they were never able to return to their homeland.

"Roll up your window!" yelled Les Williams as he jammed on the brakes. He was barely able to stop before colliding with a dark Volga that had pulled into their path.

The oncoming car, filled with burly men in dark coats and fur hats, had shot out of nowhere, forming a roadblock in front of them on the narrow street. The occupants leaped out and ran toward the two CIA officers' green Toyota.

Gina Tolbert quickly rolled up her window. "It's KGB! Lock the doors!"

She remembered for a fraction of a second the training they had received in the months before they departed for Moscow. There had been two weeks of instruction in defensive driving skills—how to handle hostile roadblocks by crashing through them; how to do a reverse 180-degree turn while the car was still moving forward and drive away from danger—but there had been no time to employ either of those or any other tactics they'd learned.

As more cars swooped in, they found themselves surrounded by more than a dozen Russians. Camera flashes were going off, blinding Williams and Tolbert even more than the headlights that illuminated the dark street.

One of the Russians rapped on the driver's window with a hard object, demanding that Williams open the door. Others were pressing against the passenger's side of the car, trying the doors in an effort to get inside. More camera flashes.

"Sit tight," Williams said through clenched jaws. "Maybe they'll go away."

From what she saw, too frightened to move, Tolbert didn't think so.

The men outside started rocking the car, slowly at first, then violently. The man at the driver's window was still banging his metal tool and yelling in Russian. After half a minute that seemed much longer, someone shouted an order. The rocking stopped, and two bulky figures stepped up with clubs. They commenced to smash the car windows.

Williams moved protectively toward his partner. "Cover your eyes!"

Tolbert screamed as the men, seconds later, reached in through the broken windows and unlocked the front doors. The two CIA officers were yanked out of the car as strong arms and hands grabbed and pulled at each of them. The same hands clawed at their clothing and reached for their faces and ears, searching for ear inductors from electronic transmitters or receivers, disguise materials, miniature cameras, and any other "spy gear."

As they were led to the waiting cars, the CIA officers were able to exchange a brief look. Williams silently mouthed the words *He's dead,* and Tolbert nodded that she understood. Their local asset, code-named DOLPHIN, was the only other person who knew the drop site for this evening. It had never been used before and had come out of the CIA's new Moscow inventory that had only recently been made available for operations. They both knew that the local agent would not have given up the information to lead the KGB to the site. The previous year he had asked for the "L" pill, in case he was ever apprehended, and had been fully prepared to take his own life rather than endure what his own country-men would put him through before executing him. Williams and Tolbert had every reason to believe that their asset had done just that when the KGB closed in on him. But then—how had they known to come to this site?

Gina Tolbert looked down at her new spring suit. They had just come from an evening at the ballet watching an enchanting Bolshoi performance of *Swan Lake,* and it was the first time she had had a chance to wear it. The pale gray suit jacket was ripped down the front, and two of the buttons were missing. As she tried to shake off the heavy hand holding her right shoulder, she was suddenly enraged. "You goddamned thugs, get away from me!" she cried. "Get your filthy hands off of me!"

She could not bear to think of what had happened to DOLPHIN, or what his sweet wife, Olga, and young son, Sasha, would have to endure. She found her legs had gone weak and her breath labored; Tolbert was more scared than she had ever been in her life.

Williams decided not to make it easy, and struggled with his captors.

The head of the KGB group spoke gruffly in Russian, issuing an order.

"Fuck you," Williams responded in perfect Russian.

The dramatic arrest was the typical practice of the Second Chief Directorate, the internal security division of the KGB, complete with cameras to document thoroughly their successes against foreign spies. The KGB museum in the block of buildings behind Lubyanka featured a series of exhibits documenting the arrests of traitors and spies—all punctuated with dozens of flash photographs of "criminals" with frightened eyes surrounded by flailing, grabbing arms. Williams and Tolbert would be taken to Lubyanka for their interrogation, but they wouldn't be given the honor of touring the counterintelligence museum.

Their pictures would be displayed in the museum shortly, and their photographs would be published in the newspaper the following day, thereby ending their covert operational careers, at least in the Soviet arena. Also part of the new museum display would be something Tolbert had thrown out the window at the drop site just before all hell broke loose. It looked like a weathered piece of board, but was actually tradecraft. Some of the "spy material" found in a hidden cavity would be carefully laid out among the museum's artifacts.

The KGB had kept their recent winning record against U.S. intelligence intact.

FIVE

WASHINGTON, D.C.

Spring 1987

Tony

The phone lines in the laboratories of OTS's South Building complex were smoking. Furtive looks were exchanged in the morning staff meeting—was today the day? And then it happened: the first fine spring day had finally arrived.

"Marina Day" was spontaneously and unofficially declared throughout the office. A single word was spoken into the telephones like a clandestine code: "Marina." Everyone knew what to do.

By 12:30 PM sharp, everyone in the Graphics and Authentication Division (GAD), who could be counted on to respond en masse to the beauty of the day, had rearranged their calendars, tidied up their in boxes, filled out their leave slips, and passed through the heavily guarded security gates of our CIA compound. This virtual motorcade of technical officers specializing in clandestine operations did not stop at the motoring marina on the Pentagon side of the parkway. That was the domain of OTS's Electronic Operations Division, the OTS audio-boy, ninja types, and a smattering of the Special Activities Division—the para-military, bang-and-burn guys. We left them to themselves.

Our caravan traveled seven miles south of Memorial Bridge on the George Washington Parkway, turned left just past National Airport, and assembled at the sailing marina on the Potomac River. The Free World was just going to have to limp along without us for an afternoon.

My GAD group claimed ownership of the sailing marina. Sometimes members of Jonna Goeser's former division, the Clandestine Imaging Division (CID), where I had been division chief a few years earlier and where Maria Santori was now working, would join us. CID was made up of a group of two distinctly different disciplines, photographers and chemists, trying to work harmoniously on operational photography and secret writing techniques. Members of our SST were also starting to be included. Spring had officially arrived when the techs hit the marinas.

When I arrived at the sailing marina that day, I saw Jonna sitting with Maria at a wooden picnic table under the trees. Maria had her head thrown back and was laughing loudly at something Jonna had just said. Then they leaned their heads together and both began to nod in wonder at the next bit of news or gossip they were catching up on.

Jonna had been back in the States for a week to attend a worldwide management conference I was putting on at an off-site location in rural Virginia. GAD officers from both disguise and documentation disciplines—with a smattering of forensic specialists—had come from around the world to attend this meeting.

Jonna had not seen Maria until now, however, so I gave them some space, even though I was anxious to debrief Jonna about her recent overseas activities, something I had not yet had a chance to do.

Maria and Jonna had been a formidable pair of women to reckon with ever since they had worked together for the director and the deputy director of OTS. Maria moved up to be the director's secretary after Jonna became an assistant in the Operations Group. After Jonna had worked her way into a technical operations assignment in Germany, she served as a European Operations clandestine photography specialist. I first worked with her after I took over the Clandestine Imaging Division in 1982, and visited her CID section. I was immediately impressed with the great job she was doing in handling agent operations.

In the fall of 1984, upon her return from Germany, Jonna was selected for a prestigious career development course—which would involve special training in all of OTS's technical disciplines. The way she had gotten into the class was characteristic.

Our OTS deputy had stopped her in the hallway while he was visiting her technical unit in Europe and had asked her what she wanted to do when she returned home. She told him that she wanted to go into the ultraexclusive career development program—a program that had not included female officers up to that point. She talked to him long enough to convince him that she would be a good candidate, and he subsequently sponsored her application. The quiet, direct approach, backed with a truckload of confidence in herself, served her well. Once she graduated at the top of her class, I persuaded her to choose a tour as a disguise officer in GAD, where I would be returning as chief in the fall.

As I watched Jonna and Maria at the picnic table, I was struck by how similar the two women were. Now in their early forties, they were tall, slim, long-legged, and attractive. They were a type; they had a style, and the intelligence to back it up. Their classy toughness came from surviving, with lots of humor, the continuous onslaught of male attention in an organization filled with machismo. Jonna and Maria had both become technical officers at a time when there were few females in the office, and they had to make their way into a primarily male hierarchy.

Finally I decided it was time to interrupt their private moment.

After all, this was Marina Day—time to drink some beer and solve some problems. I stood over the table with a pitcher of beer in one hand and two frosted mugs in the other.

"Top of the season, ladies," I said, sitting down across the table from Jonna. I filled the two mugs with beer and reached over and gave one to her. Then I topped off Maria's mug.

"Jonna, I need to borrow you for an informal information dump. I've been trying to catch up with you during the conference, but there has been too much going on."

I had heard her presentation on the state of our operations in her part of the world, and she had sat through several of my meetings on where our technology was going. But this was the first time we had had time to exchange more than a few words.

Maria understood. She picked up her beer, gave me a slight bow, and moved over to the next table, where she sat down with a group of disguise officers who were noticeably pleased to have her join them.

"Finally, we get a chance for a one-on-one," I said.

Jonna was tanner than I remembered, and appeared to be relaxed and relishing the day.

"How are things out there since Woody tried to ground you?"

"Under control for the moment. Thanks for everything you've done, Tony."

It seemed as if Tom Smallwood had gotten the hint after I'd had the OTS director send a privacy channel message telling him to back off with Jonna and let her do her job in the field. Still, I didn't expect it to last for long. Bureaucratic critters like Smallwood knew how to adapt to circumstances and bide their time.

I caught a glimpse of some of the strain coming back to Jonna's china blue eyes.

As usual, she was dressed in casual but attractive clothes. The material was raw silk, and from the way it fit I could tell that the suit had been tailor-made. This had always been one of the perks of the job—while waiting for a clandestine contact in Bangkok or Singapore, one could have something wonderful made for a song.

I suspected that Smallwood had an ulterior motive: to show that Jonna's technical specialty in disguise and documents was no longer required. Since overseas slots were at a premium, it was always a battle for each technical discipline in OTS to prove their worth to field operations, or they'd not receive their share of overseas billets.

"He still wants me out of there short of tour," Jonna said, "but I'm not going to give him that satisfaction."

"Good for you. Just keep your eye on him."

Jonna nodded, never breaking our gaze.

"Did you hear about the dustup after the op?" she asked.

"Tell me."

"The Soviets brought in a special Aeroflot flight, full of technicians and large boxes of equipment. It must have been the equivalent of our FBI lab—to see if they could find prints or anything. Of course, there were no prints, no physical evidence of any kind. The scene was as clean as a whistle. They yanked the staff officers out and sent them God knows where. Maybe Siberia."

I smiled, leaned forward on folded arms, and looked at her intently. "Tell me about TUGBOAT."

Her blue eyes grew slightly larger before she caught herself and settled back into a steady gaze. "Woody told me I wasn't to discuss it with anyone who is not on the BIGOT list for the operation. Not now, not ever."

I told her I understood the importance of a BIGOT list, which restricted information on a need-to-know basis. "But from what I've been able to tell from the cable traffic, we prepared a major technical penetration operation of some sort using our best disguise technology. And after it went down, we exfiltrated our asset, TUGBOAT, and his family out of the region. If I'm right, this means you committed major division resources. So someone back here in OTS has to be in on the complete plan. That's how it works."

I let that sink in.

"Jonna, listen closely and think about what I say." I lowered my voice a notch. "I've been snooping around a bit, and I believe SE Division is up to their old antics of double compartmenting and spoofing, and perhaps downright lying about their operational interest in this case. Miles Rhenquist, the chief of SE, as much as admitted it when I confronted him. Here's what I think. I think that your TUGBOAT operation was nothing more than a distraction—a sham to throw the opposition and the rest of the CIA off the real target here."

I had her gaze locked with mine now, and I could see her mind working.

"Think back to the operational plan they presented to the local CIA chief out there. No operation goes forward without an ops plan sent in to headquarters for approval because the Operations Directorate demands it. Did you see it? If I am right, you did not. They probably told you it was too sensitive, not available, stuck in commo, something like that. Did you ever actually see it?"

There was a pause, a beat, as she looked down at her beer. "No," she said softly, explaining how Woody had held out on showing her any of the actual traffic and had simply paraphrased the requirements as they evolved.

This was not unusual. In their operational zeal, many of the CIA's field or headquarters operating components would attempt to limit the knowledge of some of the officers involved in the most sensitive operations. SE Division was the worst in this regard. Although a final operations plan is filed and approved before any operation goes forward, those who actually see it are limited in number. Sometimes those who are excluded have the biggest stake.

In OTS, we drilled into our officers not to succumb to the smoke and mirrors of need-to-know, but to make every effort to be adequately briefed on an operation beforehand. Our technical people knew that no field operative has the same perspective or expertise that we have in these matters, and they might sacrifice our valuable sources and methods without a second thought. In a year, a technical officer might gain more experience than a typical case officer about the ins and outs of tough technical operations. The average case officer wouldn't necessarily gain this kind of know-how in a career.

When I was dealing with a case officer who was about to proceed in a reckless manner with some of our sophisticated documents or disguises, I used to make my point with a challenge: "As soon as you guys start inventing new countries to support our alias cover or better our disguise technology, then we can start throwing away our options. Until then we need to weigh in on your ops plan, or we don't provide the goods."

Smallwood had broken the cardinal rule here and had not deferred to Jonna for the final call on what the true operational stakes were in this case. Had he been bamboozled by some slick talker? Maybe the Citadel guy who headed the team?

I laid my head down on the table, covering it with both arms.

"Damn it!" I moaned. "We've been had."

The techs at one of the tables close-by were starting to notice my antics and began to laugh, so I picked up my beer and looked over at Jonna, trying to slip back into my manager's role.

"Never fall in love with your operation, Jonna. Or your asset. This is the first rule of our business. Now, tell me all about TUG-BOAT."

Another beat, several of them, in fact, and then she did.

I sipped my beer slowly while she related the details of the operation.

When she finished, I put my hand on hers. "Okay, Jonna, this is where it gets real. I'm going to give you the other half of the story."

I explained to her that I thought she had been led down the garden path. And that at the same time, TUGBOAT and his family had given up their whole past life and their country for a potentially bogus operation.

"I don't think we needed the KAPELLE device," I said evenly.

Jonna's eyebrows shot up in surprise.

"It looks to me like the purpose of the operation might have been to conceal the fact that we already have someone in the KAPELLE program working for us," I went on. "Maybe things started to get hot for him. We could have stolen the device to divert attention away from our source and to keep the KGB from discovering that we had penetrated their ranks."

"Stealing the device to cover our tracks?" Jonna said with disbelief. "All that effort and planning and we didn't need the damn thing?"

"The KGB will regroup and redirect their efforts elsewhere. In the meantime, our source is off the hook and keeping us apprised of any new developments."

It sounded to me like a twist on the USS *Pueblo* operation. This had been a diversion run by the KGB using the North Koreans in 1968. John Walker, who worked in a U.S. Navy code room, was supplying the Soviets—for payment—with the Navy's code machine key settings every time they were changed. However, the Russians needed a code machine from a U.S. Navy ship in order to read the traffic, so they had persuaded the North Koreans to capture the *Pueblo.* With the subsequent loss of one of its code machines, the Navy began changing its codes immediately—not realizing, of course, that the Soviets were getting the new codes from their well-placed spy. The *Pueblo* incident precipitated an international situation, with U.S. Navy personnel held hostage for eleven months and President Johnson reportedly contemplating the use of nuclear weapons against North Korea. At the time, who would have thought the motive behind the taking of the *Pueblo* was to capture a Navy code machine so the KGB could use Walker's key settings to decipher our submarine traffic for the next sixteen years? While chairman of the KGB, Yuri Andropov described Walker as "number one." Indeed, during the many years that Walker provided the Soviets with the ability to hear our "strike orders" to submarines, he canceled out the major deterrent the U.S. had against a surprise nuclear attack by the Soviet Union—a very dangerous imbalance, and something that the Soviets knew and we did not.

The KGB had mounted a similar operation 1955, with their overriding concern to protect their British intelligence source, George Blake. In that case, the situation was the reverse; the Soviets knew from Blake that we had successfully tapped into their underground communications lines in Berlin. The Soviets feared that if they shut down their land line traffic, it might make us suspect that they knew about our top-secret tunneling operation—code-named GOLD—and possibly lead us or our British cohorts to Blake. To protect their spy, the Soviets allowed us to read some of their military and GRU (military intelligence) communications for more than a year, making sure that no sensitive information traveled over those lines.

Both the *Pueblo* and Berlin cases demonstrated the extraordinary lengths to which intelligence services would go to protect valuable sources.

I cautioned Jonna that she and I were potentially the only officers outside of a handful in CIA's SE Division and the Citadel who were aware of the true nature of the operation. It was likely, I told her, that we had a highly placed agent in the KAPELLE program—someone far more valuable than TUGBOAT and all the resources brought to bear on this case.

"You and I have to protect our resources and capabilities," I explained. " No one else in the Directorate of Operations is going to care."

"If those are the ground rules," Jonna said, "somebody had better tell Woody to play by them. I should have known."

"Yes, you should have. Undoubtedly, Woody did."

"I would have done some things differently. Woody didn't even tell me it was a disguise operation, and I didn't bring all my materials. He's a loose cannon. He doesn't respect what we do with disguise and documents."

"Smallwood wasn't just ignoring the rules—he might have been setting you up for a serious fall. It's only because the operation came off so well that you won't get any blowback."

What I was saying was sinking in very quickly; Jonna had a look of astonishment on her face. I had worked with SE Division long enough to know that their paranoia about operational security routinely led them to extreme measures when hiding agents-in-place. A Soviet KAPELLE officer would be an unprecedented source that would warrant all kinds of twists and turns to maintain compartmentation. Without Jacob Jordan's help from inside SE Division, we probably wouldn't have known the truth ourselves.

"There's more." I continued.

I told her things were upside down in Moscow, with operational techniques no longer effective and our officers barely able to work on the street under the overwhelming, but largely invisible, surveillance they were experiencing.

"Last week, two of our ZEPHYR officers were rolled up in a KGB ambush while putting down a drop outside Moscow. Their asset took his own life rather than be interrogated. And a few days before, one of our female officers thought she had been alone on the street for hours but was suddenly surrounded when she reached the operational site. Because they had already caught the agent, the KGB was not there for an ambush, but just to humiliate and demoralize her. They escorted her all the way back home on foot, following at a short distance and taunting her."

I went on to explain that a clear message had been delivered to our CIA contingent in Moscow that they were ineffectual and impotent. Meanwhile, the good assets were disappearing or being executed. Additionally, it appeared that some Marine guards might have compromised the security of the old U.S. Embassy in Moscow, and the new building being built to house our embassy had been found riddled with sophisticated listening devices.

Jonna had put her drink down and her chin rested on her intertwined fingers as she listened intently to this avalanche of information.

I picked up her mug and set it beside my own, refilling both.

I continued with my description of the enormous threat our Moscow officers were working under. In addition to the harassment, there was the possibility that, because of the Marine guards' security lapse at the embassy, the KGB could read all of our CIA communications. And now, I explained, it was beginning to appear that they could track our officers remotely in Moscow with the mysterious tracking material called spy dust.

I explained we had been finding the whitish powder around Moscow since the 1970s, but much more often recently. A KGB defector, Vitaly Yurchenko, told us that the KGB was working on a whole program of such surveillance and tracking techniques.

"Things are going so wrong in SE Division and our Moscow office that we are just about out of business," I said.

I told Jonna that I was involved in helping to invent new silver bullets for our operational work in Moscow and about all the long hours I'd been working with the ZEPHYRs and SST in an effort to develop new capabilities.

"I need someone who can handle the chief of SE Division and his officers and take on this global problem," I explained. "We don't know how widespread our Moscow problems are, but there are many more fish to fry in other hostile operating areas as well. I think this is something you and I could work on together. I'd like to create a senior position for you called the 'denied area focal point officer.' I would like you to work with me solving this

Moscow riddle for starters, then take the lessons we learn to other places in the world where it is needed."

Jonna had heard enough of my speeches in the past to know that this was the kind of sweeping worldview that I specialized in, especially when I was holding forth on Marina Day. She sat there at the picnic table for a moment, bathed in that lovely blue light spilling through the trees, silent and, I thought, a little overwhelmed. Minutes passed while she absorbed what I had just said.

Then she met my gaze across the table, and smiled. "You know, Tony, I'm actually having an excellent tour overseas, all things considered. Almost everything about it is what I have worked for over the past four years. I am not sure I want to wade into the quicksand that Moscow has become. Thanks for the offer. Let me think about it and I'll let you know."

She picked up her mug and walked off.

I had just offered her the assignment of a lifetime—a chance to become a player on the front lines of the Cold War spy game. And she was going to *think* about it?

Aldrich Ames turned onto the Via Veneto and drove two blocks to the U.S. Embassy and his office. The steel gray XJ-6 Jaguar purred quietly as he sat in the noonday traffic. Glancing at his Rolex, he noted that he was late again, but he really didn't care.

He was mulling over a discussion he had had recently with his Russian handler. They were pressuring him now for more names, at a time when he thought he had named every Soviet agent he could think of who had ever worked for the CIA. They wanted more. Shifting gears clumsily—the alcohol didn't help his concentration—he inched the car forward in the bumper-to-bumper traffic. Then the name hit him. *Fedorenko!* He had not told them about Sergei Fedorenko, his friend from the time he had spent in the CIA's field office in New York. He would give them Fedorenko.

He knew they would shoot his old friend, as surely as they had shot all the others. It was a sad piece of work, but he couldn't turn back now.

SIX

SOUTH ASIA

Spring 1988

Jonna

Sitting in the second-floor study of our house, in front of the bay window that looked out over the street, I had a panoramic view of both the traffic on our heavily traveled road and the garden. The study was my personal island, a cool reprieve from the heat and the dust and the incredible glare of the sun. It was furnished with antiques that the British had left behind and a matched pair of six-by-nine Isfahan rugs from Iran, my favorites. On one side of the bay the windows were covered with bamboo blinds, but the view to the street was left open.

And what an incredibly rich view it was. On any given day I could look up from my desk to see a parade of camels, elephants, dancing bears, or the royal military guard on their matched white stallions parading down our street. There were women balancing large jute baskets full of cow dung, fuel for the evening's fires. There were even troupes of monkeys, all leashed to their owner and available to perform for a few pennies. I always handed out bananas for the monkeys after the performance, but it was clear from their gaunt little frames that they weren't getting any of these extra rations. Their owner, on the other hand, was suspiciously plump.

Our *chokadar*, Naresh, was in his place at the gate, fending off vendors and "protecting" our residence. In fact, Naresh had one of the cushiest jobs in town. He lorded it over the crowd on the street, comfortably slouched down in the cheap rattan chair that we had provided, proudly wearing his western khaki uniform, while everyone around him was dressed in the local fashion. A small herd of wild pigs came sauntering down the street, ever hopeful of finding a tasty pile of garbage, and Naresh poked them away with a stick. Then a *wallah,* one of the door-to-door merchants, showed up with rugs from Afghanistan, and Naresh sent him away, too. On another day I would have invited the *wallah* into the garden to spread out his wares. I was going to miss this place.

It had been a year since my conversation with Tony at the marina, and now, finally, things were about to change for me, as I would be undertaking a new and challenging assignment.

I filled my favorite fountain pen and took out a sheet of stationery from the Regent Hotel in Hong Kong. I maintained an extensive stationery collection. It had started out as a joke—I never quite let anybody know where I was, only where I had been—then I started accumulating hotels around the world. Many of the planet's best hotels were located in the Subcontinent and the Far East, and I had attempted to explore as many of them as time and money would allow.

Dear Jennifer,
    We are almost out of here! The movers will come for the furniture next week, and then we go to a hotel until our actual departure

date. This moving business is not exactly rocket science—it is all done for us.

The hard part is going to be figuring out what to do when we get home. I know where I will be working, and the people I'll be working with, and am looking forward to that. A man named Tony Mendez will be my new boss, and he is a great guy.

It's John that is troubling me—that is, John and me. We're going to have to make some hard decisions back in the States. We talk about it some, but it is mostly left hanging—neither one of us wants to hurt the other, and none of our friends even know there is a problem. It's going to be like a bomb going off when they find out.

> *Love you always,*
> *See you soon,*
> *Jonna*

I moved around my second-floor room consolidating some books and papers into small boxes. It didn't matter that there were packers to do this work; there were some things that I wanted to pack myself, and my books were in that category. I wanted to know exactly where they were when we got back to Washington. My books and my oriental rugs—I could happily live anywhere as long as I had them around me.

I stopped and looked in the mirror. I was thinner and more tanned than when I had first arrived here, and some gray was starting to show in my hair, but all in all the damage done was slight. *Woody did his best,* I thought, *but he didn't win.* I had managed to hang on at the field unit, declining Tony's offer of a quick rescue by departing short of tour. I hadn't wanted to give Smallwood the pleasure of chasing me off. Despite his continuing efforts to derail me, I had continued to work on significant cases and traveled throughout the region, and had finished out my assignment. Along the way, I had discovered an ugly stubborn streak that I had not known I possessed.

At one point, our regional chief, Richard Singer, came through to chair a promotion panel, and I was one of those being considered for advancement. Smallwood had purposely scheduled Singer, an old friend of mine, so tightly that there was no time for one-on-one conversations. And the evenings were taken up with guys-only activities to which I was not invited. So, I did the only thing I could do: I interrupted a meeting of the promotion panel and handed Singer a note. It told him I needed to talk to him in private before he left town. We met for lunch at the American community pool, and I gave him a cursory review of my problems with Smallwood, including the back-channel cables that he had sent to headquarters about me, and his threat to "shut me down." Singer and I had worked together when I first started at the CIA, and he was outraged. He asked me if I wanted to file an official complaint or talk to the CIA inspector general. I told him I did not, that I believed either course of action would be professional suicide. All I wanted him to do was call off Smallwood. That had been several months ago.

Not surprisingly, I was not promoted at that particular panel. I would learn later that it had been a very close call for me, professionally. Singer told me eventually that he had not been convinced that Smallwood was the entire problem because I refused to bring a case against him within the system, thereby making my charges look weak. Avoiding confrontation at almost all costs—a habit engraved in my heart by my mother—had nearly cost me the career that I loved.

Washington, D.C.
Three months later

Having returned to Washington a few weeks earlier for my new assignment, I was sitting in Tony's office on the third floor of the new Headquarters Building at Langley. We had just come from a meeting with SE Division where we had been informed about the premature return from tour of two more ZEPHYR operatives because of another unexplained operational compromise in Moscow.

Tony paced slowly across his office; behind him a brilliant sunny day was streaming through the double-paned wall of copper-screened windows. He was a dark silhouette against a green shimmer of foliage.

The new building was totally encased by double panes, a security measure that was supposed to eliminate emanations, both in and out. The copper screens gave the exterior of the building a slight greenish hue that inspired the SST to assign the Headquarters Building the nickname Emerald City, which they used in open code over their radios when referring to Langley.

"You know, the old hands who have visited Moscow recently say things really do seem to have changed for the worse," Tony said. "Not just the atmosphere. The crew there has always been really paranoid. But there's a sense of overwhelming surveillance that we have simply never seen before. Not that there are larger numbers of them—there aren't. But they seem able to anticipate us. We just aren't able to shake them anymore."

"Sounds like the report I got from Bill and Judy Johnson," I said. The Johnsons were a husband-and-wife technical team who supported operations in Moscow and had just been in Washington on a short temporary duty assignment (TDY). "They said that even at the end of a three-hour surveillance detection run, when they felt sure they were no longer being followed, they would discover them again, sometimes in front of them, almost like they knew where they were going."

OTS had vacated its cozy South Building complex in Foggy Bottom the previous summer and moved into the new Head-quarters Building, which had effectively doubled the size of the Langley complex. At about the same time, Tony had been made deputy chief of the Graphics and Identity Transformation Group, another step up. We all missed our old South Building location. It was hard to leave those historic offices at 2430 E Street, with the view of the Potomac River and the Kennedy Center, and move into the streamlined steel-and-glass structure in the middle of nowhere at Langley. Instead of the closely knit community that OTS had always been, with a legendary esprit de corps, we were being scattered among the various floors of the dreaded Headquarters Building, and were losing our office identity.

I was now serving as Tony's denied area focal point officer for Disguise and Documents Division operations. It was a long title, but basically my main account was Soviet and East European Divi-sion—most of the denied-area activities took place in the Soviet Union and the Soviet Bloc countries of Poland, East Germany, Czechoslovakia, Hungary, Yugoslavia, Romania, and Bulgaria. But it also included such far-flung capitals as Havana and Beijing. In other words, the most difficult places to operate with the highest concentration of foreign counterintelligence services were all mine.

Tony's idea was that I would develop close relations with all Directorate of Operations divisions with a denied-area compo-nent. His hope was that because I would work closely with SE Division and have daily contact with the case officers and man-agers, I could stay in the loop on their current operations in my geographical areas. I would also be in constant contact with the ZEPHYRs—the group of case officers in training for Moscow or other denied-area assignments. As another set of eyes and ears in

SE Division for OTS, I would be involved in the day-to-day detailed planning of SE's covert field operations.

The ZEPHYRs were generally chosen every year from the large group of case officer graduates coming fresh out of the Operations Course (OC) at our remote training center, the Camp. The group was observed by all of the area divisions: East Asia, Latin America, Europe, Africa, and SE Division. First choice always went to SE Division; it was important that they chose well. No matter how strong the candidates, many ZEPHYRs would subsequently be defeated by the year-long training course they had to take after coming back up to headquarters from the Camp. This second course was called the Internal Operations Course (IOC). Only after successfully completing both the OC and IOC courses were the ZEPHYRs taken out by the Special Surveillance Team for final postgraduate exercises, typically in the last week before they boarded the flight to their assignment.

Tragically, one of the trainees had made it through both the OC and the IOC before having his behavior called to the attention of management. Edward Lee Howard was a name that brought shame to those CIA managers who had directed his career, and inspired loathing in the rest of us. After being accused of petty thievery and lying, Howard had been dismissed from the CIA in 1983. The following year, he volunteered his services to the KGB. Tipped off by the high-level KGB defector Vitaly Yurchenko that Howard was working for the other side, round-the-clock surveillance was placed on him, but with his wife's help Howard had gotten away and promptly fled to Moscow.

The first defector to the Soviets from the ranks of the CIA, Howard divulged to the enemy all of the classified information that he could dredge up, including the names of some of our Soviet agents, who were arrested and summarily executed. He also gave up the names of his CIA classmates and colleagues, and described to the Soviets the special disguise techniques that the

Agency had for years been using with great success in Moscow, rendering those techniques all but useless. Because of Howard, our SST disguise training was now incorporating new and sometimes heretical methods and techniques in their street exercises, desperately attempting to invent new ways to work on the streets of Moscow.

The old techniques, or silver bullets, had been powerful operational tools—and so highly classified that in the interest of national security they still cannot be fully detailed. In any case, they had for years allowed us to elude KGB surveillance long enough to put down a dead drop, leave a signal, mail a letter, or meet with local assets.

"Things in Moscow really started going wrong in 1985 and 1986," Tony said. "We've lost several local agents, and three of our CIA colleagues have just been declared persona non grata and kicked out of the country. At first, we chalked all of this up to Howard's being plugged into our methods. But it's been more than two years, and there's no way that Howard could still be the problem. Besides, we're losing people and techniques that he never *knew* about. There's something else going on now."

Tony crossed his office and sat down next to me on the sofa. His eyes, which I had remembered as green, appeared to be hazel with brown flecks. I also noticed more gray in his mustache and at his temples. The job was not without stress, and we all showed it after a while. At the same time, I thought, *He's going to age nicely.*

"Do you think it could be the case officers?" I asked, swinging my focus back to the problem at hand. "Do you think they could be making mistakes that allow the KGB to anticipate the drop sites? Could they be too obvious when they photograph and case drop sites ahead of time?"

"I wish it was that easy," Tony said. "But I don't think so. It's happening way too often to too many people. KGB teams are coming out of nowhere, or waiting in ambush. The guys in

Moscow are calling it ghost surveillance. It's clear we don't understand what's going on."

"Is there a traitor in our midst?" I said, asking the question that no one in the CIA ever liked to consider. "Another Howard?"

Tony sighed. "Could be, I suppose. Anything is possible. But even if there is, we've still got to find ways to function in the field or else have our operations shut down."

We exchanged long looks as we considered the ominous possibilities.

I had recently realized how difficult it could be at times to tell what was going on inside of Tony. His Zen-like exterior was a great cover. *He'd make a terrific poker player,* I mused. Come to think of it, that's just what he did for a living—on a global scale.

We had been wrestling with the Moscow problem ever since my return to headquarters and had not come up with any great ideas. The KGB was eating our lunch, over and over. CIA operations in Moscow were being rolled up, our Soviet agents were captured and frequently executed, and either our case officers were being "bumper-locked"—a harassing move in which vehicular surveillance follows so closely that the surveilling car's front bumper is almost locked to the target car's—or the KGB teams, confident in their ability to play catch-up, were not visible for long periods of time before suddenly appearing out of nowhere. The mysterious and vexing ghost surveillance was woven throughout all of our problems, and may have been the catalyst for these events.

Tony looked at his clock and smiled. "Let's go to lunch," he said.

Lunch, in typical Tony fashion, had nothing to do with real food or drink. I had begun to join him on his daily stroll around the campus, a two-mile loop through the shady paths surrounding CIA's Langley compound, fortified with only a piece of fruit and a bottle of water. We both enjoyed the fresh air and the exercise after a typical morning of meetings piled on top of more meetings.

"Okay, let's start over," he said, as we headed away from the building and down a hill into a shady, cool area. "We have a partial list of counterintelligence capabilities that they must have and how we can defend against them. I think that we have to expand the threat assessment to include more unconventional ideas. We have to think new thoughts—whatever they are doing to us might not be on any list we have created yet."

We continued down the path while the conversation headed into the mirrors and smoke that was the essence of all espionage and counterespionage activity. Often it was hard to get your bearings.

"We shouldn't forget how our adversaries have misled us more than once with their dangle operations," Tony said.

I knew that was a real possibility. We could easily have recruited a KGB double agent—someone who was pretending to work for us but in reality was still loyal to the Soviet state. Such a "dangle," sent to us by the opposition, could be providing us with bogus information while picking up valuable details about how we handle foreign assets.

"Some of those who are volunteering to work for us in the Soviet Union these days might well be under enemy control," Tony went on. "We're starting to realize that the same thing has been going on in places like Cuba and East Germany. We could be looking at a group of double agents in Moscow."

He paused. "And there's always spy dust. That nasty stuff is still around."

Tony gave me a bit of its history. We had managed to collect several samples of the odd material between 1976 and 1982. It was finally identified, in 1982, by its proper chemical names: nitrophenyl pentadien (NPPD) and luminol. Eight more samples were collected in 1985. Early testing showed the substance to be possibly dangerous, and that prolonged exposure to it might cause cancer.

Although this was later determined not to be the case, at the time, DCI William Casey, incensed that the KGB would be risking the health of U.S. diplomatic personnel assigned to the U.S. Embassy in Moscow, wrote to President Reagan about spy dust. Deputy Secretary of State John Whitehead subsequently protested to the Soviets in August 1985, but to no avail. KGB defector Yurchenko, who defected to the U.S. that same year, had confirmed that the KGB not only continued to employ spy dust, but was also experimenting with other powerful tracking substances and techniques under a top-secret umbrella program called METKA.

We understood that spy dust could be used to track the Soviets' own citizens as well; it could be very useful in picking an individual out of a crowd, even at night, or in bad weather. A special light was used to illuminate and spot the tiny chemical particles, which, when used in small amounts, could be nearly invisible to the naked eye. Typically the technical readout would be performed at a chokepoint that the KGB controlled. The entrance to the U.S. Embassy compound, manned by the Soviet Militia, or a bridge over a well-traveled corridor were the sort of locations where a light and optics unit could be mounted.

OTS had begun testing various METKA countermeasures, but we knew that the Soviets and their surrogates had spent millions of dollars on their tagging materials, and that we were playing serious catch-up. Countering each potential threat was a formidable undertaking, and one that could end up tying our office and budget in endless knots.

After our lunchtime stroll, Tony and I went to see Daniel Schumann, an SE counterintelligence officer. Schumann had the reputation of having a quick mind, and a temper to match. He was inventive and open to new ideas, though, which made his short fuse more tolerable. Schumann was a big, somewhat burly man with bushy eyebrows, a large forehead, and a South Boston accent. Intimidating upon first meeting, he looked and acted more like a dockworker than a Harvard graduate who had aimed all along for a career in the intelligence field. The gruffness went away once he had the sense that someone understood the problem and wanted to become part of the solution. Tony and I had been working with him, trying to pry out information and get fresh ideas.

Schumann walked back and forth across his office as he talked and used his hands extensively. He was striding around his basement office now, arms flapping this way and that, as he explained information that was just surfacing from agents located in Moscow and other denied areas.

"There are defector reports from East Germany that the Stasi is using man-and-dog teams to track individuals and to detect dead drops that have already been put down. And some of our officers in Moscow have reported sighting man-and-dog teams as well."

Tony's own LexisNexis database research had found information on ways downed pilots during World War II had tried to outsmart man-and-dog teams following their scent. The research showed that the dogs could follow a human's trail in a forty-knot gale in four feet of snow even when the trail was forty-eight hours old. One could slow them down for a while by planning routes that were like closed figure-four configurations. The only way to actually elude such a search team would be to break the trail—board a bus, ford a stream, get in a car.

"We're also aware of the possibility of active or passive electronic devices that could be hidden in our cars or on our person," Schumann went on. "You'll recall the famous Czech service audio device placed in the heel of one of our diplomats' shoes that he had sent out for repair. In some such way, it's still pretty easy for a hostile service to track one of our officers electronically without his knowledge."

We knew about passive and active infrared tags used in industry to mark inventory. Forward-looking infrared (FLIR) devices were a mature, commercially available technology—FLIR could visualize thermal information, making it easy to see cold and hot spots. Some of the devices could actually see into buildings and through walls, revealing the warm human bodies on the other side.

We had heard from Yurchenko about some other wild programs the Soviets were attempting—such as the use of insect sex pheromones to mark human targets. A female pheromone could be applied when someone crossed a doormat treated with the substance. Then any kiosk or other chokepoint that contained a box of the appropriate male insects could detect if a marked individual had passed by because the male insects would almost go crazy reacting to the pheromone.

"Such markers would clearly invalidate any disguise work you might do," Schumann said. "The cricket, moth, or cockroach wouldn't give a damn about what someone looked like—only what they *smelled* like."

I fought back a smile; somehow, I couldn't see KGB officers carrying around boxes of male insects.

Moving through other METKA possibilities, Schumann explained how we were being forced to consider the uses of parapsychology as it related to intelligence collection. While it was still controversial, we had to factor it in because we knew the Soviets had poured a tremendous amount of money into research in this area.

I knew that years earlier the CIA had sponsored parapsychological research that had yielded tantalizing but incomplete data. The work had been confined to psychokinesis and remote viewing. Psychokinesis is a person's ability to interact at a distance with a machine or other object, perhaps affecting the output signal or the internal magnetic field. Remote viewing is similar to clairvoyance; a "sensitive" research subject—one who had demonstrated some ability in the paranormal field—would be asked to discern people or places geographically removed from him.

Along with many of my colleagues in OTS, I had approached the field of parapsychology with suspicion, too pragmatic by nature to consider that there might be another dimension in which information could flow and invisible networks could connect. The OTS research soon led me to discard my disbelief and follow the experiments with awe. I vividly remembered one such test in particular.

Most of our experiments were performed by the Stanford Research Institute to ensure objectivity and to maintain total control of the events. Kendrick Press, one of our senior scientists who had been given permission to do some blue-sky R and D, ran them. Kendrick selected a series of subjects, one of whom was a famous psychic who we quickly dismissed as a charlatan. Others, however, proved to be very interesting.

One of the sensitive subjects was put into a lead-shielded room and given a piece of paper, a pen, and a set of geographic coordinates: "somewhere on the planet" was about all he had to go on. Working from satellite photography, we knew what was there, of course, and had multiple images of it. The sensitive was able to make uncannily accurate sketches of a remote site halfway around the world with nothing more than the compass coordinates. He had drawn a picture of a giant crane—he knew it was big, he said, because he saw a person walk by who came up to the axles on the crane's wheels. Later, we asked him why he had not drawn the four derricks that we knew were there. He closed his eyes and a few seconds later answered that he had not drawn them because they were no longer there. In fact, our next satellite imagery revealed that two of the derricks were partially disassembled, but basically all four were still there. And therein lay a major problem. The sensitives worked in "a noisy channel," as the researchers called it. They revealed information that was often correct, but incomplete; information upon which we could not risk an operation or an agent's life.

Another sensitive was able to enter remotely an embassy of a hostile nation and correctly locate the code room. We already knew where the code room was and had even entered it; we were just interested in seeing if our subject could find it. He did. But several further tries at the same experiment with different subjects yielded useless results.

We had brought one of the researchers in to talk to us about the program, and he described a demonstration with one of the sensitives at a lunch with a former deputy chief of SE Division. The two had never met, and neither knew the other's true name or affiliation. The SE officer had brought along ten unmarked photographs of Russians he knew about, but didn't let on to the remote viewer who they were. The sensitive proceeded to name them all and give details on their current locations. The SE officer was convinced, but confessed he was reluctant to go back and tell his boss.

The CIA research in this area had been closed down because some conservative managers in the Science and Technology Directorate were embarrassed that we were even dabbling in such a subject. Like the deputy chief of SE Division, they were reluctant to pursue such esoteric research, and so the program died. We were aware, however, that the KGB had a long-standing and robust program still under way, as did certain elements of the U.S. Defense Department.

While the Soviet METKA program was already extensive, we were learning new threats weekly. It was going to take a while to work through all of the possibilities and all of the defenses. But it was one of many paths to solving the problem of how to operate in Moscow, and we had to pursue it. We had to continue, discarding each potential threat to get to the real problem, and it was tedious going.

Schumann concluded his review of Soviet capabilities with a caution.

"We know some of the things they are doing," he said gravely, "but it's what we don't know that we are most worried about."

Later that night, Tony and I were sitting together at McKeevers Pub in McLean.

We had had an exhausting evening with the SST and had gathered at this favorite watering hole to review the evening's lessons. The team had been sluggish; they had not made several of their timing points and, midway through the exercise, Tony and I had realized that we were pushing them too hard. Following a brief critique, exhausted team members had filed out of McKeevers, leaving Tony and me alone in a booth.

"Let's rest them for a week and retool before we take them back out," he said. "We've been working too hard, too."

I knew he was right. Tony was almost a driven man when it came to finding new surveillance methods, as well as ways to counter for them. It was important work, yes, but I also suspected that part of what was driving him was a need to fill up empty time and space in his life. Since his wife's death two years before, he had been working ridiculously long hours. It was going to affect his health if he didn't slow down.

"Sounds like a plan to me," I said, smiling across the table at him and putting my hand on his. "You need a mother, Tony. Somebody to tell you when to come in for dinner and when it's time to stop playing."

He looked at me intensely. "You're a good friend. A *true* friend. A person doesn't run into many of those in a lifetime. In fact, you're lucky if you can count on a couple of fingers your really true friends. Those are the only friends you let in on the knowledge that you can only share with those you trust."

He stopped for a moment, sipping his beer.

"The Japanese say our hearts are like circles of knowledge and truth," he continued, "and that we all have three hearts, one inside the other. There's the first heart, which is the knowledge you share with the public at large. The second heart is the knowledge you can only show when you are sure that your secret truths will remain between you and a trusted friend. Inside of that heart is another ring of knowledge, the third truth, that you share only with yourself and perhaps, if you're lucky, one other person. That person would have to be a soul mate, the rarest of all friends."

I found myself unable to reply to such a profound truth, somehow shaken by the depth of his feelings, so we sat silent for a moment. After years of emotional isolation and numbness, feeling my husband and me drift apart and having few friends that I wanted to share that with, I felt swept away.

He laughed softly and took my hand. "Let's shake on it—to real friendship, to a search for knowledge, to finding a rare friend, to a quest for soul mates, and all that good stuff."

We clasped hands, and a little tingle shot down my spine.

I wondered, at that moment, what his secrets were. He had just discarded another layer of the onion, and I was starting to see the heart of the real man.

I shook the moment off, and we rose to go.

As we approached the door, another couple entered the pub, drenched with rain.

We stepped through the doorway and stood under the striped awning at the entrance. The parking lot was one large puddle of water, and it was clear that we were both going to get wet getting to our cars.

I turned to Tony to say good-bye.

We were standing close together, shivering in the cold.

He smiled. "True friends can hug, can't they? A friendly, good-friend hug?"

"Of course they can," I said.

We put our arms around each other and held on for dear life, standing in the silver mist of a fine rain. It lasted maybe ten seconds.

As I moved away to my car, there was no way that I could have known that my life, as I had known it, was over. That a friend, a very good, *true* friend, was about to change my life forever.

I turned on the windshield wipers and drove home to my husband.

GRU General Dmitri Polyakov—code-named TOP HAT, one of the most productive agents the CIA has ever run—is led into a small room where he is made to kneel on the floor. He is shot in the back of the head by a KGB executioner. A form letter is sent to his wife and two sons informing them of his untimely death.

There is no announcement of his execution.

SEVEN

VIENNA, AUSTRIA

July 1988

Tony

The early evening view from the balcony of the safe house was like a picture postcard. Rising high on the horizon to the north was the great Ferris wheel of the Prater amusement park, an icon of Vienna if ever there was one, known for its cameo role in the movie *The Third Man*. Nearby, to the south, rose the spires of the Stephensdom, the cathedral of Vienna and the heart of the city with its brightly tiled roofs and gothic intensity.

I walked back into the apartment, wondering about the American woman who had rented this place, then allowed the CIA to use it by appointment for meetings too sensitive to take place anywhere else. I had been told that she was a professional astrologer. She obviously had money—the apartment was furnished lavishly in the baroque style of old world Vienna. The crystal chandelier alone would have consumed half of my annual salary. The apartment exuded an air of comfort, charm, and privacy.

I had taken my time on the surveillance detection run this afternoon, spending several hours moving across the city to this very sensitive piece of real estate that we wished to protect from

inquiring eyes. Starting out beyond the Opera Ring, part of the
road system that girdled the inner city, I had proceeded down the
Kaerntnerstrasse, one of the main shopping streets. I made a point
not to go into the area of the U.S. Embassy for fear I might run
into another American who would recognize me. Having made
this trip often, I knew it was best to keep a distance.

In a foreign country, usually the only member of our embassy
who knew our true affiliation was the ambassador. But other
embassy employees—who often took delight in trying to "spot
the spook"—had the potential, through casual recognition and
inquisitiveness, of endangering an operation.

Following Jonna's suggestion, I had strolled down Mariahilfer-
strasse and then over to Demel's, a well-known café, to grab a
light lunch. The café had been dazzling—a fantasy of butterscotch
walls and mirrored rooms filled with cases of pastries and choco-
lates. Lunch had not been light, but it had been wonderful. From
her travels, Jonna obviously knew the city well.

As I stood at the open balcony doors of the borrowed apartment, Gerald Swazie appeared with a scotch for each of us. We
moved inside to a sitting area on the other side of the room. Set-
tling into the tapestry-covered sofa, we were silent for a moment,
each of us composing our thoughts and our priorities.

Swazie looked up suddenly, startling me with his blue eyes,
pale and penetrating, set deep under a prominent brow. Of
Scandinavian descent, he had light skin and close-cropped hair
that were unblemished and intact, and his tall, wiry frame
looked as fit as ever. I knew his physical mannerisms and profile
like I would those of a close friend or family member. I had
spent hours with him in 1978 examining his traits from every
angle and coaching him in altering them in subtle ways. Swazie
had been the first officer to deploy the highly secret disguise
technique I had created after Mary Peters had been ambushed
in Moscow. We had named that technique DAGGER. I had

watched Swazie become a highly successful ZEPHYR after I had spent many months prepping him for his Moscow assignment.

Back then, ten years ago, three of us had worked closely on perfecting the DAGGER technique: Jacques Dumas, then head of SE Moscow operations, Swazie, and me. As part of my final demonstration of the technique to them, I had transformed myself from a businessman into a Russian babushka, complete with shawl and shopping cart. They had been amazed, and had quickly adopted the technique as a proprietary tool, issued to Moscow-bound case officers only. Even before then, Dumas had been a true believer in the power of disguise, especially when it went hand in hand with deception and illusion.

During our long, shared experience in Moscow operations, Swazie, Dumas, and I became friends. Although it had been years since Swazie and I had crossed paths, it felt as comfortable as ever; we spoke the same language. Swazie had risen to become the chief of Vienna, and I was here because Dumas, chief of Moscow, needed help. It was like a reunion of the Three Musketeers.

Swazie, always one to get to the point, asked how he could assist me.

I told him I was here to see him on a courtesy call, since I was using his good offices to help "cleanse" myself en route to Moscow and back. Vienna was a perfect town for a spy to get lost in, without bothersome surveillance. Despite the fact that it had been a center of intrigue from the days of the Austro-Hungarian Empire, neutral Austria was not considered a hostile arena in which to work. I planned to switch identities while here and become Robert J. Violante, an old identity I had used in previous travels. On my return, I would park Violante in Vienna, and pick up my true-name documents to travel back to Washington.

I explained that Dumas had asked for my assistance in Moscow again. "He took the Moscow job at the personal request of the

DCI," I said, "following all the disasters caused by the Edward Lee Howard defection."

"Jacques has his hands full," Swazie acknowledged.

"Sure does," I said. "I just did a quick trip with him to the West Coast, like I did for you before you went to Moscow."

"We visited your Hollywood consultant—the master of makeup and disguise. What's his name?" Swazie asked.

"Jerome Calloway."

"Right. Great guy, and what fun going around to those studio lots and meeting the stars of *Mission: Impossible.*" With a grin in place, Swazie hummed part of the popular theme tune.

I chuckled. "Art imitating life, huh?" If only the TV writers and producers knew how close they sometimes came with their disguises to what we really did.

I told Swazie I'd done the same drill with Jacques so he could see the latest stuff coming out of Calloway's Academy Award–winning special effects laboratory. "You'd be amazed with what's been developed in the past ten years. Too bad you don't need any of the sexy stuff here in Vienna."

I grinned at Swazie, knowing that he would be itching to play with some of our new techniques if only he knew what they were.

I assured him that Dumas was still the same crisp, no-nonsense professional with the intensity and bearing of a former Marine officer and the mind of a Harvard graduate. A talented officer, Dumas had highly refined language capabilities in both Russian and Chinese and had already served in both countries. Besides that he was always an introspective, thinking-feeling sort of person, quite unlike the stereotypical case officer profile of the highly extrovert man's man.

"During our flight to L.A., Jacques reflected on the fact that we'd been knocking the socks off the KGB's Second Chief Directorate and Seventh Directorate for about seven years until Howard went over. Those Moscow rules of engagement we created back in the seventies held up well."

I related how for weeks before our trip Dumas had been quietly seething. That day on the transcontinental flight, he contemplated the turn of events once more over Jack Daniel's on the rocks, then declared suddenly, "I'm going to issue every officer in Moscow a Browning nine millimeter, and whoever sees Howard first will take him out!"

Swazie laughed heartily. "I can just hear him saying that."

Although the KGB would never hesitate to execute a traitor, we both knew that Dumas had only been speaking from frustration. But we understood his sentiment. The turn of affairs in Moscow, thanks to Howard, was that devastating.

While assassination was never part of our CIA bailiwick, there had been a couple of botched attempts in the early part of the Cold War because of pressure from the White House. Since then, President Gerald Ford had signed an executive order that explicitly prohibited us from planning assassinations of heads of states, and we were now subject to intense scrutiny from four oversight committees of Congress. Nobody at the helm these days would seriously suggest assassination as an operational tool, but we knew this could change if the U.S. found itself fighting a global war and it became politically palatable.*

Swazie and I agreed that the box score for the intelligence wars between the KGB and the CIA had been changing in favor of the Soviets. The year that Howard defected to the Soviets, 1985—dubbed by *Time* magazine as "The Year of the Spy"—had been, for both sides, a year unlike any other in the intelligence game.

"Many of those cases that year had a Vienna connection,"

---

*The memorandum of notification signed by President George W. Bush in the aftermath of the September 11, 2001, attack on America overturned the earlier executive order, and gave the CIA authority to use lethal force in combating global terrorism.

Swazie pointed out. "The Soviets staged meetings here so often with their western agents that the FBI called the routine the 'Vienna Procedure.' It was in Vienna that Howard walked in to volunteer to the Soviets, and he came back here at least once for meetings."

Swazie went on to enumerate the events of 1985 in his soft clipped way of speaking, pointing up the Vienna connections to many of those unprecedented counterintelligence episodes.

First, in May, the FBI had arrested John Walker, who had had at least six meetings with his KGB handlers here. After his capture, Walker described to the FBI the "Vienna procedure" he had gone through. He was told by his KGB handler to rent a specific vehicle from a certain car rental agency and, after driving around town for hours, to park in a designated spot. Then he was to walk a corkscrew route that spiraled him through at least twenty double turns. He had to time his route so he arrived at the "brush pass" site at the right moment to meet his contact. They brushed by each other and exchanged camera cases. Walker's surreptitiously contained the Navy's latest code machine settings.

Next, in August, KGB Colonel Vitaly Yurchenko, head of its foreign counterintelligence, defected to the CIA in Rome. One of my alias documentation specialists from OTS had helped him leave Italy and accompanied him back to Washington. SE Division had assigned CIA officer Aldrich Ames to debrief Yurchenko, who told us about two spies in our midst. Ironically, as we discovered years later, Ames began selling secrets to the Soviets that very same year. The fact that a disillusioned Yurchenko re-defected the following year did not diminish the value of much of his information.

According to Yurchenko, one spy, Ron Pelton, had worked for fourteen years for NSA. Three years after retiring in 1979 from the National Security Agency headquarters in Fort Meade, Pelton had had two meetings with the enemy in Vienna and came back for a third, but when he walked around his meeting site, the gardens of the Schonbrunn Palace, he was not contacted.

Another spy, whom the KGB code-named "Robert," was identified by Yurchenko as "a former CIA officer trained to serve in Moscow but who was fired before he departed for the field." We now knew "Robert" to be Edward Lee Howard.

In an almost inexplicable set of circumstances, in June of 1985 there had been another KGB coup. One of the CIA's most valuable assets in the Soviet Union, Adolf Tolkachev, code-named GTSPHERE, who had provided some of the most detailed information on Soviet aerospace and weapons, was arrested by the KGB. He had first volunteered to work for U.S. intelligence in the late 1970s by passing a note to an American diplomat in Moscow. As an engineer, he had access to some of the Soviet Union's most important technical secrets. Over approximately eight years, he had provided some of the most important intelligence on Soviet aerospace and tactical radar. He was usually met by a CIA handler using the silver-bullet disguise technique GAMBIT to elude KGB surveillance. GTSPHERE would typically hand over many rolls of exposed film. Just one of the scores of meetings with Tolkachev was later judged to be worth $4 billion in savings to the U.S. taxpayer in defense research and development. It was believed Howard had identified him at an early meeting with the KGB here in Vienna. Before his firing from the CIA, Howard had been trained to take over as GTSPHERE's handler in Moscow. Following a yearlong interrogation by the KGB at Lefortovo Prison, Tolkachev was executed.

In July and August, the balance shifted slightly as western intelligence scored two successes of its own. Our British counterparts successfully exfiltrated their agent Oleg Gordievsky from Moscow. Gordievsky had been the KGB rezident in London and had been called back to Moscow under suspicious circumstances. It was believed that Howard had not been privy to the Gordievsky operation, but he may have been digging around in the SE files before he was fired. Then came the arrest of a longtime CIA officer, Larry Wu-tai Chin, who had been spying for Communist China for years.

"The Year of the Spy" concluded with the insult of the Sharon Scrange affair, in which a young CIA secretary had been caught providing intelligence information to her Ghanaian boyfriend. Scrange, a young, lonely black American, found herself a long way from home in Ghana, an isolated outpost under the best of circumstances. A handsome and charming Ghanaian intelligence officer was targeted against her, and she fell for it. After some sort of seduction scenario, she began providing him with the secrets of our local operations. This was a classic setup, and the CIA makes a point of cautioning its women who are going abroad to be on the lookout for this type of approach. Sexual entrapment, of course, worked in both directions.

Swazie rose and went to the lavishly stocked bar on a Biedermeier chest at the side of the room. "Something more than mere coincidence is going on here, Tony."

The clink of the glasses and ice had a comfortable, familiar sound to it. He handed me my refilled glass and made a slight adjustment to the radio. Oesterreich Drei, the Austrian national radio station, was playing the soft waltzes and polkas of the Strauss family, beloved by all Viennese. The radio was on to mask our conversation, of course, but the music was quite soothing.

The long-standing Cold War espionage battles between the CIA and the KGB had definitely heated up. In 1986, only a few months after Dumas had been put in charge of Moscow operations, a Soviet scientist, Gennady Zakharov, who did not have diplomatic immunity, although he was working for the United Nations in New York, was arrested after being drawn into an FBI sting.

In retaliation, the KGB arrested a nonaccredited American newsman in Moscow, Nicholas Daniloff, who had been unwittingly implicated in a local spy case. Although Daniloff was not a spy, the Soviets had a case against him.

Later that year, Zakharov, who *was* a spy, and Daniloff were swapped; each released to their respective ambassadors on the same day.

"That poor bastard, Daniloff," Swazie said.

"He was just caught in the crossfire."

After the exchange of volleys from U.S. Secretary of State George Shultz and Soviet Foreign Minister Eduard Shevardnadze, Reagan and Gorbachev took turns firing broadsides. Reagan soon ordered, by name, twenty-five KGB officers from the Soviet Mission at the United Nations in New York to leave the country.

The Soviet response was to declare five Americans from our Moscow embassy persona non grata. The initial U.S. reaction was to expel first five, then fifty, Soviets from theirs. The U.S.S.R. followed by expelling five more Americans, and then pulling out the hundreds of Soviets supporting the U.S. Embassy staff.

"It was a pretty robust tit for tat, wasn't it?" Swazie smiled wanly.

In December 1986, as Dumas was still catching his breath in his new assignment in Moscow, Corporal Clayton J. Lonetree, one of the previous U.S. Marine Corps guards at the U.S. Embassy there, who was by then serving in Vienna, confessed to having been entrapped by a KGB "swallow"—a female KGB officer who used sex as a tool. He had been turning over classified information to his KGB handlers for more than a year, and there was some question about whether he and other Marines caught in the honey trap had allowed KGB teams into the embassy's secure areas, including the communications rooms.

And now, I pointed out, Dumas found himself saddled with a constant flow of counterintelligence technical teams from Washington hoping to sort out these problems.

"Enough!" Swazie protested. "I know Jacques has had a hell of a ride in Moscow so far, but this place has been no picnic either, let me tell you."

Swazie was finishing his second scotch as we completed our review, and I was keeping up with him. We had both loosened our ties and rolled up our sleeves. The light outside was fading on the winding narrow street below us. The sunset was glancing off the tiled roof of the cathedral in an exquisite series of reflections and shadows and dancing into this secret space, gilding the room in a warm, golden glow. I wondered if the astrologer had realized there was this wonderful bonus when she rented the place. I wished we could go out and enjoy one of the sumptuous restaurants the city was known for, but my alternate-identity status and need to drop out of circulation complicated social engagements with my colleagues for the time being.

"I've been up to my eyebrows in the Felix Bloch case since I arrived here," said Swazie through tight lips. "For several years he has been the number two State Department guy here in the U.S. Embassy and is briefed on everything we have going on. The ambassador is a political appointee and doesn't want to dirty his hands. We are sure Bloch has been reporting to the KGB, but he appears to have been warned off. We have had hordes of FBI and CIA surveillance on him but to no avail. It is getting so blatant that the press has taken to following us following him."

It would be seventeen years before we discovered that it had been Robert Hanssen, the FBI mole, who compromised the investigation by warning the KGB, which subsequently passed word to Bloch, who, without being charged with any crimes, was allowed to retire with a minimal pension.

I smiled a pained acknowledgment of Swazie's difficulties.

"In a way, I wish I were going with you," he admitted.

"Back to the belly of the beast in Moscow?"

"It'd be like the old days."

I understood his feelings. Moscow was where the action was;

the center of the universe for Cold War field operations in the arena of intelligence work.

Swazie's comment was a perfect opening for me to bring up the most important reason I came to see him. "Remember that survey of yours in the Moscow netherworld?"

"How can I forget? Nasty job that turned out pretty well, thanks to your help."

"I need to talk to you about that, Gerry—in detail. I could use some diagrams, too, of what to expect down there."

Before leaving Washington, I had debriefed an OTS technical officer I had sent to Moscow for a week. I had some inkling as to what requirements awaited me at my destination, and knew that Swazie was the perfect guy to pump for information.

Swazie sat forward in his chair. He knew better than to ask what I was planning. "Let's refill these empty glasses and get to work."

Moscow
Two days later

Jacques Dumas was already seated in the Bubble when I arrived. I could see him through the Plexiglas walls as I entered the airlock and climbed up the three steps to the elevated room within a room.

I noticed that his closely cropped hair had gotten grayer since I had seen him in the summer, but the sparkle in his eye had not diminished, and his boyish grin was firmly in place.

It was cold in the room, and I felt a sudden shiver.

With Dumas were his wife, Suzette, a pretty, petite brunette who worked for the U.S. Mission as a personnel officer while handling occasional assignments for the CIA, and two others. The large, fair Slavic type I recognized as his deputy, Mikhail Skalov, a cherubic man of about thirty-five. The darker, more compact fellow was Luke Swisher, an OTS engineer with infectious energy and enthusiasm. He had been assigned here at Dumas's request as a "new concepts" guy. The four all sat quietly at a large table and looked rather serious.

Once I secured the thick transparent door with the two latches and turned toward them, they immediately stood to greet me warmly with smiles and handshakes.

Suzette and I gave each other a hug and a peck on the cheek. She and Jacques were the same attractive athletic couple I remembered. Her dark hair and shy smile complemented his quietly forceful and penetrating demeanor. It had been twelve years since we had first met here in Moscow, and we had seen and experienced a lot in our respective careers and travels since then.

I vividly remembered one night in August 1976 when he had gone out to meet the CIA Soviet agent TRINITY. Suzette and I were part of a small team that nervously remained behind at a safe site after playing certain supporting roles in the landmark *CLOAK* deception that allowed Jacques to elude his KGB surveillance. Since her husband would be "in the black"—free of surveillance— for several hours before he returned safely, it was tough for Suzette to wait quietly, not knowing whether he was safe. It would have been foolish not to acknowledge the danger of these operations.

I had filled some of those anxious moments by chatting with her, learning a lot more about Dumas and his highly disciplined approach to his craft. I had witnessed his many hours of preparation getting ready for the meeting with TRINITY, so I knew how precise he was. Suzette told me that, when studying Russian for the assignment to Moscow, Jacques took no time off—even for holidays. Even now, if he couldn't find someone to speak Russian with during the day here in Moscow, he would call a wrong number on the telephone just so he could speak Russian for a few minutes.

When he returned to Washington after a two-year tour in Moscow, he was tested by the CIA's language school and scored a "five," which was native proficiency. There were very few foreigners who qualified as a native speaker in the Agency's very tough language program. It was like being awarded a medal.

"I'm only here briefly to welcome you once again to Moscow," said Suzette. "This is the only time I can act like I know you, even though you're going to be around the American community for a couple of weeks."

Suzette was gently reminding me of the rules of engagement here, where members of the CIA contingent weren't able to acknowledge one another outside a secure facility like the Bubble. Since they all had different overt affiliations in order to keep the enemy guessing as to who the real intelligence officers were, they had to play the cover game even inside their offices and residences. Virtually every location was considered to be bugged with audio and sometimes visual surveillance devices. Suzette excused herself, and then went out through the door and through the airlock.

Dumas answered my question before I asked it.

"Since you'll be here for the Fourth of July, as an American you are invited to the celebration at the U.S. Embassy dacha. We can speak to one another casually there as we move outside about the grounds," he explained. "Otherwise, conversations with any officers or their spouses, or Suzette and myself, will take place here in the Bubble. Luke will be the exception. Since he is single and has a different set of cover and operational duties, and you're here conducting your ostensible admin review of the facilities, you and he can meet and move about as if you have some common interests. You should use that time sparingly, though. You'll want to reacquaint yourself with the populace and the environment, as well as hear our stories. I'm sure, as in the past, you'll spend much of your time on the streets and you'll visit the various attractions. Best you do that on your own, Tony. However, I do want you to go out with Luke so you can see how the KGB is treating him. He has established a rather quirky pattern and profile."

I was exchanging looks with Swisher and Skalov as Dumas

spoke. As with every ZEPHYR, I had spent considerable time working together with the two of them in the final days before they had launched on their assignments here. I could sense we were all anxious to catch up on experiences and compare notes on how the reality of their operational life here matched the postgraduate simulations we had done in Washington against the SST.

I could also tell that Dumas had some other matters to discuss with me. He looked as if he was about to open the red-striped file on the table in front of him. He fixed the other men with his no-nonsense gaze, and they both stood to leave.

There were handshakes again with the two; we made arrangements for our next meetings, and they excused themselves.

All field officers typically held down two jobs wherever they served. Their cover job had to be a real job with real hours, or the local counterintelligence service would see right through it. Their operational job had to be worked into an already full office and social schedule, so they more than earned their government pay.

After the two had cleared the airlock, Dumas opened the folder and took out a manila envelope marked "Top Secret/Special Compartmented Information." He laid this to one side and proceeded to remove another sheaf of forms from the folder. Each had an ID-sized, black-and-white photograph attached to it on the upper right-hand corner.

Dumas rested his hand on this stack of papers. "Each of these represents the bio data sheet out of an agent 201 file," he said gravely. "There are ten agents here who have gone missing sometime in the last three years. The fate of some of them we now know because the KGB has seen fit to announce their executions publicly. For the others, we fear the worst. You have to know that some of those we have lost, like GTSPHERE, are among the best we've ever had—as good as TRINITY, or even Penkovsky."

Oleg Penkovsky, known as "The Spy Who Saved the World" during the Cold War, was a legend in western intelligence circles.

A GRU colonel, he had high-level access to Soviet strategic intentions as well as weapons capabilities. He first volunteered to work with British and U.S. intelligence in April 1961 in Moscow, through a British businessman. He provided MI6 and the CIA with more than four thousand pages of secret documents over the next eighteen months. When the Cuban Missile Crisis erupted in October 1962, the U.S. was able to recognize the SS-4 missiles being installed in Cuba because of information provided by Penkovsky. More important, President Kennedy knew, thanks to Penkovsky, that the Soviets had no capability to stage an all-out nuclear war owing to the fact that the U.S. missiles far outnumbered the Soviet ones. On November 2, 1962, a CIA case officer in Moscow was ambushed unloading a dead drop from Penkovksy, and Penkovsky was arrested that same day. The CIA officer was expelled from the country. Penkovksy's execution was announced on May 17, 1963.

"Howard could have burned one or two of them, particularly Tolkachev, but not all ten," Dumas said. "We are under siege by the KGB. We don't know what they are doing to us or how exactly they are going about it."

Dumas went on to explain the countermeasures they were taking. "We're going to extraordinary lengths with our communications and are altering our M.O. every time we suspect a new potential threat. This Soviet program, METKA, has everyone acting more paranoid than ever. We're trying to understand how their surveillance is operating, and we need your help."

Dumas had always been one to get to the point; identify a problem and move to a solution. He was a good choice to run our operations in this time and place.

"We need to invent some new illusionary disguise techniques so we can operate effectively—new silver bullets for use only in Moscow. We need some of your best and brightest ideas. There may even be a traitor at headquarters, but there's nothing I can do about that out here. All I can deal with is the here and now. We have to continue operations, and we have to protect our agents. These bastards are not ten feet tall, and you and I know it!"

He reached for the manila envelope and slid it over in front of him.

"I want you to know we are by no means out of business. We're experiencing a flood of new volunteers, and some of them might be dangles, but others are clearly not. We are taking all precautions. However, there is one agent above all others who must *not* be caught before we can get him out. And before we can do that, we have a final piece of important work to accomplish with him."

Dumas reached into the manila envelope and exposed another file of papers. As he slid it around in front of me, I caught sight of the ID photograph attached to the top sheet of the thick 201 personnel file.

I caught my breath.

I knew him! I had disguised that face in Indochina in 1973 when his code name was SAPPHIRE. I remembered he had been a KGB specialist in the local Soviet Mission, and I had provided him with a disguise that he could put on for nighttime meetings with his CIA handler. I had also begun planning for his and his wife's exfiltration from the host country, should that have become necessary. When I transferred back to headquarters in 1974, I lost contact with the case, and never knew what became of him.

I explained to Dumas my history with SAPPHIRE.

"He's still working for us," Dumas said. "He's now a major in the KGB's KAPELLE program and has worldwide cognizance of their collection and security practices. Once he resurfaced here in Moscow, his cryptonym was changed to ORB for security purposes. He took a long time to recontact us, and then he demanded that nothing about his case be put into staff communications channels. Since his expertise is in technical security, we decided to listen. This guy can get us the crown jewels if we can keep him alive and in place, especially given the events of late."

Dumas admitted ORB was still alive probably only because he took charge of his own case and laid down the security plan. "He initiates his own meetings. We have no control of his commo plan, and he will accept no spooky spy gear or any other potentially compromising materials. His instinct for clandestine tradecraft is uncanny, and his product is fantastic, as you might imagine given his access. The bad news is we could still screw up and lead the KGB to him. Headquarters almost let the cat out of the bag last year by sharing his information too widely in the intel community."

I asked what kind of operational plan was needed for ORB.

"To keep him safe a while longer," Dumas said. "His time has about run out, and we need a current exfiltration plan. But before he leaves our good services, he's willing to do one more chore for us. Believe me when I say it's worth the effort. Well worth it. We have to find a way to meet with him safely and put together what we need to carry off this last operation—then, get him, his wife, and their boy the hell out."

As I heard more details about ORB's idea for his last operation, my pulse quickened. It was daring, and it had the potential to be a masterpiece of spy work that would make up for a lot of our recent failings in Moscow.

But was it possible to do something so complex and dangerous in the current environment here, where the KGB seemed to know our every move in advance? If we couldn't shake them through skill, cunning, and misdirection, it would end disastrously, not only for ORB and his wife and son, but for the rest of the ops team as well.

I was standing at the corner of Kalinin Prospekt and Prospekt Marksa, just one block from the Alexander Gardens and the Kremlin, looking across the eight lanes of traffic on Kalinin toward the Lenin Library. It was seven o'clock and the evening summer sunlight, always more intense this close to the Arctic

Circle, was glancing off the three-story-high, blazing red banner with a stark black-and-white portrait of Lenin in its center, hanging above the entrance to the library.

On two sides of the library there were four Metro entrances at street level and two lines and four platforms directly below. Also, I knew of four underground intersecting pedestrian transfer tunnels leading from the two lines to two more lines, and four more platforms from which there were eight ways back to the street. This entire underground warren was stacked four stories deep below the street and the library.

At this hour the foot traffic of Muscovites and foreigners on the street and in the Metro was turbocharged by the world's longest escalators leading up from and down into the Metro. Below all this snarled anthill of rush-hour humanity, we in the CIA believed, the Soviets had for many years been burrowing even deeper, bolstering and expanding the underground bunkers that had been dug during Stalin's times. They had plans for survival if the Cold War suddenly became hot.

Including the ancient sewers, some of which dated back to medieval times, there were probably as many as fifteen stories of tunnels radiating out from the Kremlin. Some of these tunnels extended as far as Ring Road, several miles away, on the outskirts of Moscow and beyond, probably all the way to the dachas of the leaders of the Supreme Soviet. The city aboveground was larger than New York and had a population of twelve million. Underground there was no telling how large it was.

I was on my way to an off-season performance of *Giselle* by the Kirov Ballet Company at the Palace of Congresses, located inside the walls of the Kremlin. But for the moment, I stood watching the intense foot and vehicular traffic on this "million-dollar mile" of Kalinin Prospekt, the so-called economic showcase section of the city.

A light gray Russian-made Zhiguli Lada, the Soviet version of the boxlike small Fiat, sped down Kalinin Prospekt from the right. It skidded to a stop at the curb directly across the street, as the driver violently threw his door open, seemingly oblivious of the rear-end collision he had narrowly escaped with the car behind him, which also screeched and lurched to a stop.

While the irate citizen driving the car in back shook his fist and yelled obscenities, the driver of the Lada bailed out and began running just as another burly type came dashing up the middle of the street from the rear of the car and quickly jumped into the Lada's driver's seat. In the same motion, like in an Olympic relay, the first man was passed a brick-sized radio transceiver from the hand of the second as the first man continued forward and dashed around the front of the Lada.

Now up on the sidewalk he quickly made his way to the Metro escalator just in front of the library entrance and disappeared like a rat down a hole.

In another blink of the eye, a third tough-looking man came chugging up the sidewalk. I could see he was frantically keying a transceiver-sized lump slung below his right armpit and hidden underneath the thin cloth of his short-sleeved white cotton shirt. He was shouting into a radio mike concealed under the corner of his shirt collar as he disappeared down the escalator on the heels of the first man.

In the meantime, the man who had assumed the role of the wheelman had sped off in the Lada. He made the first right down the side street, which led down the Kremlin side of the behemoth, block-sized library to where I knew there was another Metro entrance.

The crush of the evening rush hour seemed to part naturally to allow this spectacle to take place, and then, just as easily closed in behind it. It was as if such a chase were a normal part of everyday life; no one seemed to notice or care.

To me it was a rare opportunity to witness the KGB's Seventh

Directorate (surveillance division) in action from a front-row seat. It was clear that a prized target had gotten away down in the Metro's rabbit warren. The man who had taken over the wheel of the Lada must have been too close to the target for too long. He had probably been in front, in the point position, had made eye contact, and felt he could have been identified as hostile surveillance if he had continued into the Metro with the target.

The problem the first and third man were now facing was staying with the target so he didn't get lost in the crowded Metro underground and end up being whisked away on a train without them.

I knew the trains came like clockwork every two minutes. The Moscow system transported more than two billion people a year through several hundred kilometers of tunnels punctuated with stations that were each an architectural marvel decorated with a different motif and style—another tribute to Russian abilities to create an underground world.

In three trips to Moscow through the years, each lasting several weeks, I had spent considerable time on the streets. I had ridden hundreds of hours on the multifaceted transportation system and had a fair idea of the problems that a surveillance team would have keeping track of a target while still remaining discreet. This was especially true in the Metro.

But circumstances seemed different now, which was why it was valuable for me to scout them in the same way a football coach takes a look at his team's next opponent.

We were going to face off against each other very soon, and it would be a case of winner takes all.

Luke Swisher and I sat on our haunches in the dark.

We were in a storeroom on the back lot of the new U.S. Embassy compound. The embassy facility was being constructed on a large plot of low-lying land. It was poorly situated in a location that fronted on Bolshoi Devyatinsky Pereulok, a side street off Chaikovskoga, one of the broad thoroughfares that formed concentric rings radiating out from the Kremlin and Red Square. The building was down the street from the much higher ground where the old, seven-story U.S. Embassy commanded a view of the eight-lane boulevard. There, at least, we had a half-decent chance of intercepting local Soviet communications and telephone traffic. At the site of the new embassy, this far down the Moskva River embankment, there would be a much-impaired opportunity to receive any radio intelligence. By contrast, the new Soviet Embassy in Washington, D.C., commanded the highest ground in our nation's capital and their compound bristled with antennae.

The U.S. State Department had been outmaneuvered by the Soviet Foreign Ministry when each party had sought to negotiate for a location for a new embassy in the other's capital. The Soviets got the high piece of ground, good for intelligence purposes, and the Americans got a low site. This was attributable to the difference in the relationship between the Soviet Foreign Ministry and the KGB on the one hand, and the U.S. State Department and U.S. intelligence on the other. Because the Soviet Foreign Ministry understood the importance of spying, the KGB were consulted on many matters, including the prospective sites for foreign embassies in Moscow. The U.S. State Department, however, looked upon spying with a certain disdain, so U.S. intelligence had no such influence.

We had crept in here hours before, using an infrared point light source and infrared goggles to see our way. We avoided making noise in the pitch darkness.

I had liked Swisher as soon as I met him. He had a slight build and a quick mind that was constantly in high gear. His size gave him an almost boyish profile, but his longish brown hair and unkempt look let him blend uncannily into any street scene. He could pass for a Russian without any additional work. Swisher had worked for a week with my group before he left headquarters, and I knew a lot about his ways. I was told to expect from him expert proficiency wrapped in an easygoing personality, and had found that description to be very accurate.

In our crouching positions, we were leaning our right shoulders against a masonry wall located behind one of the embassy air handlers. Swisher was listening to the wall with a stethoscope. He handed the earpieces of the stethoscope to me and continued to hold the contact probe against the wall where he had it placed it earlier.

I listened for several minutes before I picked up the stirrings that could have been rats moving on the other side—or men in cloth-covered shoes moving quietly?

I nodded and handed the earpieces back to him.

Swisher motioned to the bottom of the wall above his head and traced a rectangle on it with his point light source. While I could see nothing remarkable about that particular part of the wall, I knew he was indicating the spot where there was a hidden hatch he had discovered with a portable sonar device.

We had been spending the past few days together while he familiarized me with his activities inside and outside of the compound, trying to characterize the types of threats being mounted by the KGB's Second Chief Directorate (internal security division) against the Americans. One of the threats was a network of tunnels near the embassy compound that Luke had discovered using his portable sonar and by special tasking of our national security satellites. He believed these tunnels were being constructed by the KGB to burrow into the foundation of our new embassy chancery so they could access the various listening devices already precast into the building elements.

He believed, as did several other members of our counterintelligence force, that our embassy was monitored by the KGB from an abandoned Russian Orthodox church, which was directly across the street from the front gates of the U.S. Embassy compound, and on higher ground. They had dubbed that church "Our Lady of the Antennae." The church steeple had a dusty round glass window, which would make a convenient observation post (OP). Next to the church was the multistory Mir Hotel, suspected of being another OP and a place for a rapid-response mobile surveillance team to be positioned.

Between the old U.S. Embassy grounds and the new U.S. Embassy grounds was a tract of land occupied by a multistory apartment building. On the ground floor of this apartment house were rooms used by the construction workers to change clothes and shower. This would be a good place from which to stage special penetration operations, since the KGB would have the natural cover of the other construction workers. The building had convenient windows that looked down into the new embassy compound and potential OPs as well. We suspected that this building also contained the Seventh Chief Directorate's "warming rooms" to house on cold, wintry days the various surveillance teams covering the members of the American community assigned to work and live on embassy grounds.

Presumably, Swisher and I had happened along when a KGB team was moving about in the tunnels. He had explained before we came here that the hidden hatch in the wall was there to allow them to come out under the cover of darkness. If they were to gain access to the embassy this way, they might be able to enter other hidden passageways precast into the walls of the chancery, which is an eavesdropping technique centuries old. Theoretically, they could stand in any wall and listen to and perhaps see what was going on in each of the rooms. All this was in addition to whatever they had done to the structure of the building itself.

State Department security people were also working after hours every night to try to figure out what the Soviet construction workers were installing during the day. Using many special devices, they probed for evidence of new eavesdropping technology and reported back to headquarters daily, where there was a full-time team of scientists modeling the countless threats by computer.

Early on we had intelligence information warning us that the Soviets had penetrated the architectural firm in San Francisco that was designing the building, long before construction had been started. American authorities, headed by Secretary of State Henry Kissinger (discussions on the new embassies began in 1969), chose not to take the threat seriously because of detente and a somewhat arrogant attitude that we could find and remove anything the Soviets did to our embassy anyway. So while the precast structural members for the Soviet Embassy were made in the Soviet Union and shipped to Washington, D.C., and assembled there under heavy guard, we allowed the Soviets to cast the structural members unsupervised in Moscow and to erect our building by themselves; the whole structure was one big microphone and the foundation a perpetual battery.

As part of the search for the new procedures—the new silver bullets that would work in Moscow against our very formidable foes in the KGB—I had been with Swisher at all hours making probes in and out of the compound. Among other places, we had visited the U.S. Embassy's two dachas—two recreational sites on the outskirts of Moscow in the woods.

When I was out on the streets riding with Swisher, I could see he was subject to the conventional discreet surveillance, three or four cars with three or four people to a car. The trailing cars would hand off the point position now and then. The car on point typically hung back a block or more and would hide behind a bus or other large vehicle when possible. Meanwhile, their other cars would run parallel on the side streets and on occasion come out in front or in back of us. Sometimes, there were several persons visible in each car, but other times only the driver was—the passengers, or "foots," were probably lying down on the seats out of sight.

If we tried walking at a place like the Saturday flea market, where there were miles of paths through the grounds of a monastery and great crowds of people, the foot soldiers would come in close. Each of them carried something like a briefcase or a shoulder bag with a hidden camera, hoping to get a picture of us making a brush-pass contact with a Soviet citizen.

Alternatively, when I was on my own on the street at all hours, including late at night or early in the morning, I generally saw nothing. Either I was without surveillance or they were always over the horizon. As in my previous trips to Moscow, or anywhere else in the world, my routes were varied and well traveled. After several weeks of using all forms of mass transit and making long, wide-ranging solo walks, I had established a dynamic but predictable pattern. I tried to make sure my trips made some sense from a cover standpoint. But I endeavored to provide enough variety in my movements to provoke and sometimes erode surveillance if it was there.

Quite often, I was conveniently the last one aboard an evening's final excursion boat departing from the landing on the Moskva River by Borodinskiy, ostensibly headed for the landing at Gorky Park and the amusement arcade. Sometimes, I would wait until I'd made sure everyone had left the boat at Gorky, then decide to go on to the next stop, thus allowing for a long walk back on the other side of the river through narrow winding streets before I chose to find a Metro to take me downtown to a favorite "dollar bar," where Americans congregated.

Occasionally, I'd stand on a busy street corner and time the traffic while I counted the number of cars with red diplomatic license plates and yellow commercial plates that went by in a five-minute period. At the same time, I tried to pick out the surveillance cars in the traffic stream—they often followed cars driven by foreigners.

It was during this trip that it hit me that perestroika and glasnost had radically changed things here. There was something new in the wind. People were smiling more. They were wearing brighter colors. They were showing more affluence. There was more going on. Lately, there were a few small private restaurants opening up where you could actually go for a good meal, rather than stand in line at a state-operated restaurant hoping for a cancellation. There was a whole line of cars with Western European license plates parked in front of the hotels on Gorky Street and in the outlying campgrounds. None of this had been here ten years earlier.

The KGB's Second Chief Directorate had to deal with an enormous explosion of potential foreign threats to national security. They could not possibly be doing business in the old ways. The command-and-control problem involved in watching all parties of potential interest had to be enormous. The typical Seventh Chief Directorate mobile surveillance team was not going to be effective by itself. There had to be many more people and resources at work here, and maybe we were looking at a truly "denied area" on the streets, with some sort of vastly improved monitoring system. Maybe our competition truly *had* become ten feet tall.

I also spent hours in Moscow talking to each of the ZEPHYRs about their experiences inside and outside of the American community. I observed the comings and goings of these intelligence officers, looking for anomalies in their patterns and profiles that would give me some clues as to our weaknesses.

We postulated about the ways surveillance could suddenly appear after a target had been in the clear—without surveillance—for many hours. It must have had something to do with the subject venturing through a chokepoint where some kind of marker or tag triggered an alarm and another team was scrambled.

Another theory we discussed was the two-surveillance-teams concept—the idea that there was a ghost team just over the horizon that you never saw. It was always there, surrounding you but always out of sight. The watcher team was the one seen as discreet surveillance—it appeared and disappeared but was actually being directed by the ghost team. I decided we should attempt to develop this concept in our SST simulations back home and experiment ourselves with these surveillance techniques.

During the Fourth of July celebration at the larger of the U.S. Embassy's two dachas, I had the unique experience of seeing our own officers mixed in with hundreds of the other members of the community. I could now compare our overt profiles with the profiles of the larger population. It was quite common for our own operational doctrine of behavior to yield an unintended cover pattern. It was easy to lag behind the times and changes in the environment and therefore cause ourselves to stand out. This was one of the things we always looked for in our exercises with the ZEPHYRs in Washington.

Of this wider group, the most interesting were the American graduate students in Russian studies who were here on contract with the U.S. Department of State doing the menial chores formerly accomplished by Soviet employees in the embassy. They had a wide-ranging pattern and profile that gave them opportunities to move around that the more tightly controlled members of the community didn't enjoy. That particular day a group of students had launched a rubber boat down on the Moskva River very early in the morning. They had somehow navigated their way through a series of reservoirs and canals and traveled many kilometers to a tiny canal behind the dacha. Here they boisterously announced their arrival like Vikings, counting cadence and stroking their oars in unison while propelling their seagoing dragon boat. I could just imagine how this must have driven the KGB wild, since it was outside their doctrine of operational behavior. I'm sure they had no contingency plan for rubber boat surveillance. Jonna would have loved it, and I made a mental note to tell her the whole story when I got home.

In sharp contrast, I noticed that every road intersection on the way out to the dacha that day was manned by the Soviet Militia, who make up the national police force. This heightened security was to ensure that no American car went astray, but it had not factored in a rubber raft off the security chart.

Luke Swisher was a lot like the student population in that his personal pattern was quite unlike that of an intelligence officer. A free spirit, he had all sorts of far-out ideas that still needed work but were scientifically sound. Like many of our OTS technical types, he was a blue-sky R and D guy who liked to think outside the box. In addition, he had great operational instincts. A perfect combination when you needed to reinvent the world.

We developed a mental blueprint between us, which included all the ways that the KGB could be surveilling us without being seen. A major part of what was driving our planning was the proposed project at hand: How could someone move clandestinely to a secret rendezvous point to meet a highly placed agent, continue onward through the most formidable security apparatus on earth, then perform an unprecedented technical penetration, and, finally, carry out a successful exfiltration of that agent and his family.

In order to meet these narrowly defined operational requirements, a new set of Moscow rules was needed that would allow us to carry out our mission quickly, quietly, and surreptitiously.

Careful not to tip my hand on the streets of Moscow, I planned to bounce some ideas off Jonna as soon as possible.

The thought of Jonna made me smile. How I missed her being with me, sharing these experiences and ideas. We had become close collaborators in recent months, and this had made the long hours and sometimes lonely work of intelligence much more pleasant.

The night before leaving Moscow to return to Washington and work out the final details for the upcoming Moscow operation, I had a vivid dream. Jonna and I were walking through an evening landscape somewhere out in the country. It was dark, but there was enough moonlight to make out the features of her face and the shine of her eyes. The landscape seemed to be filtered through a pale green lens, and when I looked up, we were walking toward a sky painted with the northern lights. It looked like a large velvet drapery, sheets of light falling to the dark horizon in deep folds and shades of green. It seemed to move and sway in the heavens, and we simply walked into it.

I wondered what the dream meant.

Edward Lee Howard sat in a chair in the living room of his tiny apartment in downtown Moscow. The furniture looked like something out of a Motel 6—cheap, modern, and uncomfortable. The apartment was relatively bare and devoid of any personal items except for a single photograph of Mary, his wife, and Lee, his son.

Though his wife would visit him occasionally in Moscow, she had decided not to abandon America, and remained there to raise their son. The U.S. government never chose to prosecute her as an accomplice to her husband's daring escape.

Howard was making notes on a pad of paper, letting his Russian handlers know which faces in the field of photos in front of him were CIA officers. They had been taken by KGB surveillance of Americans as they entered and departed various U.S. embassies around the world, including Moscow.

Of three he was certain, and two others looked familiar, so he included them.

His anger at the CIA had not abated. He was not finished with his war of revenge.

EIGHT

LUBYANKA, MOSCOW

1988

Petr Leonov sat in his seventh-floor office in the tower in Dom 2 of Lubyanka. It was 0830 hours, the beginning of a normal business day for him.

He had just arrived and hadn't yet opened his safe. He was contemplating a photo of his wife, Lara, holding their son on her lap. Dmitri had been two years old when the picture was taken; he was now eight, but retained the sweetness and good nature of that toddler. Lost in thought, Leonov was considering the past, and wondering about the future—for Dmitri, Lara, himself. Would they make it?

Located at No. 2 Dzerzhinsky Square, in the center of Moscow, Lubyanka was the traditional home of the Committee for State Security: the KGB. It was also known as the Center. The tower in which Leonov worked was nicknamed the "Appendix," and one of his windows overlooked an inner courtyard. Like all the windows in the tower, it was covered by a white sheer drape, partly for security reasons, partly to keep employees from looking out and seeing things best left unseen. In the old days, many Soviet citizens, including more than a few KGB officers, had been put to death for treason in the courtyard. No one was supposed to know exactly what took place there, but the grapevine never failed—

and some had felt compelled to take last, forlorn looks at former colleagues as they met their deaths.

In 1972, while Leonov was overseas, the headquarters of the First Chief Directorate of the KGB, the organization's foreign intelligence arm, had moved from here. On the outskirts of Moscow, near the village of Yasenevo, a new building had been built in a dark pine forest, and was thus known as the Forest.

Not long after their return to Moscow, while on a long walk that afforded the only certainty of their conversation's not being monitored, Lara had first brought up the subject that had been on both their minds for some time. Through the years, she had supported Petr's work with the Americans, hoping he could do his part to rid their beloved motherland of the oppressive Communist system that held it captive. As they walked hand in hand past Red Square, she first verbalized the possibility of their leaving Russia— of defecting to the West with their son and bringing him up in a free society where he could grow up to be anything he liked. On their overseas assignments, they had had their first real taste of freedom—they found it addictive. And now, to dream of a life in America? Since that day when they first discussed the possibility, the pattern of their lives had changed greatly. It was no longer just about what work he could do and how to prevent himself from being discovered. The idea of their son's future—indeed, his very freedom—was the beacon that now guided their every move.

In his job in the Science and Technology Directorate, Leonov was in charge of technical security for the KAPELLE program. His section's mission was to ensure secure KAPELLE operations for all the KGB, but mainly for the First Chief Directorate to and from the Center, and all outposts worldwide. Because of his assignment, Leonov had access to all secret Soviet communications around the world. During his seventeen-year career, he had done well professionally, and on the face of it, he had no reason to be concerned. He had joined the KGB as a young man and had been posted abroad for a few years as a KAPELLE operator. Although he had been trained in one of the Soviet Union's scientific academies and had much greater potential, they had wanted him to get his hands dirty in the field, doing the actual work, before advancing him in rank. He returned to Moscow in 1980, and began working his way up the chain of command. By now, at the relatively young age of thirty-eight, he had earned the rank of major and was a section chief with offices in the Appendix.

His short blond hair and pleasant, smooth face made him appear to be in his late twenties. His heavily muscled torso and trim waist amplified his ramrod-straight military profile. While he did not know it, the secretaries of Lubyanka called him "the Gymnast," acknowledging his physique, good looks, and charisma. There were many pairs of female eyes on him as he moved through the offices during the day—admiring eyes that he did not acknowledge except with a courteous smile.

Sinking back into his chair, he thought back to the events of last year. The Americans had proved to him the extent to which they would go in order to protect him, and he was both amazed and relieved. Pressure had begun to build the previous spring; he had noticed security in the directorate offices increasing and had noticed that his own routine surveillance had been reinforced. He remembered the butterflies in his stomach and the month of interrupted sleep as he worried about being apprehended. But then, suddenly, it had stopped. His friend Natasha in the division secretariat had been the first to enlighten him. She told him that they had been worried about a leak in their KAPELLE network, but had finally discarded the idea after the Americans had spirited one of the devices out of a KGB stronghold on the Asian subcontinent. The increased security and heightened surveillance had then ceased. Why on earth, she had asked rhetorically, would the Americans steal a machine if they had an agent inside of the KAPELLE network? It made no sense.

Leonov smiled at the memory. To him, of course, it had made

great sense. His friends, the Americans, had stolen the machine to get him off the hook.

But now, a year later, things were heating up again.

Outside, the gray stone building that was Lubyanka formed one side of Dzerzhinsky Square and took up a whole city block. The joke was that Lubyanka was the tallest building in Moscow, and that on a clear day you could see all the way to Siberia from here. Those who witnessed the revolution could never forget the building as a symbol of terror. It had served as the Cheka headquarters, as well as a prison and execution center. The predecessors of the KGB had occupied these quarters over the years, all through the various name changes of the secret police and intelligence arms of the U.S.S.R.

During the purges of the 1930s, the condemned traitors were taken down to the cellar of Lubyanka to one of the death cells, where they exchanged their garments for a set of white underclothes. Then, they were positioned in a kneeling position and shot in the back of the neck with a Nagant revolver. After they were declared dead, their remains were removed and the tarpaulin on the floor of the cell was taken out and cleaned by a woman employed expressly for that purpose. She was never seen except following one of these executions. In fact, she had become something of a folk figure in the KGB, and the promise of a visit from "the Cellar Babushka" was a thinly veiled threat.

Today, the cellar of Lubyanka was no longer used as the execution center for enemies of the state. Although the very efficient technique of a pistol to the head was still employed, the executions had been moved to Lefortovo Prison in Moscow. Leonov and his colleagues knew there had been a significant number of these executions carried out in recent years. Shockingly, many of those executed were traitors found inside the KGB itself.

He seldom allowed himself these thoughts; if he dwelled too long on the risks he was taking—not just to himself but also to

Lara and Dmitri—he could become overwhelmed by the potential danger and paralyzed into inaction.

Although the details of many of those cases were not widely known, Leonov had picked up the usual office scuttlebutt. The division secretariat, the distributor of all mail and communications, served another function as the main office rumor mill. Leonov was on good terms with the ladies in the secretariat. He had just returned from there this morning, picking up his mail along with unofficial details of yet another traitor in their midst, who had just been executed.

Leonov closely scanned the round disk of soft gray oil-based clay mounted on the door joint of his safe. It bore the undisturbed impression of his personal seal, as it should. The disk had two pieces of cord embedded in it that were strung across the crevice of the safe door and attached to the door itself. If anyone had entered his safe he would know. He tore the cord from the disk of clay and used two different keys to open the safe.

His official files and other classified documents were inside. There was also a small notebook. He reached in and removed the notebook and began thumbing through the pages. This was his book of addresses and telephone numbers. It also contained a few pages of his private financial accounts. Being a technical security officer, he had developed a note-taking system that disguised important information so it appeared to be part of the other innocuous notations in his notebook. This was how he concealed very sensitive notes to himself. Sometimes these notes pertained to his official duties and missions, and sometimes not.

This was the only piece of physical evidence of his work, including his efforts for the Americans, that he allowed himself. This was how he was keeping track of the details of the net that he had been feeling closing in ever tighter these last few months. He found the page in his accounting records for his and Lara's retirement funds and goods, and went to the entry for items they had planned to stockpile at their dacha. This was not considered hoarding in Soviet society; every citizen spent a great deal of time during their daily lives standing in line in hopes of buying goods that were scarce on the market. Often, they would use these items to barter for other goods not easily obtainable. The Soviet economy under Gorbachev was improving somewhat as reforms were implemented, but it had a long way to go. Until then, every citizen needed to build a hedge against the day when he or she would have a diminished cash flow, such as in retirement—forced or otherwise.

Disguised as part of this list was a secret record he had been compiling of the names and particulars of those who had been subject to arrest by the KGB in recent years, including sketchy notations about each—details such as their names, the circumstances of their trials, and eventual sentences. Anything he was able to piece together from the public record or from the rumor mill. He also had friends in the Second Chief Directorate who owed him favors and on occasion enjoyed talking shop. From them, he found out details available nowhere else.

Now, in this notebook, he made another entry, which, according to his personal shorthand, indicated the twelfth entry of its sort since 1985. The notation, like the others, would appear to anyone's curious gaze as simple groups of numbers and Cyrillic words of little consequence.

This last entry in open code would have translated to read: GRU POLYAKOV 15.3.88.

This was the affiliation, name, and execution date of the man he would later learn was one of the most harmful to the U.S.S.R., one of the most productive spies ever in the U.S. arsenal. A general in the GRU, Dmitri Polyakov had worked clandestinely for the CIA for eighteen years—handing over enough classified information to fill twenty-seven file drawers at CIA headquarters—until his retirement. Following his arrest in July 1986, he had been interrogated for nearly two years after making a deal with the KGB: in exchange for their leaving his family alone and allowing his wife to keep their dacha, he would tell them everything he'd given the Americans. Then, in March 1988, he had been executed.

The entry right above this last one would translate from the code to read: KGB MARTYNOV 28.5.87.

This entry was a little more personal. One of Leonov's early colleagues, KGB Lieutenant Colonel Valeriy F. Martynov had been a tall, friendly, happy-go-lucky fellow whom he had always been glad to see. They had been friends only briefly, however, as their careers had diverged early on. Leonov had spent six months in intensive English language training with Martynov; enough time to get to know him and for them to have a few drinks together. Then, Valeriy had married Natalya, and they had two children. Leonov had lost track of them when he and Lara had started dating, but had eventually heard through the grapevine of their posting to Washington, D.C. Leonov had felt a twinge of envy at such a choice assignment for his friend, but wished him and his wife well.

When news reached him of Valeriy Martynov's execution, Leonov was helpless to pursue the details. Any undue attention paid to the case might have raised suspicions. He could do no more than make this terse, encrypted note in his personal book and affirm to himself that he was doing everything he could to protect himself and his family from a similar fate. He could not bear to think of Natalya without her husband, and her two young children without a father, forced to live in shame for the rest of their lives.

Above Martynov's entry was that for another KGB officer named Motorin, also executed last year. Leonov had not known KGB Major Sergey M. Motorin personally, but had known of him many years previously. His friends in his KGB entry class had called Motorin "the Gentle Giant." He came from the north of Russia, and had the Nordic good looks of a Scandinavian. While he was a giant of a man physically, with an athletic build, his claim to fame in the young KGB class had been his roving eye and his entourage of good-looking young women, whom he showed up with at every social occasion, oftentimes with one on each arm. Leonov was aware that Motorin had also been assigned to the Soviet Embassy in Washington, D.C. He was a line officer, collecting political intelligence, and the U.S. assignment was an indication that his star was on the rise. Leonov had no knowledge of what had happened to cause his execution, but he had been arrested and shot almost two years after his return to Moscow.

On his list were six KGB officers and three GRU officers; two more KGB officers, he knew, had managed to escape to the West shortly before they could be arrested. There was one civilian on the list: Adolf Tolkachev, a scientist from the institute where Leonov had been trained. Word was he had done grave damage to the Soviet aeronautical weapons systems effort during the years he worked for the CIA.

Now, Leonov feared his time was approaching. He had to make some sense of this disturbing pattern that seemed to have begun in 1985, a year after he'd made the fateful decision to recontact the Americans, following his earlier work with them. His, Lara's, and Dmitri's future depended on it—not to mention his chance to change for the better the future of his country.

He sat and stared at his list, trying to figure out what it all meant. He recalled the time in April 1985 when this spiderweb of cases had started to appear to him.

Back then, a KGB foreign counterintelligence officer, Viktor Cherkashin, who was at the time posted to Washington, D.C., made an unexpected trip to Moscow. He had made arrangements to brief the head of the First Chief Directorate, Vladimir Kryuchkov, on a matter too hot to put in staff communications channels. Kryuchkov had immediately taken Cherkashin to the chairman of the KGB, who then took him to Gorbachev. The head of the Second Chief Directorate was summoned and Gorbachev was livid—angry, it was said, that the large birthmark on his forehead disappeared into his bloodred complexion for several long moments. The recounting of this tidbit was invariably followed by belly laughs, for Gorbachev was without many friends in the KGB.

The whole matter was kept very tight, but the tremors could be felt through both the directorates concerned. Leonov's friends in those sections opined that there must have been an enormous counterintelligence problem in the Soviet intelligence apparatus. But whatever brought it to light was so important that Cherkashin made a series of trips to Moscow in the following months.

Leonov interpreted the increased activity to mean that there had been some new source of threatening information—perhaps a defector from U.S. intelligence had revealed the names of Soviet citizens and officials working for the Americans?

Since then, the careers and lives of more than twenty Soviets had been ended either by execution or banishment to the gulag. Somehow through it all, Leonov had survived. He was not sure whether it had to do with luck or his decision to lie low for a time, and thereafter, to make his own decisions regarding tradecraft.

Petr and Lara knew about surveillance. Lara, for all her beauty and youthful looks, was a skilled countersurveillance part of their team. Whenever they were out for a walk and one of their private discussions, it was invariably Lara who called out the approaching surveillance team members. She would stop him in the middle of a sentence, putting her hand on his shoulder, and simply lean over and spontaneously kiss him, thus providing cover for her action, as well as a tender moment. She seemed to have a sixth sense, an ability to intuit when something was out of place or when the scene did not add up. She had steered them away from danger more than once. Petr loved Lara with all of his heart, and from the beginning she had been his primary motivation for his activities with the Americans. He would never have done it without her support. In fact, it had been Lara who had initially raised the idea of working for the Americans and of helping to change the horrible system that controlled life in their country.

As a member of the KAPELLE program, Leonov was subject to intermittent surveillance mounted by the Seventh Directorate—the surveillance division. Mostly, this was conducted routinely and was not a cause for alarm. In the same way, he had been assigned a personal security escort when he was abroad as a KAPELLE officer—not because he was under suspicion but because his defection would be a disaster. Each member of the Sixteenth Directorate was paid 20 percent more than others of equal rank in the KGB, but they were also put under more scrutiny and tighter restriction. This was because they had potential access to all the secrets of the KGB, the Party, and the Politburo by virtue of their mission to protect the secret technical networks.

One of the common threads Leonov had found in the cases of those who had come under suspicion and been discovered to be foreign spies was their tradecraft. Almost all of them used the classic techniques that spies use to communicate. In order to accomplish this, they had to possess some kind of spy gear or evidence of their activities. Also, they had to adhere to the planning of another intelligence service and the actions of those officers responsible for handling them. Limiting knowledge within an organization about a particular case was exceedingly difficult in these situations. Too, when your life was at stake, depending on the professionalism of just any one officer was unacceptable. For these reasons, he had taken charge of his own case and laid down the ground rules to the Americans. No spy tools. Few personal meetings, and only those that he asked for.

Years ago, back in Indochina, he had also established the rules of dissemination of his information to the Americans in an attempt to design a compartment that would give him the highest measure of protection from a leak within the CIA or the Citadel, where his product would surely end up. His CIA handler had assured him that anyone in his position recruited by the U.S. would receive this kind of compartmentation. The product of other agents, such as the doomed General Polyakov, received wider, political dissemination because they reported on broad-based issues that were of interest to many U.S. agencies and departments, even the White House. Whereas his own product was very specific technical security intelligence that would be consumed only by a highly compartmented group in the Citadel. Potentially it could allow the U.S. to read all secure Soviet communications worldwide, but he had been assured that fact would never be widely disseminated in the U.S. government and would stay compartmented.

Coincidentally, Polyakov had been in Indochina about the same time as Leonov, and had established his own rules of engagement, which had kept him alive for more than twenty years. Leonov's rules had succeeded for nearly that long as well. He and Polyakov weren't aware of each other's CIA activities during the time they were both active, but with the information Leonov had gleaned in recent weeks, he had been able to study Polyakov's techniques.

Polyakov had been receiving some of his communications by dead drop and had a system of secret, coded writing. He had the capability to receive communications about dead drops via an open code used in classified ads in *The New York Times*. Polyakov also had a very sophisticated technical device made for him by the CIA that could be used to make quick exchanges on the street without making visible or physical contact. Not lost on Leonov was the fact that each of Polyakov's techniques required that he possess tradecraft items that could, if discovered, compromise him. It also required that physical items had to be exchanged. All of this only reinforced Leonov's determination that his own rules should continue to forbid his use of spy tools, such as miniature cameras and the like.

One of the missions of his own directorate was to intercept hostile communications, so he was well aware of the kind of convoluted tradecraft involved in making successful exchanges via technical devices without being "seen" by an alert counterintelligence service equipped with scanners.

Leonov had also heard that his colleagues in the Second CD were working on a number of tagging or tracking systems that would allow them to trace the transfer of materials from suspected or known intelligence officers. They incorporated all of the techniques possible into the program called METKA. This was another reason he insisted on self-initiated personal meetings only. He was capable of setting them up ahead of time in the sites he chose so he could observe the approach of his handler and determine if there was anyone trailing him. He made sure that the only contact between himself and his handler was when he passed something over without touching the CIA officer. He accepted nothing in exchange. Having personal meetings was the one thing Polyakov had refused to do in Moscow because he considered it too dangerous. He had used them in the Third World, but insisted upon impersonal means of communication here at home.

On their walk the previous night, Petr had expressed to Lara his unease, and reminded her of the words of Jack Maxwell, his first CIA handler, back in Asia: "If it feels wrong, it probably is wrong." She nodded sympathetically, and said she trusted his intuition.

And feel wrong it did; he knew in his gut that the time to leave was drawing near. The rules of engagement had changed. Something was different about the surveillance they had become so accustomed to seeing. It was as if the KGB *knew.*

There had long been plans, ever since his early work for the Americans in Indochina, for his exfiltration should he be discovered. Leonov knew this and took heart that he, Lara, and Dmitri could take flight before it was too late for them all.

Leonov appreciated that at least two of those on his list of traitors to the Soviet cause had succeeded in escaping to the West, no doubt with CIA assistance, rather than face execution. Above all, he wanted to ensure that Lara and Dmitri were out of danger.

As long as he could do that and continue to work against the perverse regime that was ruining his country, he would be content. But he sensed he didn't have much time left. Before he was finished with this kind of dangerous work, he wanted to leave something behind—a legacy of his and Lara's service, something that would continue to serve the cause of freedom, as they had tried to do for so many years.

He had hatched his daring plan over several weeks. He knew that he could make it work if he had enough time to pull things together. He had contacted the Americans and told them his idea, and they had, of course, been quite excited.

Now, still sitting in repose at his desk, he glanced again at the sheer drapes covering the windows to his office. He rose and walked over to the window, the one looking out toward Dzerzhinsky Square. He reached up high, behind the drapes, and pulled the roller blind down almost one meter. It was so simple. This was the signal to the Americans, specifically to one American who checked that window every morning on his way to work at his cover office. This signal meant only one thing: *Emergency— get us out soon.*

Then, Petr Leonov, the man the Americans had once called SAPPHIRE but now called ORB, picked up the telephone and dialed the number for his KGB counterpart in the Second CD.

It was time to begin his day's work.

NINE

DULLES AIRPORT, WASHINGTON, D.C.

August 1988

Jonna

Tony and I were standing so close to one another that light could barely pass between us. He was quietly telling me something important about the upcoming flight to Los Angeles, but I couldn't focus on the words. I was almost dizzy with his nearness; the sensation was like being somewhat tipsy and knowing you are about to get into trouble, only you can't turn back.

When they called our flight, we walked through the United Airlines departure lounge at Dulles and filed down the walkway that tethered the plane to the gate. Our first stop on this trip would be L.A., before I headed on to Hong Kong, then China. Tony and I would be meeting in California with several specialized contractors he had worked with for years, looking for new answers to our current problems in Moscow.

I took my seat in business class and looked back to see how far away he was sitting. I spotted him quickly, looking for the Harris Tweed coat and the black-and-gray-striped shirt before I looked for his face—an old habit from surveillance exercises. Only three rows back. *Good, I can keep track of him without being too obvious.*

I was sitting up front in business class because this was the first leg of an international trip and the office would pay for business class either if the trip was long enough or if you were going to work right after getting to your destination. As I was to end up halfway around the world, that put me solidly in the "long enough" part of the travel regulation. I would be visiting Guangzhou, Beijing, and Shanghai—a trip I had wanted to take almost my entire working career. It would be a two-week survey, a relatively easy visit, to see what each city and region looked like, to observe the people, and to survey the operational lay of the land. I would be visiting with our operations officers along the way, but a lot of the time I would be out on my own. This was a type of work that I particularly enjoyed. I knew that some professional women didn't like traveling alone, but I did. It was almost like running—I got a lot of mental work done when I could tune out the rest of the world. Besides doing the survey, I would also be trying to solve some other problems, both professional and personal.

Foremost among those in the latter category was what to do about my marriage. At this point, I felt as if the marriage was just a shell—picture perfect on the outside but empty within. While John and I could and did talk about our work, we actually discussed little else. Our passions lay elsewhere, outside of our marriage. Sports, in fact, were at the top of his list, and books were at the top of mine. It wasn't that I was miserable. In fact, I was so comfortable in my big Victorian home in Reston, Virginia, and so pleased with my garden that there was no impetus for me to take the final step and make a break. We had just completed a real library at the front of the house, a place full of glass-fronted bookcases that could hold all of the old classics and modern first editions that I had collected for years. The rugs were down on the dark-stained hardwood floors; the antiques I had collected in Europe and the Far East were finally in place. Life was pleasant, and John and I had been coasting in this way for years. On the other hand, if my feelings for Tony continued like this, I was looking at a real dilemma. That was exactly the kind of situation I had many times watched from the sidelines, and marveled at how people made such stupid mistakes in their personal affairs and ruined their lives and careers.

I turned to look at him. He was immersed in his reading—a biography of Winston Churchill called *The Last Lion* that he had been telling me about for weeks.

Turning back to my newspaper, I tried to shake off the butterflies in my stomach. What in the world was happening? This is my *boss* and I am getting giddy when he gets close? Sounded like a problem I had heard about from a few friends over the years, but surely not one I would encounter. I picked up *The Washington Post* and dived into the Style section. I was about halfway through the last piece when I sensed someone standing by my seat.

He was kneeling down on one knee in the aisle beside me.

"I got a book for you last night," Tony said. "I was at Olsson's bookstore down by the Metro downtown. I think you should read this."

I took the thin volume from him and turned it over. *The Art of War.*

"Why?" I asked, a bit mystified.

"It was written by a Chinese general named Sun Tzu nearly twenty-five hundred years ago. It's the most brilliant philosophy on espionage, strategy, tactics, and warfare that I've read."

He looked at me with a slight smile, eyebrows raised. "We are at war, you know. We're the generals who are developing the strategy for a counterattack. Why don't you look it over and see what you think."

Tony rose and returned to his seat.

I sat there, perfectly still, my heart beating too fast. I felt a blush sweep up my neck and envelop my face. I flashed to all of the stories of those who had beat the polygraph machines by failing to register their true emotions when tested. I summoned up a picture-perfect image of the terrace at the Oriental Hotel in Bangkok, with a soft wind and endless sun streaming through the palms. It worked. I could breathe again.

I picked up the book and began to read:

> *If you know the enemy and know yourself, you need not fear the result of a hundred battles. If you know yourself but not the enemy, for every victory gained you will also suffer a defeat. If you know neither the enemy nor yourself, you will succumb in every battle.*

I was still reading as we began our descent into LAX. The flight had been uneventful, the food the usual mystery buried under a cream sauce, and the dessert inedible. And I was aware of his presence with every turned page.

"The first order of business," Tony proclaimed as we deplaned, "as important as all of the rest, is to have a good time while we're out here. It's going to get very intense, and in the moments in between, you have to be sure to enjoy the place."

I *liked* this man's style.

Los Angeles

The Hollywood Roosevelt Hotel was something special. Built in 1927, it was a true luxury hotel in the heart of Tinseltown, designed in the popular 1920s Spanish-Moorish style, complete with tile roofs and elaborately carved beamed ceilings in all of the public rooms. The lobby was a grand space with iron chandeliers, arched windows, and marble floors. Just about the best part of the hotel was the pool area, which I could see once we walked down the corridor and exited the back side of the facility. It was lushly planted with tropical blooming plants and had a large pool and an enticing hot tub at the far end. I filed away this information; the hot tub would be a great place to seek out after a long day of meetings.

We dropped our bags in our rooms—cabana rooms, they each faced the pool. I noticed that Tony's room was almost directly across from mine. We freshened up and met again in the bar at five o'clock.

"We're meeting Jerome Calloway for drinks at six and going to the Magic Castle for dinner," Tony said.

I knew Jerome was an award-winning makeup artist whom Tony had worked with before on some operational problems. Hollywood had provided expertise in materials and techniques on several previous CIA operations.

"The Castle is a real treat," Tony continued. "It's a private club by and for magicians, and friends of magicians. They perform for each other in a small intimate setting. You'll never get closer to a card trick or a stage show."

The Castle was within walking distance of the hotel. As we exited onto Hollywood Boulevard, I realized that we were on the famous Walk of Fame. The pink granite stars in the sidewalk were engraved with the names of famous entertainers.

We crossed the street to see Mann's Chinese Theater.

"Look, there," Tony pointed, slowing down. "That's Jerome's star—almost right smack in front of the theater entrance."

We walked one block over and two blocks down. From the exterior, the Magic Castle did not disappoint. We approached it from Hollywood Boulevard, heading up a steep incline. Perched high above us was a large Victorian building with the appropriate turrets and gingerbread. It was painted a creamy, buttery yellow, and closely resembled something from the set of *The Addams Family*. At the top of the turret in front, on the third floor, was a window displaying a skeleton in a rocking chair busily moving back and forth and peering out onto the parking lot.

We were met at the entrance by an older man in a tuxedo, the maitre d', who looked at me with a slight frown. "Excuse me, madam, but our dress code requires evening dress for women. Do you perhaps have a jacket that goes with those trousers? If you have a jacket, we could call it a suit and I could admit you."

He looked me up and down again—a little arrogantly, I thought.

I felt the blush sweeping over me, my second one in less than twenty-four hours. I was surprised, then embarrassed, and finally angry at the situation.

"Sorry," I said. "I didn't realize it was a dress occasion."

My bags were full of the casual working clothes I planned for China, but I was turned out in silk pants and a hand-knit silk sweater with pearls and low-heeled Bruno Magli sandals. Evidently my ensemble did not quite measure up.

Jerome Calloway, who had joined us, was clearly mortified and began spluttering an apology to me. Tony turned to him and easily and gracefully defused the situation.

"That's okay, Jerome. Jonna and I will just get a quick bite to eat and head back to the hotel. We're both tired from the flight. We'll meet you at nine in the morning."

Jerome readily agreed to this new plan, throwing a final glaring look at the doorman. Jerome was feeling personally slighted; he was a man of some stature in this town and not used to being denied his way. Besides, this was the equivalent of his private club. The doorman held his ground, though; he had enforced the rules and his authority had prevailed. I thought that he would make a good Indian of the kind that you find at the airport in New Delhi. The British had taught them all about enforcing the rules, and it was now a large cottage industry there.

Tony and I departed.

"Thanks," I murmured. "Nice save. Now, where shall we go? Do you know your way around this town?"

We drove down Hollywood Boulevard in our rental car, heading east. We took the ramp to the 101 South to cross Los Angeles. We left Hollywood behind, shooting across the city, and emerged on the east side; some would say the real Los Angeles. It was clear that Tony was intimately familiar with the city and its freeways.

"We'll go over to Olvera Street, if that's okay with you," he said. "Olvera is on this side of town, the wrong side, surrounded by darker and quieter streets than those we have been seeing so far. It looks a little menacing, but the place I'm taking you to is perfectly safe. I haven't been there in a long time, but I think you'll like it."

We exited from the freeway, and the streets did have a different character. They were not the well-lit, bustling thoroughfares of Hollywood and Beverly Hills but more subdued, with closed storefronts and darkened windows facing the street.

I thought it was a little ominous. "This is how *Bonfire of the Vanities* begins, I ventured."

Tony said he hadn't yet read it.

"They exit a highway in New York City and get so scared that they run over a couple of young men who are trying to help them," I explained. "Be careful and don't run anybody down. Tom Wolfe isn't here to write us out of it."

I smiled at him to show that I was only kidding, and got a nod and a beaming smile in return. We were driving by cars sitting on blocks and boarded-up apartment buildings. Then, a couple of blocks ahead, there was a shimmer of thousands of small lights in the trees.

"That's it," Tony said, pulling the car into a nearby parking lot.

We walked across the deserted street and entered a walkway that was out of a fairy tale. Olvera Street is constructed like a Mexican village, with all of the restaurants, street stalls, and shops you would expect to encounter south of the border. We passed a group of

local musicians on their break and wandered down one side of the
street, examining all sorts of Mexican products for sale in the stalls.

"Just a little farther," Tony said, "on the left-hand side."

We stopped outside La Golondrina ("The Swallow"), and he
motioned me in. The restaurant was dark with a lot of glistening,
highly polished wooden surfaces, and ceiling fans stirred the air
from above. We took a table in front of the fireplace, where we
had a splendid view of the entire room and there was a fire going
just a few feet from us in the chilly evening.

"What color would you call these walls?" I asked. "Sienna?"

"Well, let's see. Not raw sienna or burnt sienna or red sienna,"
replied my boss, an artist. "The color is really called Indian Red.
Can you guess why?" He paused a beat. "Because it is the exact
color of the makeup used to make Cherokee and Cheyenne Indi-
ans in the movies."

I didn't believe him and thought he was just trying to be amus-
ing. But he finally convinced me that he was telling the truth. His
oil paints, he explained, came in large tubes, and the one containing this hue was labeled "Indian Red."

"How in the world did you find this place?" I asked.

"I didn't. My mom and dad found it. They came here from
Eureka, Nevada, on their honeymoon in 1937. They were eighteen years old and newlyweds. Kids really. My dad died working
in a copper mine in 1943, when I was three. I was too young
to remember him, but I've seen his photos and he was a great-
looking guy. He played guitar and often joined in one of these
kinds of bands on the weekend. In fact, they were a great-looking
couple. My mom always talked about their trip to Olvera Street
while we were growing up. She had six young kids back then, and
she used to tell us a lot of romantic stories about the two of them.
She said this place was just like vacationing in Mexico."

Tony had a sad smile at the thought of his mother here as a
young woman.

I looked around. Although it was summertime, the Christmas decorations were still up and the lights still on. *They probably never take them down,* I thought, *just like in the bars in the Philippines.* Through the open door and the wide windows we watched a steady stream of families and kids strolling past, many on their way to dinner.

A young gringo waitress appeared out of nowhere to take our drink orders. Tony ordered a Dos Equis amber, and I succumbed to their house special, a huge margarita. While we were waiting for them, Tony gave me a thumbnail sketch of his L.A. connections, most of which involved a lot of travel from Washington consulting with Hollywood. He told me about his grandmother, Lucia Serrata Gomez, who was buried in an unmarked pauper's grave somewhere in the city. He wanted to come back someday and find her—he had inherited a lot of family lore from his mother and was very interested in her family history. He said that she had been a beautiful woman. Many months later I saw a photograph of her: a sad, attractive young girl with a gardenia behind one ear. She was a world-class beauty.

We were approached by two guitarists, dressed to the nines in the kind of mariachi outfits that made my teeth ache. I grimaced to Tony, hoping he would wave them off. To my horror, he motioned them over. They knew a live one when they saw him. They happily launched into a song that charmed us both—a song neither of us had heard before. It was soft and melodic and a little melancholy and in Spanish, which meant I didn't understand a word.

When they finished, we applauded them and asked their names.

"Raul and Moises," they said, bowing.

"What was the name of that song?" I asked. "It was really lovely."

"The song is called 'Sabor a Mi,' " replied Raul, who so resembled Jabba the Hutt that it had seriously detracted from the music.

I had listened to them sing while watching Tony, wondering if he understood Spanish. He looked at me, shrugged his shoulders, and raised his hands palms up in the universal I-haven't-got-a-clue gesture.

Raul leaned down to the table. "It means, 'A Taste of Me,' " he whispered.

I looked at him, rather blankly, I expect.

"Like in a kiss," he said, gently smiling at our apparent lack of romance.

Tony handed them some money, and they moved off across the restaurant.

We remained silent for several minutes, each lost in our thoughts.

"This was the first Mexican restaurant in Los Angeles," Tony finally said. "It dates back to 1924."

I could see he was reading from the back of the menu. No doubt he was trying to lighten the suddenly awkward mood, but it was tough going.

The evening deteriorated from there. On the way home we both tried to make light conversation, but it didn't work. Finally, I asked what had been on my mind all evening: "Did you and Karen come here often?"

I had begun to feel that Tony was still so vulnerable after his wife's death that his actions and words had to be taken with that in mind. I was afraid that he might be trying to replace her, and no woman wanted to be someone else's stand-in.

"What does that have to do with anything?" he asked, irritated. "I was trying to show you a place that is special to me—a place that I thought you would love—and all you can do is question my motives?"

He drove on in silence, going faster. We got back onto the freeway and picked up speed, hurtling back across the city in a mass of traffic.

When we got back to the hotel, we both went directly to our rooms, avoiding the bar, where we would normally have had a drink before retiring. I found myself unable to sleep and sat on a small sofa in my darkened room with the drapes open, looking out on the pool that had looked so tantalizing earlier in the day. I could see that the lights were on in his room, but the drapes were drawn.

Why did he have to get so angry? I was uncomfortable with the feelings that Tony was arousing in me and did not trust my own judgment at this point. He was putting me in a difficult position. On the one hand, I admired him as I had admired few men. He was the complete package: intelligent, balanced, clever, and funny. He was a romantic at heart, an adventurer, and an artist who thought with the right side of his brain, the creative side, as well as a skilled negotiator. He was kind and warm and real.

Both of our marriages had ended; his suddenly and tragically, mine sadly and incompletely. There would be no rush on my part to jump into another relationship, and no need to do so with Tony, especially since it might spoil our professional partnership and wonderful friendship.

Maybe what bothered me most was the thought of jeopardizing our friendship; the chance that it might end abruptly. Already, I couldn't imagine not having Tony in my life.

I finally fell asleep, fully clothed, sitting on the sofa.

I was awakened the next morning by the glare of California sunshine shooting through the opened blinds.

It had been a long night—so full in the beginning, and so lonely at the end.

We went through the security formalities at the entrance to the studio lot in Burbank, and parked beside a group of stucco buildings surrounded by palm trees that looked faintly reminiscent of Hollywood in the 1930s.

Strolling down the narrow streets of the studio complex, we came to another group of buildings that served as offices for a variety of producers, directors, and administrative types; these buildings were less grand than the earlier ones. We kept going, finally turning a corner and finding a slightly run-down building with an outside staircase.

Tony led me up the stairs and along a balcony into what turned out to be the right office, but with no one in it. "He must be in his laboratory."

We went down the stairs and across the street to enter a large, hangarlike building with a row of trailers parked in a line outside.

"Wardrobe, catering, and the stars, if they are famous enough, get a trailer of their own," Tony explained. He had been here many times and was comfortably familiar with the surroundings.

We went down a long, dark corridor, emerging into a two-story room that was obviously a working lab. I saw immediately that it bore an uncanny resemblance to our own labs back at head-quarters. It even smelled the same, except here all four walls were lined with rubber faces of characters and monsters from many of the classic movies of our time. I felt like a kid in a candy store.

Jerome Calloway came striding through a doorway and greeted Tony the way he had last night, with a bear hug. He was a large and affable man with thinning gray hair and heavy, black-rimmed glasses. He looked like an aging postman, tanned and fit, but getting a little heavy.

"Sorry about last night," Calloway said. "We'll get you in there another night." Turning to me, he said, "Jonna, do you have any idea what you're in for today?"

"I think so, Jerome, and I can't wait to get started. It's not often that I get to work with a living legend."

"That has a faintly ominous ring to it." Calloway smiled at me, the first of many kindly smiles from this good-natured gentleman as he guided us through his processes.

After Jerome's tour, Tony wanted to get down to work.

"Jerome, here's our problem," he said. "As always, we're going to ask you to treat this information as privileged."

"Of course."

"We need your expertise for some special effects we want to perform. The goal is to have two individuals disappear in a crowded room without a trace—into thin air. We've all seen it done by magicians and on the big screen; maybe you can show us how to create that same effect without the benefit of lights, retakes, and hours of makeup."

"You know my methods pretty well by now," Calloway said. "Whether I do the work or you do it, it goes back to the same principles. You have to know where the stage is—that is, where your actors will be performing. And it is a performance—you can't treat it as anything less. You have to know exactly who your audience is, and then pick the right time. You've picked the stage. Oh, this is very important: the illusion is usually over with before the performance begins. Let's sit down and define these areas; then we can make a start. First, how tall are they and how much do they weigh?"

"Individually or together?" I asked, smiling.

Jerome cracked up. "We'll treat each one as a single unit, if you please."

That evening after dinner, Tony and I found ourselves sitting on the terrace by the pool at the hotel. A glass of champagne in my hand, I leaned back in the chaise lounge and said, "What an amazing day. I can't believe what we are talking about."

Tony smiled at me. He raised the glass in a toast, then took a sip and set it down. "It is pretty interesting stuff. And wait until tomorrow—the 'Wizards' are going to throw technology into the mix. Right now, though, I just want to relax."

"Good idea. Look over there, across the pool. They have a hot tub. I think I'm going to put on my suit and slip in. I've been thinking about it since we checked in."

I stood and headed for my room.

"I'll race you," said Tony.

Ten minutes later, we were sitting in the tub up to our necks in bubbles and steaming mist. We sat close together in the cool evening air, enjoying the jet stream coming over the ledge, and were silent for a long time.

"This is heaven," I said.

"Pretty close to it."

Tony looked steadily at me.

I looked back. *I wonder who invented this man? Who cobbled him together? He's the most interesting man I have ever met. He needs to be kissed, he is so lonely.*

I leaned over, put my hand on his shoulder, and kissed him lightly on the lips.

There was a moment of recognition by us both.

"That's not a kiss," he said, putting his glass down on the side of the tub. He pulled me toward him, through the steam and bubbles. *"This* is a kiss."

The meeting with the Wizards started at nine-thirty sharp the next morning.

Assembled in a conference room at a private facility were a group of scientists and theorists who represented the state of the art in their fields. Chemists, engineers, computer gurus, research heads, all brought together under one roof. Tony had called this high-powered brainstorming session to help solve some of our problems in Moscow.

Ted Giles, a former Navy submarine commander, chaired the meeting. Retired from the U.S. Navy and now working in private industry, Giles was one of those bald men who look totally cool without hair. He had broad shoulders and the command presence one would expect from a man with his military background. On the other hand, he was a little hard to handle. The submarine commander in him liked to take charge of the subject, any subject, and run with it. He had been with a think tank on the East Coast for several years and now headed a research-and-development element of a large corporation. Tony and I had worked with Giles for a number of years, and we admired his ability to bring focus to a project and to execute it with precision.

Months earlier, Giles had been in my office at headquarters going over a program that I had him undertaking for Disguise Branch. When I had insisted that he give the men in his research area their head and let them do some blue-sky research on our project, he had balked. I remembered how Tony had brought him around, talking him down off his imaginary podium. "Ted," he had said, "turn it off. I'm transmitting, you're receiving." Giles had gone mute, finally hearing what we'd been trying to tell him.

"Gentlemen," Giles said now to the roomful of specialists, "thank you for coming. We all know the rules, but I will review them just to ensure that everything is crystal clear. One, anything said in this room today does not leave this room. Two, the only written record of what goes on here will be kept by our client. Three, once we are finished, this meeting never happened. You all know Tony Mendez. He has brought one of his OTS colleagues with him, Jonna Goeser. They have another puzzler for us, and this one has a short fuse. Let's get to it."

"Good morning," Tony said. "Please bear with me while I try to set the stage for this problem. Somewhere in the world near one of our cover installations, there is a doorway that we have never opened. What if one were interested in finally opening that door, but wanted to do so undetected? Once it's open, what if one found a dark corridor on the other side and wanted to enter that corridor without anyone knowing? What if there are no lights in the space—just a dark, mysterious burrow of unlimited size and shape?"

The room was silent; the scientists leaned forward to hear Tony's every word.

Tony continued, explaining that he hoped the group would consider what might be in that corridor that could be a threat, and what countermeasures designed to guard the burrow's contents might the entry team expect to find.

In truth, there was no installation exactly like this. But the scenario was very close to some operational contingencies that Tony thought might be faced in Moscow.

"Let me also add that going into the corridor is not optional," Tony said. "However, if we go in unprepared, some lives may be at risk. That is unacceptable. We have given it some thought ourselves, but rather than prejudice the experiment, we will reserve our ideas until we see what you come up with. We will share with you some raw data on what our enemies might have been trying to do to keep track of us and why."

Tony nodded at me with a smile so warm that I was worried that others in the meeting might notice. I felt as if I were floating on air, just like in those cloying songs about young love. Last night had been something that I would characterize as "a significant emotional event." And I was finding it difficult to focus on the business at hand.

I circulated through the room, handing out numbered copies of a classified document: a ten-page, letter-sized list that contained a lot of the known, or suspected, threats from the KGB that we now faced while operating in Moscow—such as ghost surveillance and spy dust. There was a small sheet attached to each document that had to be signed and handed back to me immediately. Rules again, only this time from the CIA's Office of Security, and to my liking. I felt Tony's eyes on me as I moved around the room, and it took some work on my part to stave off the blush.

Giles pulled several large newsprint pads into position, each on its own three-legged easel. Felt-tipped pens were on a side table, and the coffee machine was gurgling, the crew having already finished what would be the first of many pots of coffee.

"You'll notice that the obvious threats are itemized first, and that the ideas get more exotic as we move down the list," Tony said. "For instance, the first items up for discussion are called 'Sensing Devices,' which are then spelled out in more detail. We can start out with optical systems. The first question, then, is, What is the threat to our officer or agent from optical-sensing systems? Exactly what is the state of the art today?"

Disciplined and thorough, the specialists walked us through the numerous disciplines they represented—physics, chemistry, electrical engineering, computer science, biology, parapsychology. Each expert brought to the table cutting-edge technologies. They all accepted our design goal—to enable a man to enter the burrow undetected and travel a good distance through it—and did not stray from that mission. That so many of their ideas and strategies were eventually put to good use by us and other CIA field operatives attests to the fact that the Wizards did not disappoint that day.

Hours later, at the end of the session, Tony and I had hung back while the rest of the crowd left in small groups and clusters. I was gathering up the paperwork and getting my purse when Giles briefly stepped back into the room. He was pleased with the day's progress, as were we. We thanked him for all of his help, and he turned to go, then turned back around and looked at us.

"Stay out of mischief, you two," he said sternly before his face lit up with a beaming smile.

There was no way the ex–submarine skipper could have known that it was too late—that Tony and I were already up to our ears in mischief.

Two days later, I was at LAX again, boarding a United commuter flight for San Francisco, where I was to begin the long trip to China. Tony boarded with me, holding my hand, and we found seats together near the front of the plane.

When Tony had learned I was spending a day in San Francisco without an official tour guide, he had volunteered to escort me there and show me the city. I was beginning to wonder if he knew his way around every major city in America. I would find out later that he could navigate in almost all of the major capitals of the world.

At the car rental counter, I was down for a midsize car, following CIA travel regulations. The fact that we upgraded it to a Chrysler LeBaron convertible would be an out-of-pocket expense for which I would reimburse the U.S. government. Paying strict attention to the rules and following them to the letter had kept my conscience clear and my record straight for many years. Knowing when to enhance the rules creatively came only with experience.

Tony placed our bags in the trunk of the car, lowered the convertible top, and took the keys from my hand. "Destination?" he asked.

"The Hilton Hotel downtown," I replied.

And off we sailed into the most perfect twenty-four hours of my life.

Checking in at the hotel, we got the giggles as we stood in line at the registration desk in the beautiful sunlit lobby. By the time we stepped up to the desk, we had trouble rearranging our faces into a businesslike demeanor.

The hotel employee did not seem in the mood to join us in our obviously frivolous moment. "And how many will be staying tonight?" he asked.

"Two," I responded weakly.

"Twin-sized beds or a king?"

"Oh, a king would be fine." I tensed, trying to maintain a hold on my professional façade, what with a line of other people having formed behind us.

Tony showed superb control as he looked at the floor, composing himself. We could have been a pair of ten-year-olds planning a prank.

"How will you be paying for the room, Mrs. Goeser?"

Well, *that* certainly sobered me up.

I recognized in that instant that I was in the process of physically leaving my husband, that the brittle shell of the marriage had finally shattered. I knew now that I would leave, and that John and I would finalize something that had been hanging in the air for years. It would be a burden lifted, perhaps for both of us. It would be a relief. In that moment of clarity I wanted to talk to him, to call him and tell him this decision. But of course, better judgment took hold. That conversation could only be held in person, and it would have to wait until I returned from China.

"Visa," I barely whispered.

Tony and I walked out of the hotel into a perfect day of sunshine and light breezes. Back in the car, we headed for Ghirardelli Square and lunch. As we sat outside at a café, he described the years he had spent in San Francisco. Tony's mother had once managed a hotel on Lombard Street, and we walked over there to take a look at it. On the way, we bought matching navy blue cable-knit sweaters to combat the early morning chill and silly Dick Tracy baseball hats at a gift shop. We wore our tourist disguises the rest of the afternoon.

We worked our way through Chinatown, then went to Golden Gate Park. We drove out of San Francisco over the Golden Gate Bridge, then turned around and drove back—all so that we could experience, on the fog-encased bridge, the sensation of flying. We parked the car and walked down to Seal Rock, a coastal rock shelf right on the ocean, where we sat for a good part of the afternoon watching seals frolic in the surf and getting sprayed by foam from the Pacific. We sat quietly, not talking. Tony sat behind me, shielding me from the cool ocean breeze, his arms wrapped around my shoulders. It felt fine.

That evening we were going to eat at a restaurant named Shadows. "It's a famous place," Tony said as we got ready. "Our reservations are for seven-thirty—and don't worry about what to wear. In San Francisco, your silk pants and sweater will do just fine."

Alas, I will never know what culinary delights I missed.

We never got out the door that night, never got any dinner at all. We were both acutely aware that I was leaving the next day for a long and solitary journey, and we began saying good-bye well in advance of my departure.

The next morning came too early and too bright. What had been delightful sunlight just the day before now felt more like a blowtorch burning through the hotel window, waking us up abruptly.

We had one last stop before the airport—across the bridge and through the fog again, to a restaurant down by the Sausalito marina. I found myself thoroughly charmed with the San Francisco Bay Area, especially as presented by my personal tour guide.

Totally content from breakfast and deliriously happy in each other's company, we headed for the airport, the ragtop down and the wind in our hair. Tony held on to my left knee all the way to the airport, as though it were part of the gearshift. We didn't talk much, but we were both thinking a thousand miles an hour. At the airport, I checked my bags at the curb and made a dash for the gate. There was a hurried good-bye and much waving and some kissing—and then we parted.

He was gone, and I was alone again.

Flying into Hong Kong's Kai Tak Airport was the same exciting ride it had always been. We came in low and fast, over clotheslines, hopping over billboards, and setting down prematurely, it seemed, until you saw the end of the runway rushing toward you and the South China Sea just beyond. In other words, a normal landing.

My taxi driver made his way through the sea of cars to China Airlines, where all travel into mainland China is arranged through the national airline. The first leg of my journey would be by rail, traveling from Hong Kong to Guangzhou on the train, then by air to Beijing and Shanghai. Once I had attended to all the formalities and had my tickets in hand, I was issued a travel visa. I made mental—and later, actual—notes of all the various procedures for entry into the Communist country. Whenever it was possible, I pocketed extra forms to give to our document operations people in Washington in the event they ever needed to make forgeries.

The train ride was not particularly interesting, but the border formalities were, and a little intimidating at that. There was a lot of security and countless military guards at the border, where each passenger was closely scrutinized through the controls. As we disembarked from the train, I fell in purposefully with an American family I had noticed earlier—a businessman from Chicago with a wife and two small children who were relocating to China for his company. I chatted with the wife and even helped them with one of their bags. The five of us slowly moved through the formalities as a group. It was a nonalerting way to arrive on the mainland.

Guangzhou was only a stop on the way to Beijing. I had a nine-hour wait before making my way to the airport for my flight, so I spent most of the time with my camera in hand, walking through the city and taking photographs. I happened on a group of elderly men and women in a park, playing mahjong. The game triggers incredible passions. To my surprise, fights broke out and people were yelling at one another; it was a very aggressive atmosphere. I was glad to see that the women were holding their own, though, and shot photos at close range. The players were so engaged in their strategies that they didn't even notice me snapping pictures of them.

Beijing and Shanghai were amazing and mesmerizing and utterly exotic to my professional and photographic sensibilities. The sheer volume of foot traffic on the street was incredible. The crowds never seemed to taper off; no matter how far out of the city one drove, you never seemed to get to the edge of the population.

As the denied area focal point officer, I was in China doing a "passive probe" of one of the venues of my global domain. I had to be alert in case the Ministry of State Security decided to perform one of their entrapment operations on me. They wouldn't think twice about sticking an American citizen in jail and throwing away the key. Rumor had it that at least one CIA officer had died in a Chinese prison. I was on my own, with no backup or lifeline.

I was there to examine the fabric of the society—the woof and the warp and the texture of the weave. Everything was interesting to me, including the ethnic diversity, which ranged from the clearly Mongolian features of some citizens to the almost Caucasian skin tones of others. Their clothing was uniform: dark pants, blue-gray jackets, flip-flops worn by almost everyone, and straw hats by the older ones. I studied their bicycles and accessories, and looked closely at the things they carried—bags, umbrellas, baskets, glasses, cigarettes, and pipes. No detail went unnoticed or unfilmed; thirty-six rolls of exposed film—well over a thousand images—would be my final tally for the two-week trip.

Our officers in China had work to do and were having difficulty finding places to do it. While there are many occasions when a crowd is useful—for masking the action you are performing, for instance—there are many other acts that can be performed only when you are alone: putting down a drop, mailing a letter, making a phone call, picking up a drop from an asset, a personal meeting. In China, it seemed to me, being alone was a luxury that no one could count on having outside—ever. It was impossible to be in a place on the street with any assurance that you were not being observed. My guidebook told me that Shanghai, historically described as "The Whore of the East," encompassed 2,400 square miles. It didn't just *look* big, it *was* big. It looked to me as if we were going to have to rewrite our operational handbook and reconfigure our tradecraft to this teeming crowd. Mentally, I began to write my report, which would go out of Shanghai before I headed home.

The two-week trip through China was something of a blur. I was so distracted by my personal emotions and feelings that I am afraid the CIA's work suffered. If ever I have a staff again, and if one of them falls in love—madly, head-over-heels, stupidly in love—I believe I will fire that person, then and there. When you are in love, there is simply no focus, no grounding, ergo not much real work gets done. But I tried.

I missed Tony terribly. We were so entwined in our mutual work that we could almost finish each other's thoughts and sentences. I wanted to show him how a collapsible bicycle would make all of the difference outside of Beijing at the Winter Garden and to ask him what he thought of using the Forbidden City as an operational arena. We knew it was loaded with cameras and surveillance, but it also came with lots of tight turns and dark corridors that might suit our purposes. I photographed all of it, knowing we would pore over the pictures together, brainstorming.

The morning before I left Shanghai, I walked out of the Portman Hotel on Nanjing Xi Lu, and headed for the river. The hotel had been a contender for my collection of world-class destinations, but had fallen a little short. Too tall, too new, and too western to be interesting, it never made the list. I collected a few sheets of stationery, though.

The two weeks flew by, my report went out, and I headed home, stopping in Japan and Hawaii on the way back. But the fact was, I was afraid to go home. All during the trip I had been thinking about Tony, and longing for him.

There was one small problem, however: my husband.

Two weeks after my return to Washington, John and I were meeting together with a lawyer. Typically amicable, we shared the same attorney, much to the horror of our mutual friends, who warned us that this would never work. They were almost right, in the end. But at the beginning it seemed the simple and nonconfrontational thing to do.

We had decided to dissolve our childless marriage in a civilized manner, even to remain friends—if that was possible. It took us one long night, a whole night of talking, to arrive at this decision. We talked and paced and yelled and cried several times. When dawn came, we had made some of the initial decisions about who would do what and how we would proceed. We agreed to sell the house and worked out how to divide things. The biggest stumbling block was custody of our two dogs, Chloe and Joe Cocker. In the end, John kept them—they were almost like his children, and he simply could not give them up.

Looking back now, it is interesting that John and I were so terribly worried about how to break this news to Margaret, the Indian housekeeper and cook we had brought back to the United States with us from the Subcontinent and who had become almost family to us. We both considered her a friend as well as an employee. When we told Margaret our news, she was distraught, almost beyond reason. We spent the better part of an hour comforting her. It was typical of our marriage that we spent no time at all comforting each other.

I packed a bag quickly, and put a few things in the back of my car. I took some pictures of my family, some favorite music, a pile of books that I was planning to get to next, and my cameras. It was as though the house were on fire and I could rescue only about a dozen things. There was really no thought process going on—it was that fight-or-flight thing, and I knew I had to get out of there now, or I might be stuck for a long time. The rest would wait. Without looking back, I drove quickly away from my house, and from my life and the last twenty-three years. It was perhaps the hardest thing I have ever done.

Of course, no divorce is so simple or so straightforward. What began as a friendly effort to do it nicely soon became more complex. Friends of mine, or at least people I thought of as friends, had told John that Tony had gone to China with me, and John chose to believe that. The more he pondered that idea, the

angrier he got. I finally convinced him to look into the comput-
erized badge system in the Agency—every employee reporting to
work every day had to insert a badge to enter. While I had no
idea what Tony had done while I was gone, I assumed he had
gone to work. John worked in CIA security and had access to that
badge database—he must have looked and learned the truth,
because that disagreement seemed to abate.

And so, there I was—driving down Route 7 in Fairfax County
with my bags in the back, no place to go, and no schedule to
meet. It was late in the morning, before lunch, around eleven
o'clock. I was crying so hard that it was difficult to drive, and my
pulse was racing. I pulled into the parking lot of a bar I had never
heard of—Shenanigans in Sterling—and tried to collect myself. I
felt as though I had escaped from prison.

I called Tony.

He was working on an oil painting in his art studio, doing what
he usually did on weekend afternoons.

"Don't move," he said. "I'll be right there."

And he was.

FBI Special Agent Robert Hanssen sat in his basement office at home. The door was closed and locked; his wife, Bonnie, and six children knew not to intrude on his privacy here.

He opened the safe in the corner and carefully removed a black velvet pouch. Loosening the cord, he watched as a large, two-carat Russian diamond spilled out into his hand, sparkling and luminous under the glare of the Tensor lamp on his desk.

He gazed at the gem longingly for several minutes, turning it over in his palm, then slipped it back into the dark, soft folds and carefully put it away again.

He knew there were plenty more diamonds to be had where this one came from.

TEN

WASHINGTON, D.C.

November 1988

Tony

I stood on the stage of the empty theater, wrapped in total darkness, waiting for my eyes to adjust and make out the rows of empty seats, the aisles, and the balcony.

In the darkness, the sound of my heart beating seemed almost audible, and I found all of my senses heightened and on guard. I strained my ears, listening for any sound that would alert me to the presence of a security guard or a casual passerby who might give me away. Gradually, the soft glow of the exit signs and thin strips of light from numerous small openings to the outer, lighted corridors illuminated the gloom. They came from under the doors, from behind the stage curtain, and from the ends of two long corridors that led off stage left and right.

A slight shiver moved down my torso, a reaction to the tense evening and the effect of adrenaline finally beginning to ebb. I had come to this spot quickly, moving on foot rapidly through Foggy Bottom, up M Street into Georgetown, and then taking a long winding approach back down K Street through the darkened underpass beneath Whitehurst Freeway. Finally, I had sprinted toward this huge monolith of a building, across the wide lanes of two-way traffic, thereby putting space between me and those few vigorous surveillants left with me. I then slipped through the one door into the underground parking lot I knew was not locked. *Their security really could use a little work,* I thought. *They wouldn't like to know how easy it is to penetrate their building.*

As my breathing began to resume a normal rhythm and my pulse slowed, the room began to reveal itself to me. I noted the layout and the directions of the audience flow during intermission and after the finale. This theater bore a remarkable resemblance to the Palace of Congresses inside the Kremlin, where I had attended a number of ballet performances by the Bolshoi Company through the years. It seemed perfectly suited for the first phase of our exfiltration of ORB and his family, since our target area for his last espionage act was located directly beneath it. In this case, we were not trying to penetrate a building in the Kremlin but to use it as an escape hatch.

The D.C. theater was a well-known destination to the hundreds of thousands of Americans who had attended musical or theatrical events here. I had been here with Karen and the kids, attending Saturday afternoon matinees of *The Nutcracker* and several versions of *Romeo and Juliet*—the most memorable by the Kirov Ballet. Then I had always been sitting in the audience watching the performance, never up on stage, planning a performance of my own. But now we had begun crafting our special operation in this very building, and if all went well, we would export it to the Soviet Union.

On my last trip to Moscow, I had spent a considerable amount of time entering, moving around in, and exiting public edifices in the course of my cover activities. I had confirmed once again in my own mind what I had always felt about every location I had ever visited: in spite of the challenges, there is always a wealth of operational possibilities for us to exploit.

Knowing your territory intimately is a fundamental operating procedure of the Chinese philosopher and general Sun Tzu. *Knowing how the opposition is going to handle the territory* is also a precept spelled out in his book, *The Art of War.*

We expected that Edward Lee Howard had explained to his KGB handlers that we would use certain kinds of terrain to run a deception operation. Knowing that, the KGB would sometimes give us certain spaces—they wouldn't follow us into places like buildings where they didn't think we'd run an operation—and just set up around the perimeter in order to pick us up when we came out. It was now our chance to turn the tables on Howard and the KGB. *Choose the time and the place for action and overwhelm their senses,* wrote Sun Tzu, a concept that was repeated by Mao Tse-tung in his *On Guerrilla Warfare.*

Tonight was our first attempt at exploring some of the back doors, elevators, and trapdoors in this theater. Every large building had them; knowing where they were and when they were locked and when they were not was a critical part of any operational planning. Knowing the security devices, personnel, and alarms was equally important. The best way to learn these things was by developing a source inside. In the case of the Palace of Congresses, we had the ultimate source already, and he'd be the one doing the manipulations—but he would need help getting the time and space he needed.

The Special Surveillance Team would have been gathering for a parlay about now, outraged at my treacherous behavior in outwitting them earlier, when I sprinted diagonally across the speeding traffic, slipped through that garage door, and locked it behind me. We had trained them in the ways of surveillance teams the world over, and a universal rule was that the rabbit should never anger his surveillance team, never act precipitously.

In the real world, overt hindrance would be a direct challenge to the surveillance team, an insult of sorts, and they would be quick to make the rabbit pay. They would move in on him so closely, whether on foot or in vehicles, that they would lock up with him.

I had broken the rules tonight because I felt I had to. After all, we would be breaking new ground in Moscow, and the old rules were going to change in the process. I would make that point in the after-action briefing.

The end goal of defeating KGB surveillance would make it all worthwhile.

The crisp air of the Washington, D.C., autumn was a harbinger of winter.

Tonight Washingtonians were beginning to wear coats on the street, and the pace of pedestrians was becoming more brisk with the cold. To members of the SST, this boded well. Coats, hats, mufflers, gloves, and boots—all of these were just an added layer of obfuscation, which they could put on and take off as the exercise required. The cold air allowed them to add layers of disguises to their normal clothing: city trashman jumpsuits in brilliant orange, green surgical scrubs and white lab coats when moving through and around the George Washington University campus and hospital. The accelerated pace also helped: they usually moved quickly when they were paralleling "the rabbit," their target, typically one block over from where the action was. Team members blended much more readily into this speeded-up movement on the streets.

Jim Blake, who specialized in a whole series of homeless outfits, was pleased with the cold wave. "Look out for him," said Victoria Sanderson, wearing a business suit and white sneakers—a very "in" look in conservative Washington these days. "He was wearing his street-guy outfit last night, the one with the three-day stubble and the gloves with all the fingers cut off, and we thought he was being rounded up by the police. Turns out it was a van, feeding the homeless. When we picked him up, he had half a cherry pie and a bunch of fried chicken. He's dangerous in those clothes!" The other members of the team laughed, remembering the impromptu picnic in the van.

"He's wearing it again tonight," said Victoria. As she talked, she sat down on a park bench and coolly unzipped and stepped out of her suit skirt. Removing the matching jacket, she revealed the full outfit underneath, a pink Gore-Tex running top with matching shorts. As she jogged away, slipping a sweatband over her blonde hair, she turned back to the group. "Tell him to get some corn bread tonight," she called out, laughing, "I just love corn bread with fried chicken." She sprinted down the street and out of sight.

Jonna had been with me on the street this evening too. Since returning from China and going through her separation from John, she had been my constant companion on the streets during these evening exercises. No matter what else was going on, she was always ready for and anticipating the next run. I could see the pleasure on her face as we worked the SST on one of our long and wide-ranging cover runs with the night's ZEPHYR team—she liked doing it as much as I did. She had a lot of energy and a high metabolism: it seemed she was always hungry on our nighttime runs, and it had become something of a joke that we would have to find something for her to eat in the middle of executing a plan.

Tonight, we had stopped at Chadwick's on K Street, just under the Whitehurst Freeway—the same site where, unbeknownst to us at the time, Aldrich Ames had three years earlier handed over to his KGB handler a thirty-pound stack of stolen documents that named almost all of the active Soviet agents working for the U.S. and the British.

Our SST leader, John Winslow, was waiting for us in a back booth.

We slipped in and joined him. When the waiter came, Jonna ordered an onion loaf appetizer to stave off her usual "hungries."

"We're going to head off in a completely new direction for a couple of weeks," I told Winslow after the waiter departed.

"We're going to bump the ZEPHYR schedule and commandeer the team for a specific series of exercises. This is going to be new and different, Johnny, and it's very important. We've got to get the team up to speed fast, then rehearse them until you can assure us that they can do it in their sleep. There will be no second takes on this one. It has to be right the first time."

I asked Winslow to go over the old Moscow rules again for the benefit of new team members. Part of the surveillance team would continue to operate under the old rules, as some KGB members were presumably still doing in Moscow.

Another part of the team—trained by Jonna and me—would employ our new rules, formulated to counter what we believed were the KGB's new procedures, including ghost surveillance. Like our officers and agents in future Moscow operations, the rabbits would be playing by the new rules, thereby foiling, we hoped, the KGB's best techniques. The new rules included an added layer of mobile ghost surveillance that rarely, if ever, showed itself, plus a highly secure line of communications with a vast network of static ghosts who could acquire the target and hand him off to the next ghost without showing themselves. The Wizards had helped us design some of these new countermeasures, including how to handle the challenges of spy dust and the inevitable chokepoint.

As we talked, Winslow also picked out two members of the team, one female and one male, who matched the descriptions I had handed to him on a small sheet of yellow lined paper. Height and weight were what was important; we could play with the rest of it. They also had to be good, as they would be standing in for the real rabbits for the next two weeks, and I wanted them pumped up. I asked Winslow what more he needed to get the job done.

"When are we getting the operational plan?" asked Winslow.

"As soon as we finish writing it up," I said, glancing over at Jonna with a smile.

★ ★ ★

We had the plan all put together in our heads; we just needed to get it on paper and make sure it looked as good as it sounded. Jonna and I had the tired-eyed look of people who were burning the candle at both ends; we had barely slept since she had moved out of her house. We were running on black coffee, Reese's peanut butter cups, and love. We were trying to make light of our relationship and keep it away from our work and our colleagues, but it was a stretch. When a couple is in love, there is always something in the air that is palpable to people who know them well. We were almost too tired to work any harder at concealing it.

My personal life had changed dramatically after Jonna called me on the Sunday morning she left her husband. I had walked out of my studio with my pulse racing, without even cleaning my brushes. I jumped into my car and raced across the bridge over the Potomac River and into Virginia. I burned up the familiar back roads, and it took me only about thirty minutes to reach the parking lot of Shenanigans. I found her waiting for me in her car, a silver Porsche 928 that she had bought used from a friend when she got back from overseas. I could see a suitcase through the back window, and a couple of boxes. *Looks like she travels light.*

I got a great hug and a kiss as she bounded out of her car. I was looking at a face swollen with tears, ravaged by streaks of dribbling mascara, and torn between joy and pain. She was balanced precariously between happiness at seeing me and relief at having the trauma of her separation from John behind her. We stood silently for several minutes, wrapped in each other's arms, both of us letting our emotions settle into a quieter place. The soft smell of her shampoo, of her perfume, of her skin soothed me, and a calmness swept over both of us.

We dropped her car at my house and spent the rest of the day in my 300 ZX exploring the country roads around my part of Maryland and West Virginia, the part where the Blue Ridge Mountains begin, rippling like muscles under the bucolic skin of

the earth. The rolling countryside, coupled with the confluence
of the Potomac and the Shenandoah Rivers, provides spectacular
and beautiful scenery. The motorcycle guys and the Porsche Club
loved these winding back roads for their rallies. Both Jonna and I
had high-performance sports cars, and I told her that living here
meant you could commute the entire fifty-five miles to Langley
via the back roads.

We drove up through the mountains, and I showed her some of
my all-time favorite spots—the battlefield at Antietam, and the
view from Weverton Cliffs, high on the Appalachian Trail, overlooking the Potomac with Harpers Ferry in the distance. We
ended up in Shepherdstown at the Yellow Brick Bank, a restaurant of some local fame.

As fate is wont to do sometimes, it added a final irony to our
day. When we'd begun to fall in love, I had been living alone, in
an empty house. Since then, all three of my grown children had
returned and were hanging out there, with their significant others
staying over half of the time. The house had taken on something
of the feel of a college dormitory—complete with piles of laundry
and a communal atmosphere. On that first night of her new inde-
pendence, I had invited Jonna over to meet the kids, which to us
felt more like "meet the parents." Though Jonna and I continued
to have difficulty finding any privacy at my place, it was good to
be out in the open with the kids at home while we were still
attempting to keep our new relationship secret from our colleagues at work.

Jonna had rented an apartment in nearby Frederick and used it
as a place to move her things, install an answering machine, and as
a legal address. We were spending a great deal of time and effort
keeping up appearances, but the kids kept pointing out our defi-
ciencies. Evidently the tradecraft and security practices that we
used in our work fell by the wayside when it came to our personal
life. Once, we went away for the weekend in my car and left her

Porsche parked at my house, and, of course, we took her keys. When one of the young guys from our disguise shop came over to visit the kids, they had to quickly hide Jonna's car with a tarp.

Spies shouldn't fall in love should have become one of the new Moscow rules.

Several of us were sitting in the airy bar of the Four Seasons Hotel on the edge of Georgetown, rich, thick carpeting underfoot and, in the background, the soft sounds of Ella singing an old version of Hoagy Carmichael's "Skylark." We were surrounded by an extensive collection of artwork, and the elaborate plantings of palms and ferns gave the room an almost tropical feel. The late afternoon sun slanting through the glass walls of the bar suggested a noteworthy sunset in our near future.

We loved this hotel and used it often; it had multiple levels on the main floor that dropped down two levels to exits at the back onto the C&O Canal. Upstairs, off the main lobby, a puzzling series of staggered stairways, corridors, and courtyards provided a multitude of entrances and exits for the ease of its guests. We "collected" hotels for many operational purposes, and this one was particularly well suited to some of our silver bullets, but we used it only for our Moscow-bound ZEPHYRs.

We relaxed into the upholstery of the chairs and picked up our drinks.

"*Nostrovia*," I said. "To your health."

Martin Tucker, chief of Internal Operations, SE Division, lifted his glass in a toast. Clint Bradley, the ZEPHYR who was one of the operational targets for the evening, lifted his glass a little more tentatively. Another ZEPHYR, Rose Cohen, a petite brunette with luminous brown eyes, was nursing a Coke and listening intently to the conversation. She might have been a college coed or perhaps a graduate student.

Bradley and Cohen were still first-tour case officers—"virgins," in the vernacular of the intelligence community. But they had proven themselves in previous training as capable and courageous.

Bradley looked more like a military officer than a diplomatic type. His blond hair was just a bit too short, his mustache a bit too thin. His John Lennon wire-rimmed glasses gave him a somewhat hip profile, but his finely muscled upper body testified to his work ethic and discipline.

Jonna and I exchanged a glance.

She smiled at me warmly, I melted, and we both sipped our martinis.

In spite of appearances, this was not a social moment. In the dim light of the waning autumn afternoon, a surveillance team of thirty-six men and women had surrounded the Four Seasons Hotel and taken up their positions. Their goal was to keep this young couple under continuous observation for the duration of the evening, clandestinely, and they were more than happy to have the rabbits slip into the bar, so that they could regroup, reconfigure their coverage, and catch their breath.

Team members, at the same time, were constantly changing their stripes. A businesswoman was deftly pulling sweats over her office attire, and a younger man was removing his sports jacket to reveal ragged clothes. A woman handed her toddler to a man in a van and pulled a bicycle out of the same vehicle. A dog barked from inside the van, and a hand emerged with a pair of Rollerblades for someone else. A young couple, holding hands, began nuzzling each other on a park bench. Every one of these people were ours— training to blend in while on surveillance. It never ceased to amaze me how most of these actions, when done in the heart of a major city teeming with street life, drew little attention. In fact, some people on these streets were doing much crazier things than we were: one man was walking up K Street brushing his teeth.

For the most part oblivious of all this activity were the two young CIA officers sitting at our table in the bar. They were within days of boarding a plane for Moscow, where they would begin a two-year tour of duty in a country like no other in the world. Clint Bradley and Rose Cohen would have their own personal surveillance teams for the duration of their tours; their offices and homes would be bugged with both video and audio surveillance. Neither one would have an argument or intimate moment with a significant other without its being recorded and transcribed by this invisible presence.

Martin Tucker had been their boss during the two-year training period for this assignment, directing not only the courses they had taken but the tradecraft and philosophy that they had been taught. SE Division prided itself on being unique in the Agency, and Tucker carried on that tradition.

We sat, drinks in hand, as I openly disagreed with much of that tradition—SE's operational doctrine and the philosophy that supported it. I was suggesting to Tucker—no, insisting—that there was a new and better way to work in Moscow these days. "Not on my watch," said Tucker. "There's no way we are going to change gears now. Clint and Rose have been in training for two years. This idea of yours will never work. The Soviets are too sophisticated to fall for it."

"Listen to me, Martin," I said. "This is a new game. Your tradecraft is based on the historical model. My proposal is based on observations in Moscow this summer and discussions with the officers who are working there now. I'm telling you, these new techniques will work. We are ready to demonstrate it tonight."

"Tonight?" he asked, somewhat taken aback.

"Yes. Right now. The SST will surveil, and Clint and Rose will try it out. Let's go through an exercise with them using these new ideas to elude surveillance. Afterward, we'll meet with everyone and debrief them. If you don't like the way it works, or if you don't like the team's reaction, or if Clint and Rose don't think it'll fly in Moscow, then we'll forget it. But let's at least give it a chance."

I watched Tucker closely, waiting for a decision.

"All we're asking you to do," Jonna said, leaning forward, "is to sit back and enjoy the show. You'll see the whole thing from the surveillance team's point of view."

I gave her a slight nod; her lines were perfectly timed, just as we had rehearsed. Under the table, I felt her hand move over to mine and grasp it warmly. Momentarily flustered, I patted her hand, then took mine away. *Focus. Don't lose focus here.*

Outside the team was getting restless. Their normal pattern had been broken; usually a stop in the bar wouldn't go more than fifteen minutes. Our group had been in there almost half an hour. *Better send in a probe.*

One of the team members pulled out a tie and a blazer from a backpack, handed the pack to his colleague, brushed back his hair with the other hand, and entered the hotel from one of the street entrances. He walked slowly through the room to the bar, where he ordered a beer and paid cash for it. The probe sipped his beer, then set it on the bar, reached into his pocket for some change, and exited into the lobby, toward the pay phones. He was back on the street in less than a minute, reporting to the team leader that the group was in a heated discussion in the bar and they were all accounted for.

Tucker seemed tempted, but he was not yet convinced.

No other city in the world was as tightly controlled as Moscow, and no other intelligence personnel were as closely watched as the CIA officers in residence there. It had become almost impossible to work, to talk, and to perform an operational act. The simplest transaction could take months to plan, and even then, many had gone bust.

The Internal Ops chief knew things had changed, and not for the better. We had lost some of our most important Soviet sources in Moscow; the CIA officers operating there felt they were under omnipresent surveillance that could not be shaken; the old silver-bullet techniques were blown; CIA operations were being shut down right and left.

With a weary nod, Tucker gave the go-ahead for the proposed exercise.

We stood up and headed out the door to the street—with the ops chief in tow—before he could change his mind.

The scene on the street was deceptively normal.

Clint Bradley and Rose Cohen, trained to sniff out the odd and the inappropriate—the people who did not belong in the scene— swept the street visually. Not a lot of people there, most likely because of the cold. An old homeless guy was going into McDonald's, probably to get warm. A van across the street with a Tony's Pizza sign was illegally parked and the delivery guy was getting out. A woman with a dog on a leash was window-shopping across the street. An attractive couple, hand in hand, moved past our small group and headed into the bar, oblivious of mere mortals. A messenger on Rollerblades zipped by, moving with the speed and grace of his profession.

On their own now, Bradley and Cohen left us to proceed on a prearranged course.

Jonna and I strolled down Pennsylvania Avenue with Tucker. As we approached the edge of Georgetown, we stopped at an outdoor café positioned directly across from the One Step Down, the small jazz club well known to aficionados in the city as a center of excellent live music.

The three of us ordered coffee and settled into the glassed-in sidewalk portico.

I told Tucker that in just a few minutes, he would see the two ZEPHYR officers coming down the street. The SST would have them covered. They would have an "eye," the team member responsible for reporting the rabbits' position to control, and a "point," the team member who would be primarily responsible at any given time for maintaining contact. There would be "casuals," who would periodically enter and exit the exercise all evening. Out of sight over the horizon would be "control," to keep track of everyone.

The rules that had been reinforced with the team included these: any contact with the rabbits and you are out of the exercise; if the rabbits see you twice, you are out of the exercise; if in doubt, step out of the exercise. In other words, be discreet.

Looking down Pennsylvania Avenue, Tucker saw Bradley and Cohen strolling leisurely down the street, stopping and looking in several shop windows.

We could make out a lone pedestrian about thirty feet behind them.

"That's the point," I said softly.

On our side of the street, a stream of office workers moved toward Georgetown.

Bradley and Cohen stopped in front of the One Step Down and looked at the jazz schedule posted in the window. They went down several steps and ducked inside the club, emerging seconds later with what appeared to be a copy of the schedule in hand.

They continued strolling down the street.

We saw the point turn right onto a residential side street, and his place was taken by a couple of women who looked as if they worked in a restaurant kitchen.

When Bradley and Cohen stopped to window-shop, the two women moved past them and entered an appliance store several doors down.

A college student with a backpack came off a side street and fell in discreetly behind the ZEPHYR couple, and the whole entourage slowly moved into the distance.

Tucker was not impressed so far.

"Discreet, I give you," he said, "but I hope you have more than this to show me."

I sipped my coffee while Jonna watched Tucker carefully.

Tucker felt a tap on his shoulder and turned around.

Bradley and Cohen fell into two empty chairs, their faces beaming, short of breath and gleaming with perspiration.

The ops chief leaned forward to look down the street and could clearly make out the rabbits, which he had thought were the couple now sitting before him, moving slowly down Pennsylvania Avenue, taking the surveillance team with them.

"You switched," he muttered. "I'll be damned!"

The next day, escorted by Martin Tucker, we met with SE Division Chief Miles Rhenquist in his corner office at headquarters.

Rhenquist wanted to review our progress on the recommendations I'd made as a result of my trip to Moscow, the trip to Hollywood, and the planning for our Moscow operation.

I had made arrangements for Jonna to go to Moscow to help collect data regarding the KGB's surveillance package and other ways we might counter it. I felt certain that with her technical expertise, she could configure some SST street exercises that would help us better understand the KGB's modus operandi.

I filled Rhenquist in on the previous evening's successful exercise, which was enthusiastically attested to by Martin Tucker. Rhenquist tended to reject out of hand any information he didn't want to hear. But this time he listened.

Rhenquist was in a very difficult spot. There were some in the Agency who felt he had mishandled the Edward Lee Howard case, but beyond that there was the impression that he was losing control of Moscow operations. The Soviet Union he knew dated from when he was the CIA chief in Moscow, during the golden days of the late 1970s and early 1980s, when we had so many successes there. That Moscow existed no more. He seemed to know about the problems, but couldn't always fathom a solution. There were also indications that he was being kept out of the loop because of the mounting paranoia about a possible high-placed mole. In truth, he was on a shortlist of those suspected.

When I was finished, Rhenquist did not hold back his strong opinion.

"I think you're putting way too much emphasis on this 'ghost surveillance' business," he said. "I'm not sure it exists. Face it, the KGB are simply good. Always have been." He went on to say he feared I was sounding an alarm that was unwarranted. He explained that the Agency inspector general had found that in each instance of arrest or execution in Moscow, there had been a fatal flaw in the fieldwork or case itself.

"Our foreign agents are getting rolled up because of faulty tradecraft," Rhenquist said, "not because of some larger conspiracy."

I realized he had on the blinders he always seemed to keep close-by.

"And I warn you," he continued, "there are some things going on in Moscow right now that are so highly classified that even the chief there doesn't know about them. I want you to steer clear of the kind of activities that might accidentally stumble across one of those operations in progress."

Keeping on my poker face, I looked over at Tucker in time to see him wince.

Rhenquist then turned to Jonna and told her he was withholding authorization for her to travel to Moscow for the time being: the operation he was referring to could be compromised if she should suddenly appear on the scene.

Jonna shot me a penetrating look.

I raised my eyebrows in acknowledgment; Rhenquist had clearly made a faux pas. It was unusual for him to let something slip out like that.

As Jonna and I left Rhenquist's office and moved down the hallway toward the atrium of the new Headquarters Building, we were both silent. We stepped on the escalators that would take us down to our office level, and I looked at her long and hard.

"Be careful, Jonna. We're in danger of running up SE's tailpipe, and they're not liking it. Rhenquist doesn't have the foggiest idea what is going on in Moscow these days. And he's obviously forgotten that we're involved in the operation he was alluding to."

"But am I going to Moscow or not, Tony?" she asked.

I smiled. "How long will it take you to learn Spanish?"

With Jonna restricted for the time being from going to Moscow—I would fight that prohibition later—I decided on the spot that Cuba was the next best thing.

We knew that the KGB trained the DGI, the Cuban intelligence service, extensively. In terms of tradecraft training, we knew that the KGB had trained the Cubans in their favorite techniques—their modus operandi. So, questions about the techniques the KGB might use in Moscow against our upcoming operations could perhaps be answered by observing how the DGI operated in Havana. Too, by not conducting extra street activity in Moscow, we wouldn't be taking the chance of possibly alerting the KGB that something big was about to come down. Jonna's exposure could have been raised among the KGB after the episode involving TUGBOAT, if in fact they had identified her as being in-country during that nifty operation. At this point, particularly with the need to have her back in Moscow so soon for the actual operation, the less exposure for her the better.

Our blueprint of the Moscow rescue of ORB and his family was being painstakingly drawn up. In response to each of the technical threats that the Wizards had identified in our marathon session in L.A., we were busy plugging each hole in the dike. I was becoming more confident that the technical end of this operation was under control.

The Disguise Branch had allocated their best resources to the operation. Thanks to some suggestions from Jerome Calloway, we were pulling out all of the stops in engineering several new disguise systems that would fit the scenario in Moscow and elude detection exquisitely. Our rescue operation was taking on all of the hallmarks of a performance, as the famous Hollywood consultant had suggested it should.

The SST had done a superb job in preparing Clint Bradley and Rose Cohen for the upcoming scenario and in readying themselves, as we would be sending in SST team members to participate in the actual operation—something we had never done before. We had returned to the local theater many times after my first visit to the darkened stage, conducting a series of exercises during peak performance hours, attempting to refine the operation in the middle of a large crowd. Now that the team was morphing from a training tool into principal players in the operation, they were excited and ready to go.

As time went on, I had become more convinced that the Soviets were using a variation of the ghost-team watcher-team surveillance technique. The watchers would be the surveillance team that the rabbit would be aware of. They would keep a discreet distance, but would occasionally show themselves. They would allow the rabbit to get comfortable with their presence. Occasionally, the watchers would seem to be absent—perhaps a scheduling error? perhaps sloppiness on their part? or a planned event? This was the moment that our Moscow-based case officers were trained to look for, the opportunity to perform an operational act. But if my theory held true, while the watcher team may have stepped aside, the ghost team would always be there. *Always.* Just over the horizon, out of sight, invisible and highly dangerous: tracking us from static observation posts and even airplanes, known as "overhead platforms" in the intelligence world; using spy dust and other markers to follow our every movement;

identifying our own tracking and locating techniques. All of it focused on us like searchlights on the streets of Moscow.

We had to find out if the KGB was, in fact, using the ghost-team watcher-team technique against us, and if so, its strengths and weaknesses. If they were, then our officers were never safe in thinking they could go operational on the street. This was the rationale for setting the ORB escape in a large public building—like the Palace of Congresses. But in the spy game, with lives at risk, it's always necessary to know exactly what you're facing.

Of course, Cuba had its risks, too, which was why I was sending John Winslow, head of SST, along with Jonna. Our office had a history with the Cubans, and every OTS officer knew the story. Some years earlier, three of our officers had flown down to Havana to execute a bugging operation. One of the three had gone along at the last minute, literally jumping on the plane with the other two as a lark. Some lark. The three officers had been compromised some-how while they were installing some audio bugs, and they had all been arrested. Since the United States government had no diplo-matic relations with Cuba, our officers had no diplomatic immu-nity. They were on their own. They were tried and convicted and had been sent to the infamous prison on the Isle of Pines to serve long jail terms. They had conducted themselves splendidly, never breaking their cover or otherwise revealing their Agency affiliation, and several years later had been released early in a trade for tractors.

"I know what you're thinking, but don't worry," Jonna said. "Johnny will be with me, and it's only going to be a lot of walk-ing and observing. They're not going to grab us or arrest us as long as we conduct ourselves properly. I hope they surveil the hell out of us. If we can get them in the right configuration, they'll have to show themselves. I know what we want: the ghost team, if there is one. Anyway, we'll be so unthreatening that when it's over, they'll think they've wasted their time."

A two-week trip was planned, with Jonna and Winslow posing

as U.S. government administrative types doing a study for the U.S. Interests Section in the Swiss Embassy. They would supposedly be surveying the cost of goods and services in Havana in order to ensure that the U.S. employees there were receiving an adequate cost-of-living supplement. The U.S. government still had no embassy in Cuba, which meant that, like the previous CIA officers who had been arrested and imprisoned, Jonna and Winslow would have no official or diplomatic protection if anything went wrong.

At one point, I had second thoughts, and admitted them to Jonna.

"I don't like sending you off like this, even with Johnny going along. It's not just that they were trained by the KGB—they act like the KGB. That means they won't hesitate to arrest you if they think you're making trouble for them."

"Tony, don't worry so. You never used to worry about me like this."

She gave me a look I recognized. She was going—end of discussion.

We were at home on a Saturday morning, sitting in the garden behind the house. Jonna was busy planting bulbs; as the weather was getting cold, it was time to finish up the preparations for next spring. It was the first time anybody had worked in the garden since Karen had died. We had properly edged and weeded it, and were putting it to bed for the winter. As a matter of fact, the whole place was beginning to look more like a home again. I had repainted the exteriors of the house and the studio and the show pavilion. The house was evocative of a Yankee barn, and it was painted Maryland Barn Red with white trim. The studios and the deck echoed both the style and the colors.

Jonna had rearranged some of the furniture and brought a few of her things over to freshen up the look. Her oriental rugs were everywhere, adding brilliant dashes of reds to the relatively neutral palette in the house. I had done several paintings of her, and they hung now in the living room. One of my favorites was a spontaneous watercolor of her at Hawk Mountain up in Pennsylvania. We had gone up there two weekends before to watch the raptors migrate—it was like seeing a highway in the sky, and was a most impressive spectacle.

I moved around the table and took her in my arms. "You'll just have to be very careful. I'm going to worry about you until I get a cable from Miami telling me that you're out of there."

For that, I got a kiss.

And another one, in a long string of kisses.

ELEVEN

HAVANA

November 1988

Jonna

I saw the large lens of the video camera before I spotted the man standing behind it. A Cuban national, he was wearing a khaki uniform of some sort, with a black beret.

We filed up to the few open immigration counters at Havana Airport, forming long meandering lines that wound through the dark, empty space. It was two-thirty in the morning and we were dead tired. The lines moved with an exhausted rhythm, like snakes slowly going to sleep. The whole process of traveling to Cuba had been like something out of a Marc Chagall painting: one of the dream sequences with donkeys flying and everything upside down.

John Winslow and I had flown to Miami from Washington, D.C., earlier in the day, then had to cool our heels until almost 10 PM before making our way back to Miami International Airport. We reported to a certain Eastern Airlines counter, where, as the clock turned to midnight, the Eastern sign was flipped over to reveal the name of a Spanish charter airline. The Eastern employees took off their jackets and checked the passengers in, paying a lot of attention to the number of bags each of us had. We were taken out to an

Eastern Airlines airplane being piloted by one of their uniformed pilots. The flight wasn't much more than an hour. The other passengers were apparently Cubans returning home for a visit.

I kept track of the movements of the guy with the camera as my line slowly wound forward. Although he lowered his camera once we had all queued up, I had the distinct impression that he'd been videotaping me.

In keeping with procedures, Winslow had moved to a separate line and we were going through the immigration procedures separately. Even though we were traveling under the same cover, we knew not to stand together in line. Unless you have the same family name, you are considered separate travelers in most countries and will get separate treatment. In any case, this worked well for us from an intelligence point of view: we could collect two separate sets of data on the border controls being used. We would compare notes later at the hotel and write up the arrival procedures in detail. Our OTS alias-document specialists always liked to know how you were treated when you arrived in a country, what the procedures were going in and going out, and how you were treated when you left. It was the beginning of building a recipe for penetrating the border of a particular country.

When I got to the front of the line, the immigration officer maintained a poker face as he closely scrutinized my documents, then my face, then my documents again. I was traveling under an alias, *Jennifer Calloway,* and I knew that the documents were completely backstopped and would pass any scrutiny they cared to give them. The name had been carefully chosen because it had to resonate with me whenever anybody used it. *Jennifer* came from my sister; *Calloway* was a nod to Jerome. I had my cover story well memorized and was prepared to answer endless questions about my boring job as a low-level bureaucrat, but no questions were asked. He did not consult any watch lists that I could make out, nor was he using a computer database. The officer slammed down his foursquare date stamp on my passport and slid the document across the desk to me.

I had slipped into Cuba.

I met Winslow outside of immigration, and we headed off to pick up our luggage. I noted the video camera again, back against a wall in the baggage area, and was aware that the same guy was still running the camera, this time clearly taping the group that Winslow and I were walking with.

Clearly, we had already met the Cuban intelligence service, the DGI. I already knew what to expect: that they were very good at what they did. Shortly after I had transferred to the subcontinent, there had been a brouhaha in the international press about a reported DGI operation in which, it was claimed, the Cubans had run thirty-five double agents against the CIA in various operations, and we were unable to detect even one of them. They later claimed that each of their agents had been trained in biofeedback methods for defeating the polygraph machine. The polygraph was one of the Agency's primary security tools in evaluating foreign agents and was also used routinely on CIA employees. All Agency employees had to pass a polygraph examination at the time they entered on duty, and then again every five years during their employment. My husband, John, had been a polygraph operator for a number of years, and I knew how much credence the CIA placed in its ability to ferret out useful information and also to serve as a deterrent. The story went that thirty-five times the poly was defeated by Cubans working for the DGI, which meant, if true, that thirty-five foreign agents were placed in our intelligence acquisition process and thirty-five streams of false information had begun flowing into the CIA. It was also claimed that we thoroughly trained these agents in our modus operandi—the way we conducted operations around the world—then tasked them to collect intelligence for us. If this were so, it would have been clear—to the Cuban DGI and to their sponsors, the Soviet KGB—from the questions we asked the agents, what information we were holding and what information we needed. If it had been just a poker game, it would have been equivalent to showing the table your hand before the betting began.

Anxious to demonstrate this intelligence success, the Cuban government had produced a documentary for the world to see. While we had read the reports in *The Washington Post* and *The Miami Herald* about the botched operation, it was easy for us to dismiss them as speculation by the media or disinformation being exploited by the Cubans. Because we didn't have a need-to-know in our department, we knew very little. However, we soon received a videotape of the documentary that had been shown on Cuban television, and all of us had gathered one day to watch it. I went away thinking that if it was true as reported, the story would have to go in our Hall of Shame as one of our Most Humiliating Moments.

It was almost five o'clock in the morning when we arrived at our hotel. We were staying in the famous, Mafia-backed, Frank Sinatra–sponsored Riviera Hotel, right on the Malecón, the oceanfront that bordered Havana City. In fact, as we checked in, we were too tired to care that "Old Blue Eyes" had prowled this same lobby and had probably signed the same register. The book clearly looked old enough to hold his signature, and many of those before his. In fact, *everything* looked old.

Later that morning, before breakfast, we strolled around the lobby. The hotel had never made it out of the 1950s; everything that at one time had been new and modern and hip was now passé, worn, and dirty. The pool area was still in pretty good shape, and later I would be able to say that I had swum in the same pool that Ginger Rogers and Esther Williams had once splashed in when Cuba was a playground for the rich and famous.

My colleague and I had apparently done something very good in a previous life because we had a stroke of great luck. It seemed that once a year the Riviera and its comrade-in-arms sister hotel, the Metropol in East Berlin, had an exchange of cuisine and chefs. By sheer luck we were booked at the Riviera for the two weeks that the exchange lasted. This meant that instead of the rather meager fare of rice and beans and fish that we had expected, we would dine on ingredients that had been imported from Europe for this event only. The menu posted prominently in the lobby spelled out the first week's selections: chateaubriand with béarnaise sauce, caviar, Wiener schnitzel, oxtail soup, and on tap, the remarkable Pilsner Urquell beer from Czechoslovakia, one of the best beers in the world. I couldn't help but feel sorry for the poor unsuspecting souls who had checked into the Metropol in Berlin that week, as they no doubt received the worse end of the culinary exchange. The waiters were walking around in tuxedo pants and nearly floor-length white aprons, serving the luncheon menu. Reservations were almost impossible to get, restricted to hotel guests and invited VIPs, mostly government officials, including Castro himself.

Alas, Fidel never showed. Or at least if he did, we never saw him.

After breakfast, we exited the hotel to get our bearings and begin to form a plan of action. Our first impression of Havana was dramatic. The city was falling apart, crumbling, on its knees. Think of decaying colonial grandeur; beautiful old mansions and public buildings were simply melting away. It reminded me of Calcutta, only in India they were putting things back together again. Not in Havana.

And they must have the world's most antiquated auto fleet. Winslow was able to call them out because he was into classic cars. They all dated back to before the Cuban Revolution: the dove gray 1949 Chevrolet Fleetside with its teardrop streamlined shape; the maroon 1940 DeSoto with Fluid Drive and built like a tank; the 1950 Hudson Hornet in forest green with a massive grill and bug-eyed headlights; the lime green 1949 Buick convertible that looked like a huge bathtub turned upside down, and many more. All were American-made, and most of them looked shiny and new, but they were all models from the 1950s, just like the hotels.

We had entered a time warp.

The main blocks along the Malecón were rhythmically punctu-ated with billboards blaring out the proclamations of Castro's prop-aganda machine. "Viva Fidel" was spray-painted on many of the vertical surfaces. Halfway down the Malecón, about a hundred yards from the U.S. Interest Section, was a large sign with a growl-ing Uncle Sam in top hat and striped pants, and next to him a Cuban soldier with a rifle. The soldier was saying, *"Senores Imperi-alistas, No Les Tenemos Absolutamente Ningún Miedo."*

I had some Latin under my belt, and a smattering of French and German, but did not speak Spanish. Neither did Winslow, so we got out our Spanish-English dictionary. We figured out what the soldier holding Uncle Sam at bay was saying. Something like: "Mr. Imperialist, we absolutely have you." As in, I suppose, *Don't make any false moves.*

The most amazing piece of propaganda we saw was a memorial in a park to Ethel and Julius Rosenberg, the infamous American atom bomb spies who had been executed for treason in 1953—the only contemporary Americans to pay the ultimate price for treach-ery in a time of peace. The Cuban memorial noted cryptically that they had been *"asesinados 19-6-1953."* I looked up *"asesinados"* in the book, and discovered it meant assassinated or murdered.

We stood quietly in front of the brick-and-concrete edifice. I had long understood that one country's traitor was another coun-try's hero, but had never seen such palpable evidence of that truism.

That morning we continued down the Malecón, the great meeting place of Havana that served as the city's front porch. It was where you took your 1950 Buick to wash and wax and linger by it, nursing your beer all afternoon. It was where you brought your young children and let them run free on the low wall over-looking the harbor. The street along the water was also the lovers' lane of Havana. On Sundays, we discovered couples every four or five feet sitting together, holding hands, smooching, doing all the

stuff that young people in love do. I probably stopped too often
and looked too long. I missed Tony terribly and couldn't write or
call, but could only daydream.

The Malecón was one of the only places where residents could
fish, as it was forbidden to own a boat of any kind or to catch certain kinds of fish, which were reserved for export only. We were
approached by an East German expatriate who offered to sell us
the two small fish he had caught that morning. When we
declined politely, he offered to cook them for us in his home and
serve them with some boiled potatoes for a small price. We
declined again and moved on. Even on this, our first outing, we
were aware of a group of young Cubans who seemed to be moving down the Malecón with us. We paid them no attention this
first day; there would be plenty of time for that in the two weeks
to come. EVERYONE IS POTENTIALLY UNDER OPPOSITION CON-
TROL. I started automatically to apply the Moscow rules to the
situation, as I would continue to do throughout our stay in Cuba.

To our amazement, there was almost nothing in the store windows. We had known that the economy of Cuba was in pretty dire
straits, but we had not been prepared for the absence of a lot of the
simple things of life. We were going to have a tough time pretending to do a cost-of-living survey in a country with almost nothing
for sale. How do you calculate the average price of beef if there is
no beef in the stores? I was reminded of the stores in Moscow as we
moved through the commercial district. Large stores were displaying only three or four garments in a picture window; food stores
would have six bottles of salsa displayed on a shelf meant to hold
dozens. There were lines at the bakeries for bread and other baked
goods. Evidently, though, there was no shortage of rum, and we
would be able to do a nice sampling of rum prices. It seemed that
there would always be ingredients for Cuba Libres and Mojitos.

On our maps we identified several spots that were of operational interest to our Latin America Division. We were planning

to meet with the local CIA chief, and have some input into his ideas for future planning. During his last trip to Washington, he had told me that the surveillance inside the residences of foreign nationals was just as it was in Moscow, with live video and audio feeds. The U.S. Interest Section offices in the Swiss Embassy were considered insecure, so the only place to have a safe conversation was out in the open, preferably on the move.

Our plan for the next two weeks included a lot of walking, but I was used to walking many miles a day as part of our team exercises, so that would not be a problem. ESTABLISH A DISTINCTIVE AND DYNAMIC PROFILE AND PATTERN.

We threw in several of the tourist sites in and around Havana. We wanted to look at them for many reasons. Some required a car to get there, and we wanted to see what vehicular surveillance looked like and how it would handle us. These sites were also of interest to the local chief. He thought that they might provide fertile ground for some operational scenarios, but he could not go and evaluate them himself. To do so would raise the profile of the sites, and make them less useful. So we made a short list of places that we had to visit, including Hemingway's Finca (his old estate outside of Havana City), the Tropicana nightclub, the Marina Hemingway, and several of the museums in the old part of the city. We had no cover reason to stray any further from the city than those points. MAKE SURE THEY CAN ANTICIPATE YOUR DESTINATION.

After a day of recovering from the all-night trip to the island, we reported to the U.S. Interest Section the next morning. We were greeted by the local chief, Josh Barnett, a freshly scrubbed, vibrant officer, and his young wife, Ellen, a CIA employee who worked with him. They gave us a brief tour around the offices and poured us cups of excellent Cuban coffee. As we sat with them that morning describing our cover plans for the next two weeks, Ellen briefly left the office, then returned with a frown on her face.

"I had hoped to copy your schedule," she said, "so that we

could keep track of you. But the Xerox is down again." She looked over at her husband with a wrinkled brow. "The last time it broke it took a month to get it serviced."

Winslow got up to check out the machine in the other room, and the three of us continued our conversation. Ten minutes later, he returned with blackened hands and the news that the Xerox was up and running. The Barnetts had had no idea that Winslow was a highly skilled mechanical engineer with several advanced degrees, and that he could fix almost anything. They were elated, and invited him to transfer to Havana.

We headed out for a foot tour of the old city. It was the section most seen by tourists, and the part that had had the most restoration work done to the old buildings. The national museums and government buildings were very much intact, and some new construction had actually taken place over the years. The overall effect, however, was of a decaying, Third World capital. Winslow and I wound our way through this quarter, moving into and out of stores, stopping at windows, and as part of our cover, making notes on my clipboard whenever it seemed appropriate.

It was going to take a day or two to develop our eyes, to be able to see into the crowds that we were moving through and past and to pinpoint the surveillance team that we knew was there. It was not unlike hunting morels in the woods. In the beginning, all you see on the forest floor is a carpet of leaves; it takes time before you can make out the mushrooms poking up through the leaves. MAINTAIN A NATURAL PACE.

The next day, we broadened our path and began moving through some of the broad boulevards that broke up the city. We believed that there were static observation posts along these major streets and wanted to try to identify them. The first day we went out of the old city we must have walked ten miles. We had both brought good walking shoes, Rockports, but on the fourth day, Winslow started to develop blisters that became very uncomfortable for him the rest of the trip. GO WITH THE FLOW AND USE THE TERRAIN.

For the trip out of Havana to Hemingway's Finca, we picked a splendid day, with clear skies and a cool breeze. The estate was located up on a promontory with a view of Havana in the distance. I could understand the appeal the setting must have had for Hemingway, who bought the place in 1940 and used it as his official residence until his death in 1961. His wife, Mary, had later donated it to the Cuban government.

Cubans had long worshiped Hemingway. He was proclaimed a friend of the Cuban people in every publication and on every sign at the house, and was still widely read on the island. While you could not go into his house, the large exterior windows were open, and you could glean a very personal look at where Hemingway had lived and worked.

We had gone out to Finca Hemingway in a rental car. It had been easy going; traffic on the island of Cuba was not heavy, and the roads were decent. What had been hard was finding real maps to get us there—I suggested to Winslow that they were afraid of another Bay of Pigs invasion and didn't want the arriving army to know how to get to Havana. It was a joke, but the lack of good maps was a real problem.

Of course, the surveillance teams did not need maps—if they were as good as I suspected, they would know every bump in the road, every shortcut, every dead end. As Winslow drove, I watched them discreetly in the rearview mirror and in the mirror on the side of the car.

There were three cars that I could make out. They changed positions, rotating "the eye"—the car in front—so that it didn't appear that any one of them was right on top of us. As we had parked at the estate, so they had parked too, all together just inside the gate, which I thought odd.

When we left, I noticed two of the drivers chatting with the guard at the gate, while the third car was positioned to slip out behind us as we left the estate. The other two then caught up and we proceeded back into Havana, sort of like a parade out of the 1950s. This was a classic watcher-team operation, sitting back, rather relaxed, and just keeping an eye out. Nothing threatening. LULL THEM INTO A SENSE OF COMPLACENCY.

The next night we decided to do, an interior surveillance run. If we were going to change the Moscow rules, there was nothing like trying it out here and now.

An evening at the famous Tropicana was our plan for Thursday night. One of Havana's enduring legends, the Tropicana continued to provide the sort of nightlife that had been associated with the city's heyday in the 1940s and 1950s. A reservation was required for the performance, which came with dinner and a multitude of rum drinks. As we parked our car and entered the theater, the rhythm of the Cuban music was reverberating throughout the building. The floor show was on an outdoor stage, set in a courtyard of the building. The tables were all under a roof, but the show was in an open-air area. Tropical trees and dramatic footlights gave the stage area a very lush look. As the lights came up very slowly, we discovered that there were dancers on stages set up in the trees as well as down on the main stage. The room filled up quickly with an international audience—Canadians, East Germans, Soviets, some Europeans. We seemed to be the only Americanos in the room.

After the show began I excused myself to find the ladies' room. I conveniently became "lost"—at least that's what I would claim if I were discovered snooping about. I had the opportunity to explore some of the corridors and anterooms of the theater before finding the rest room and returning to my seat. I had made mental notes of the exterior doors and the corridors that led to them. Tomorrow, I would sketch them out. After about half an hour, Winslow made the same trip, and also seemed to lose his bearings, while deftly expanding our reconnaissance wider to the south. By the time dinner and the show were over, we had a pretty good understanding of how the building worked and where the security was—including the team that was surveilling us.

I would have guessed that the surveillance team would come in with us. The show, after all, had a lot of scantily clad beautiful women—what healthy Latin guys wouldn't want to check it out? Depending on how discreet the team wanted to be, they could have entered the club without alarming us. Also, they might have wanted to ensure they knew exactly where we were after thirty minutes or so—just like our SST team. But they did not come in. Instead, they set up outside and covered every exit, which indicated that they were very disciplined, and sharp—giving us no uncovered back doors to exit through.

In giving us freedom to move about undetected inside the building, however, they were playing by the old Moscow rules. This was important information.

BUILD IN OPPORTUNITY, BUT USE IT SPARINGLY.

Josh Barnett and I stood on a high point of ground in East Havana, across the harbor from Old Havana. We had driven there in his car and parked halfway up the drive to the Castillo del Morro, an old ruin overlooking the city. When we walked up to the edge of the cliff, I pulled out my ever-present camera to photograph the scene. Out of film, I reached into my purse and took out a fresh canister, but dropped the distinctive gold box over the cliff's edge. It landed on a rock ledge, about ten feet down.

"Great move," Barnett exclaimed, grinning widely. "You know, the DGI will set up on that box now, probably after commandeering a window in that apartment over there. They'll bring in a static camera, man it twenty-four hours a day, and wait to see who comes for it. If I had enough of you scattered around the island, Jonna, I could tie them *all* up in knots." He had clearly been pleased with the small drama he had sketched out, and we both laughed at the outrageous truth he had described.

We had gone to the overlook to have a secure talk. We were followed by at least three surveillance cars that we saw. Two had stopped below the crest of the hill, and the occupants were also moving discreetly around the overlook, attempting to enjoy the view. One car had gone on up ahead of them, to the top of the hill and to the castle. It had turned around and was prepared to depart as soon as we got back into Barnett's car. This was the watcher team, of course. It was pretty easy to find them—and they didn't seem to mind being sighted. They were just doing their job—making sure that we did nothing untoward. Like meet with a Cuban citizen. Or mail a letter that they could not intercept. Or leave a dead drop. They were making sure that the two of us were staying out of trouble. PICK THE TIME AND PLACE FOR ACTION.

In fact, you could contract and expand the watcher team at will. The team was like an amoeba, with you in the center. They moved around you as you moved forward. If you went into a small space, like a courtyard, they would come in with you and you could check them out. If you went through a chokepoint, like a tunnel or a bridge, they would squeeze through with you, and that would bring them in closer. If you were in a large public space, they could give you all the room you wanted because they could watch you from a distance.

We also knew that we could whittle a surveillance team away. By moving quickly and aggressively through population centers, and stairstepping through town, you could cause considerable attrition. If you really knew the area you were in and took advantage of natural shortcuts and cut-throughs, without looking as if you were trying to break free, you could, in fact, lose them. Not for long, but long enough to do something.

IF YOUR GUT SAYS TO ACT, OVERWHELM THEIR SENSES. This is exactly what Winslow and I set out to do during our last week in Cuba. If we lost the watchers, then presumably the invisible ghost team would have to come in over the horizon and see what was going on.

We were here, after all, to find the spooks.

Winslow, a former Princeton rugby player, had the build and look of a weight lifter. Tall and heavily muscled, with a trim waist and an athlete's walk, he was a pale reddish blond with a conservative haircut and no facial hair. Winslow stood out in this city of three million ethnically diverse Havanans, as he was a very visible gringo. We had decided to make use of that fact, and let it help the watcher team stay with us. In fact, Winslow hadn't worn a hat on the entire trip because he wanted them to use his reddish blond hair and pale look as a marker. It was easy to see him fifty feet ahead, even on a crowded avenue.

We had decided to split up on the street, something we had not done up to this point, a mini "star-burst" maneuver. USE MISDIRECTION, ILLUSION, AND DECEPTION.

"Let's split up in Vedado," Winslow suggested, "about three blocks behind the Riviera." Vedado was a dense residential area with lots of foot traffic on the streets and plenty of alleyways and sidewalks that cut through the city blocks. "They won't know what to do at first. I think that most of them will follow me. They are Latin and predominantly male, and probably have underestimated the female part of our team. Besides, you are more difficult to follow—you blend in better in a crowd. You have a better chance of losing them."

I thought this over. It sounded good to me. With my dark hair and almost perpetual tan, I melted into a crowd readily.

BREAK YOUR TRAIL AND BLEND INTO THE LOCAL SCENE.

"I think you're right," I said. "Those that stay with me I'll take through Vedado, then cut over to the old Hotel Nacional on the Malecón and drag them through some of those long stairs and bridges. I might be able to get out of sight long enough to give the ghost team a chance to get worried and come in and find me. *If* they are there, that is. Let's try it."

Thirty minutes later, I sat on a bench in a small plaza in Vedado, and waited.

It was a quiet time in the city, the hour after lunch when a lot of businesses shut down and the city slowed down for a siesta. The pace would pick up again later, around four-thirty, and the crowds would once again own the streets.

The bench was at the far end of the plaza, occupying the only bit of shade in this piece of urban landscape. I had moved at a brisk pace through the streets of Vedado, but not too fast, not fast enough to draw their eye. Still, I was out of breath and my heart was pounding. I knew that I had lost several of them at the hotel because there were simply too many entrances and exits to cover, and too many stairways spilling down the hill toward the Malecón. It was almost impossible to parallel me that close to the water; they would have to make exaggerated end runs around large apartment blocks to try to stay with me.

I sat with my camera, map, clipboard with my survey forms, and a tourist guide. There was nobody else in the plaza, and the only sound I was aware of was my own labored breathing and the rapid beat of my heart. I was alone. I had lost my watchers. The question now was, Would they come? Would the ghost team appear? Were they out there, and would they come in? I waited.

LET THEM BELIEVE THEY HAVE LOST YOU; ACT INNOCENT.

Five minutes later, there was a small movement in my peripheral vision. I turned my head slightly and saw a young man on a bicycle pedaling down the street. He was barefoot and dressed in khaki shorts and a T-shirt, as close to a national uniform on this island as you could get. As he approached the plaza, I unfolded my tourist map and began studying it. He continued toward my position in a straight line, then steered onto the sidewalk and began to cut through the plaza diagonally. He was moving so slowly now that I wondered how his bicycle could remain upright. He did not look at me. I discovered that I was holding my breath and made a conscious effort to breathe in.

He passed me about thirty feet away, then gradually started to move out of the plaza.

Suddenly, there was a loud clatter.

I glanced up and saw lying exposed on the concrete what appeared to be a walkie-talkie radio, with a remote earpiece attached to it by a long wire. The radio was broken into pieces. The young man jumped off the bike, dropping it roughly to the side, and ran over to the radio. He picked up most of the pieces and the earpiece, stuffed them inside his shirt, hopped back onto the bike, and sped away as if on a leg of the Tour de France.

So there it was. The first sighting of the ghost team. So discreet and so invisible that had it not been for that exotic radio and the young man's sloppy tradecraft, we would have never known. *That's once,* I thought.

Over the next three days, we set up two more scenarios designed to force the hand of the ghost team, and each time we managed to draw them out. ONCE IS AN ACCIDENT; TWICE IS A COINCIDENCE; THREE TIMES IS AN ENEMY ACTION.

The third time that the ghost team was forced to show itself, I just moved through the small streets of Old Havana trying to contain myself. I had an enormous sense of relief that we had found them and been able to manipulate them by forcing them to come in close enough to us that we could see them. This was the final piece of information we needed for the exfiltration of ORB and his family—we now had confirmation that the KGB and their sister intelligence services used more than one surveillance team on the street watching any given individual. Our plan would have to take that into account.

I could not help thinking about how much Tony was going to like these action reports. I couldn't wait to get home and share these experiences with the person in the world it mattered most to, and who could and would use the lessons learned for a higher purpose.

Now it was time for Winslow and me to let the ghost team cool off, or they would begin to suspect something was up. Our last couple of days in Havana, we acted like dumb bureaucrats, maintaining the pattern that we had established all along without the provocative maneuvers. When we departed Havana at the end of our trip, they probably looked after us and thought, *You two gringos are probably CIA pigs, but we kept you from accomplishing anything while you were here.* THERE IS NO LIMIT TO A HUMAN BEING'S ABILITY TO RATIONALIZE THE TRUTH.

Our flight out of Havana was as surreal as our flight in. The Eastern flight attendant must have counted the passengers fifteen times before local security, convinced there were no stowaways, would allow her to close the door on the airplane.

We arrived in Miami around midnight under the dark of the moon.

Our findings on the trip would make the planning for the Moscow operation more complicated, but at least we had the answer to the big question. We now knew for certain that we would perform the rescue maneuver inside—off the street. We could not count on eluding street surveillance in Moscow, not with the ghosts waiting in the wings.

At home on a cold November evening, Tony and I were walking across the yard toward a large stack of firewood that he stored underneath the deck.

Suddenly, in the darkness, he grabbed my hand.

We stopped, mesmerized by the sky unfolding above us. It appeared to be formed out of a soft green fabric and seemed to be moving slowly, at a great distance away.

Tony stepped behind me and put his arm around my waist.

We understood they were the northern lights. As long as both of us had been living and working in Washington, D.C., we had never seen them this far south.

"This is my dream," he whispered in awe. "When I was in Moscow a few months ago, I dreamed the two of us saw this together. I didn't know what it meant."

"Any ideas now?" I asked, sinking farther into his strong arms.

"Yes, dear. That we were going to be together."

Later that night, Tony and I sat on the big red sofa in his living room, and we quietly began to sketch out the final details of the escape plan.

He was smoking a Cuban Montecristo No. 4. The cigars had recently been smuggled off the island by someone who loved him dearly. Two Cuba Libre rum drinks were on the coffee table, and one of Sinatra's albums from the war years was playing. The song was "Someone to Watch Over Me."

We were in the zone.

At the same time, we had our hands almost on the lever. We were about to throw the switch, and in doing so, possibly change the course of world events.

TWELVE

MOSCOW

March 1989

On a Sunday evening, Petr Leonov drove through the gate past the mili-man and pulled into his usual parking space in the reserved lot outside of their apartment block in central Moscow. The visit with his parents had been unusual; normally they did not make the long drive out into the countryside until spring, when the weather had cleared and the days became longer. But he and Lara had other schedules and travels in mind for this spring, and had decided to take Dmitri to see his grandparents, perhaps for the last time.

Leonov had noticed tailing surveillance vehicles on both legs of the trip.

After he parked, Lara unloaded the jars of pickled turnips and beets that Grandma had sent home with them, and Dmitri took his favorite toy car out of the backseat.

"Don't worry about the rest," Leonov said to Lara. "I'll get it later."

Before heading for the apartment complex, Leonov leaned into the backseat of the gray Lada and pulled out a small shopping bag and, from under the seat, a large book about Soviet Olympic heroes they had given Dmitri last year.

Leonov placed the bright red book on the ledge of the rear

window. A distraction for a boy during long rides—perfectly normal.

He locked the car and followed his family into their building.

The following evening, Leonov climbed into his car after work and headed home, staying with his normal driving route, which would take him past Fili Park at a designated time. As he passed the filling station he knew was frequented by foreign diplomats, he saw the black car he was looking for in line to be fueled, right on schedule.

It was a passive signal that required no overt action on the part of Moscow CIA chief Jacques Dumas, who was behind the wheel of the black car with diplomatic plates. That particular car merely had to be there at a certain time to confirm that the message had been received.

Leonov allowed himself a sigh of relief. It had been a long, nervous wait all day. But now he knew that they had seen the red book on the ledge of the car's rear window—his emergency signal. It meant that it was time for the CIA to at last honor its longstanding promise to protect him and his family.

Leonov's thoughts now turned to the details of the final operation he had committed himself to—a kind of swan song that would give the Americans an intelligence coup of unprecedented and even historic proportions.

He and Lara had a late evening stroll around the apartment complex that night, and he told her that preparations were now underway for their upcoming departure. He cautioned her to do nothing out of the ordinary. They would take nothing with them, absolutely nothing, not even photographs. They would give nothing away. They would make no unusual phone calls. There would be no farewells, not even with family.

When it was time, they would simply vanish.

★ ★ ★

The trip into Russia turned into a nightmare.

What should have been a simple travel process became a series of minidramas as we proceeded east, into the heart of enemy territory.

Our troubles began as early as our visa applications. Tony and I had gone separately to the Soviet Embassy in Washington. Like Aldrich Ames, who had come here four years earlier to betray his country, we stood in front of the glass enclosure, looking down at the uniformed guard. Directed to the Consular Section, where visas were handled, we each soon discovered that the Soviets were in no hurry to accommodate our applications.

There had always been a certain low-level harassment that went on in the official channels between our two nations. We would delay our approvals of their diplomatic appointments, and they would make our officers in Moscow wait months for permanent housing. This was really just more of the same. As the dates for our departure loomed closer, we were still without visas. There was really nothing to be done but wait, as any jostling of the visa process itself would call undue attention to our applications. Finally, two days before departure, the visas arrived back at State Department, and we rushed over to pick them up.

"Robert J. Violante" and "Jane M. Campbell" were now cleared to depart.

After we wrapped up our alias-document packages and dispatched a courier to take them to Vienna, we packed our bags and picked up our tickets and final paperwork at Central Travel on the fifth floor of CIA Headquarters.

We arrived at Dulles International Airport separately.

As usual, I traveled light. I had one small suitcase and a large, handmade leather tote bag filled with newspapers and books.

Traveling through Dulles involves dealing with those irritating "people movers"—shuttle buses that transport travelers from the main air terminal to the various satellite terminals out on the tarmac. When it was our turn, the shuttle broke down halfway between the terminals, and we waited nearly an hour for another shuttle to come rescue us. Once we got to the midfield terminal, we discovered that there was no problem with our being late, as our flight had been delayed two hours due to a mechanical hold. Then we waited another two hours.

We were headed for Vienna once again, that favorite jumping-off point for U.S. spies on their way to the Soviet Union. The Soviet national airline, Aeroflot, had a convenient daily flight to Moscow from Vienna, and also, the stopover would give Tony a chance for a final quick exchange with his old colleague, Vienna CIA chief Gerald Swazie, before launching the Moscow operation.

On the last flight to depart Dulles that night, we found that we were the only passengers upstairs in the 747's business-class section. Tony and I were both exhausted, and we were prepared to sleep for a major portion of the flight.

"Do you think the rest of the passengers left because of the delays?" I asked. "Or do you think they just decided to give us some privacy?"

"Maybe they saw how hopelessly in love we are," said Tony, "and were trying to give us some room in which to operate." This made him grin, and he gave me a big hug.

About then, the flight attendant came upstairs and asked us to move downstairs, even offering to upgrade us to first class if we would relocate, as they didn't have sufficient crew to provide service to this level for just two passengers.

"We're going to make your day," Tony said with his friendliest smile. "We don't want any service—no meals, no drinks, no music, no movie. Please just turn off the lights on your way out. You won't hear from us again until morning."

The flight attendant was only too happy to accommodate us.

We stretched out full-length on the seats, using the long shelves under the windows as footrests, and for the first time that either of us could remember, we actually got a good night's sleep together.

As we were making our final approach into Vienna's Schwechat Airport, the captain abruptly came on the public address system, waking us up.

"Please fasten your seat belts and remain in your seats. We are experiencing a security problem and request that all passengers remain seated." There was another conversation going on behind his voice—a loud conversation—and some yelling.

Alone on the upper deck of the plane, we could neither see nor hear what was going on. Tony hesitated for a few seconds, then unfastened his seat belt and moved quickly to the circular stairs leading down to the main cabin. Cautiously, he descended the stairs until he could make out the scene below. There was broken glass in the aisle and several female passengers were in tears, but otherwise it was quiet.

He caught the eye of the woman nearest the staircase, who happened to be American. "It's okay now," she said. "They caught him. The crew has him tied up."

It turned out a hijacking attempt had been foiled; a lone man with a gun had tried to enter the cockpit but had been subdued by the crew.

After landing, we sat on the plane for another hour, waiting for the police to take away the would-be hijacker and sort out which passengers they needed to interview as witnesses. The baggage was off-loaded, and it must have been carefully inspected because it was another hour before we could retrieve it.

Anticipating a full day in Vienna before leaving on the evening flight, we checked into a hotel to have use of a room during the day to shower, change, and rest.

Later, Swazie had a secretary deliver our alias documents to us at the hotel. She told us the time and place for the rendezvous with Swazie, scheduled to happen shortly before we left for the airport. He had prepared some notes for us to take to Moscow, for Jacques Dumas, and some additional technical details regarding what might lie ahead of us. As a result of Tony's earlier discussion with Swazie about his exploits in the Moscow netherworld—the place that we had chosen as an operational venue—we were now retooling and adjusting the final details, a process that would go on right up until the last moment.

After a quick meeting with Swazie, it was time for us to catch our flight to Moscow.

Several Days Later
Tony

From our window table in the second-floor dining room of Moscow's National Hotel, through blowing snow, Jonna and I could see the glow of the ruby red star on top of the 190-foot Gothic-style Trinity Tower.

The dark winter night had already closed in, even though it was still early evening. The medieval Kremlin walls were barely visible through the violet gloom as we enjoyed Georgian brandy with our traditional Russian dessert of ice cream.

The curtain would rise on the Bolshoi Theater's performance of the romantic and lyrical ballet *Coppélia* promptly at 7 PM at the Palace of Congresses. After paying the check, we got back into our winter wraps and, with our personal KGB surveillance team in tow, crossed the wide expanse of Prospekt Marksa, dancing through the frenzy of traffic and curtains of white flakes.

As foreign tourists, we expected that we would receive light, almost cursory surveillance. Of course, had either Jonna or I set off any bells when we came into the country under our aliases, the level of surveillance would have been upped considerably, and we would be at increased risk of capture. If caught spying and with no diplomatic umbrella to hide behind, we could be guaranteed an extended tour of Lubyanka.

On the other hand, Victoria Sanderson and John Winslow, the SST members who had arrived earlier on a tour arranged by Intourist, the Russian national travel agency, were pretty much guaranteed to receive no surveillance at all, outside of their tour guides. But if their cover didn't hold, they very likely could be in similar difficulty.

We joined the throng of huddled citizens now moving as a snaking unit of fur hats, mittens, and bulky coats over the very picturesque battlement-laden bridge that joined the Kutafia Tower with the Trinity Tower and its gate through the Kremlin wall.

A classic chokepoint, I knew. A surveillance team could set up here and observe everyone coming and going.

It was through this gate that Napoleon's army entered the Kremlin, after a brief battle in 1812. At that time, the Neglinnaya River could be seen, flowing under the bridge and forming part of the moat system around the Kremlin walls. The deep moat on the Red Square side of the walls that had joined the Neglinnaya to the Moskva River was now gone, and the Neglinnaya, now hidden, flowed along underneath the Alexander Gardens. In the sixteenth century the czarina, Catherine, thought it a nice idea to bring in Italian architects to design a network of underground canals to contain the river. The fourteenth-century walls of the Kremlin concealed many subterranean secrets. Ivan the Terrible had hidden a treasure room there, which has never been found. Many believed he had forced a work gang to burrow hundreds of feet down and build a cavern to use for interrogations and to conceal his treasure. The story says he did away with the crew once they were finished and entombed them there. In fact, one of the towers on the Moskva River side was named the Tower of Secrets because it hid the underground passages used by the czars to escape the river.

Those secret passages figured heavily in our plans for tonight.

From the time of the czars forward, the Soviets had continued to modernize their underground city. Their sewer systems and subways were models of the revolution. Their sandhogs continued to dig even deeper, creating an ever more complex system of hidden tunnels and transportation networks. The KGB and other government entities moved in and set up shop as well. This became the plan for continuity of government during the Cold War. In the 1940s and 1950s, during the depths of the Cold War, Stalin had installed a complex many stories deep and a transport infrastructure that would quickly evacuate the Soviet elite to an underground alternate Kremlin outside of Moscow.

When I first discovered the Palace of Congresses inside the Kremlin walls a decade earlier, I would have sworn that it was a Soviet rip-off of a western idea. It looked just like the Kennedy Center in Washington, D.C.—transplanted inside these fourteenth-century walls. But while recently studying both buildings in detail, I had learned that the Palace of Congresses was inaugurated a full decade before the Kennedy Center. Perhaps we had copied the Soviets? In any case, the similarities were amazing; for instance they both had an enormous wall of glass overlooking the respective rivers flowing through the capital cities of their respective superpower nations.

The grand foyer of the Kennedy Center was one of the world's largest rooms, 630 feet long, 40 feet wide, and 60 feet tall. The Washington Monument could have been laid lengthwise in it and not touched the walls. Likewise, the conference hall of the Palace of Congresses, with six thousand seats, was one of the biggest in the world: 165 feet deep and 65 feet high. The vast Party congresses were held there, but the rest of the time the Bolshoi used the hall as an alternative space for its performances—the stage being much wider than the Bolshoi Theater stage. Both buildings had a large rooftop mezzanine.

I had learned there were two large escalators leading up to the mezzanine hall from the grand foyer of the Palace of Congresses, and two more went down to the cloakroom and rest rooms on a lower level beneath the main floor.

Perfect for what we had in mind—a good part of our drama tonight would play out on these escalators, and the rooms above and below.

Jonna

Tony and I descended the escalator off the main lobby of the Palace of Congresses to the lower cloakroom and stood in line, arm in arm, to check our coats, hats, and mittens at an enormous counter with cavernous closets looming behind it.

Since attending the ballet in the U.S.S.R. was affordable and highly popular, the room was filled with people from all walks of society. Due to the press of the crowd, it was very warm and humid, and there was a distinct aroma radiating from the crowd— the familiar scent of the unwashed Third World. There was also a lot of pushing and shoving, a common practice in most of the ubiquitous lines in the Soviet Union.

The coat-check counter was staffed with about twenty sour-looking old Russian women in black dresses with white collars, each seemingly trying to be less cordial than the other.

Earlier in the day, Tony had bought me a gray fox shapka, the classic fur cap worn in the winter by almost every Russian. I loved it, and he said I looked good in it, especially with the long black cashmere coat I had brought. I now removed my hat and coat and handed both to him. When Tony turned to me to finish a sentence, the coat-check lady almost wrenched our coats and hats out of his hand. Whether in politics or in the social graces, there was little finesse to be found hereabouts.

He was handed our coat-check token, a small round metal disk with a number stamped on it; then he purchased programs and rented a pair of opera glasses.

Like everyone else, we then stood in front of the huge mirrors that lined the walls of the cloakroom and straightened our clothes and smoothed our hair. For us, this was a handy way not only to check our appearance and adjust some vital piece of our identities, but also to get a free look at the other occupants of the room.

We didn't expect to see our own KGB watchers down here. Even if they were nearby, we assumed that there were other methods of keeping an eye on the crowd. The cloakroom attendants were not the least of this threat and no doubt were informants, and we would have to assume there were also technical devices hidden all around. There were also rest rooms on this level, which afforded additional operational opportunities, although there were attendants there as well. But despite all those pairs of eyes trained to keep track of us, it was our job as disguise officers to overwhelm the senses of the human members of the surveillance teams, be they watchers or ghosts. Our ability to do so would determine whether tonight's operation would succeed or fail.

Back upstairs and free of the crush in the cloakroom, we moved through the ornate lobby, admiring the marble, mirrors, and the gilding on every possible surface. I was able to catch our own reflection as we strolled down the hall and couldn't help admiring our dressed-up images. A more innocent-looking pair of dance enthusiasts could not be imagined. The series of crystal chandeliers overhead shimmered opulently, showering the crowd and the gilded interior with a gossamer veil of softly moving light.

As planned, we had arrived at the ballet early, ensuring time for a leisurely stroll around the lobbies and mezzanine before the crowd swelled to capacity and we had to take our seats.

We took our time, hoping we looked like tourists admiring the surroundings.

Tony

We were heading back toward the main entrance to the lobby when I signaled Jonna by pressing my hand over her arm, which was linked through mine.

I caught my breath as I realized that Petr and Lara Leonov had entered the huge hall and were heading our way. ORB was wearing a military-style cap and a camel hair coat that was almost floor-length—a very dashing appearance for a military officer. Lara was simply luminous. Her dark hair was pulled up off her neck, and she was wearing a shapka like Jonna's, but hers was a paler gray—it looked as if it was made out of silver fox, and because of the superior length of the fur, it was like a delicate silver cloud floating on her head. She was carrying a muff to match it and a dark green coat that just cleared her ankles.

It had been fourteen years since I had last seen them, but I recognized them instantly. They made no sign of recognizing me, of course, although I felt certain that they did as we passed each other. I had worked on plans to exfiltrate them so long ago; it seemed unbelievable that they had remained undetected for such a long time while continuing to work for U.S. intelligence. How had they carried it off? At what cost to their lives? There were so many questions I wanted to ask them, but I knew I would probably never get the chance. In the espionage profession, we have to constantly remind ourselves not to become too close to a local asset, because feelings can get in the way of the job that must be done. Still, I felt an emotional connection to this courageous couple. And now, I was prepared to help carry out what had long ago been promised them: an escape to freedom.

As they approached the escalator going down to the cloakroom, we stepped on the escalator heading up to the rooftop mezzanine, where we would have a sweeping view of the crowd assembling below.

Watching as the handsome Russian couple descended, Jonna and I tried to pick out the watchers who would have followed them here tonight. ORB and Lara, too, were surrounded by the same crush of fans of the ballet, and it took a trained eye to identify their surveillance. But we did, spotting several of them staying close to their targets.

We scanned the crowd for our other players in tonight's unofficial offstage performance: our ZEPHYRs, Rose Cohen and Clint Bradley. We saw them as they entered the building, quite a distance away now that we were nearly forty feet above them. A surveillance team would also accompany them.

Even in this crowd, the two of them could not have looked more American. Bradley wore a long black coat and a black Greek fisherman's hat, with one of those Burberry scarves around his neck. Cohen, in an almost floor-length black coat and matching black velvet hat, looked like something out of a Currier and Ives etching. They moved with the crowd toward the escalator to the coat-checking area.

We now had three couples in place, each under KGB surveillance.

At that moment, we spotted Victoria Sanderson and John Winslow coming up from the cloakroom. They had come in with a group of American tourists who were attending tonight's ballet as the final event of their fourteen-day visit to Russia. Because the pair had been sticking to their benign tourist pattern for two weeks, they should not have picked up KGB surveillance, as the group was safely kept in the cocoon of their Intourist tour guide's scrutiny. They moved through the crowded lobby and up the escalator to the mezzanine with their group, carrying their programs and rented opera glasses. Vicki was loaded down with a Berioska bag, a colorful plastic tote that obviously contained this afternoon's purchases. Her long hair fell well below her shoulders, and she moved gracefully through the lobby in an ankle-length long black skirt with a form-fitting, sleeveless black top.

I made eye contact with Johnny briefly, but otherwise did not acknowledge them as they strolled past us.

At that point, the lights began to flicker; the performance was about to begin.

Only a few of us knew it was going to be a double bill.

Jonna and I settled into the plush pale green velour seats in the sixth row center of the orchestra section. The overture was just starting.

I took her hand in mine, hoping both to give her reassurance for the evening ahead and to measure her emotional state. She leaned over and kissed me lightly on the cheek, then gave me one of those smiles. From where I sat, her emotional state looked just fine—she was as cool as any field operative I'd ever worked with. Some people who are otherwise in control can come apart when the going gets rough; others thrive on it. Jonna, I was learning, was a splendid example of the latter.

In the packed Palace of Congresses Theater, the large banks of overhead lights began to dim.

We could make out our Soviet couple seated diagonally from us a few rows down. Having shed his overcoat, ORB was now in a formal dark evening uniform, and Lara glowed, all pale skin and black velvet. I noticed her distinctive ornate necklace, a tall choker that encircled her neck almost like a cuff.

As the stage lights began to come up, I also caught sight of the ZEPHYR couple taking their seats across the aisle on the right, Bradley in a black tuxedo and Cohen wearing a black crepe dress that fell to the floor. Her hair was flowing down her back and across her shoulders, so voluminous that it was almost impossible to make out her features.

We certainly had chosen a handsome cast for our show.

We had gone over the timing of our performance at least a

dozen times, and the SST had proved the concept in a series of simulation exercises at the theater in Washington. The dress rehearsals had gone very well, but now, with two of the SST's own in position in the Palace of Congresses Theater, it was show time.

Johnny Winslow had turned out to be the closest male match to our physical requirements, and the other half of the SST couple, Vicki Sanderson, was our chosen female. The young electrical engineer was a natural blonde, but for this operation she had dyed her long mane a dark brown with an overtone of henna. She looked smashing. Because of their tourist cover, Johnny and Vicki had had no contact with us, the local CIA contingent, or with ORB and Lara. Before finally launching our operation tonight, we had to assure ourselves that they had no surveillance other than their tour guide, because if things went badly, they had no official affiliations to fall back on, which put them at enormous risk.

In truth, Jonna and I were no better off. Traveling under alias identities, we were not accredited members of the official U.S. community either, and could end up with an extended visit to Lefortovo if the Second Chief Directorate wanted to press the point.

We were more sanguine about this possibility at our level of seniority, but now, looking at her and smelling her perfume and holding her hand, I had an added level of apprehension—Jonna was no longer just a trusted professional colleague with whom I would confidently serve in the heat of any operation. I couldn't bear to think of her standing before KGB interrogators, who would no doubt take their time extracting any spy trade information and tradecraft from her if she were caught helping someone as important as ORB defect. I was fighting off flashes of her standing barefoot on some raised metal platform in a narrow cell, resisting the sleep that would send her tumbling into icy water, then punished with a beating or loss of a day's ration. We had heard many true stories of how the KGB treated its prisoners, and we had few illusions.

We had considered these dire possibilities before launching this high-stakes operation, but they were rarely verbalized. One thing was guaranteed if we didn't succeed tonight: ORB would have no chance of a reprieve. He was marked for arrest and would suffer an even more ghastly form of prolonged torture before his show trial and execution.

We knew that ORB had recently come under increasingly hostile surveillance. We had realized, as he did, that his days were growing short. His contingency exfiltration plan had been in place for years, ever since he first started working with the CIA, and had constantly been updated, depending on his assignment and location. This was our standard practice with all our valued sources, and we had never failed in a rescue operation once we undertook to implement the plan. We had brought out whole families time and again.

I didn't relish the idea of spoiling that record with ORB, Lara, and their son.

The final stage for the deception and escape, here at the Palace of Congresses, had been chosen because of its proximity to the Kremlin Communications Center—and the communications trunk line to all the Soviet ministries, including the KGB.

Following my last discussion with Swazie in Vienna, I had been able to pass along final details on the operational venue to our OTS engineer, Luke Swisher, and he had factored them into his planning. Earlier today, in fact, a shadowy figure, wearing the black stealth carbon fiber gear of a modern-day ninja warrior, had entered the perpetually nocturnal world of the subterranean city under Moscow by means of a small entrance on the banks of the Pakhra River embankment south of Moscow.

For twenty years a little-known band of urban spelunkers known as the Diggers of the Underground Planet have used this entrance, as have Satanists, poets, dissidents, and society's dropouts. This lone traveler had a hyper-version of the KAPELLE device—created from specifications provided by ORB—slung in a special harness attached to his black web-gear.

The ninja bristled with all the tools that only a highly motivated and enormously talented force of technologists could provide for his journey into the unknown abyss. His equipment foreshadowed the gear that would be standard issue for commandos in the wars of the next century. Among the exotic gadgets in his self-contained life-support system (designed to thwart the threats of the KGB's most sophisticated counterintel gear) were tunnel sniffers, air purifiers, and a special scrubber breathing apparatus. He wore an infrared helmet light and night-vision goggles—to the naked eye the tunnel was dark, but the ninja was able to view it through the eerie green light provided by the infrared source. The goggles also illuminated a heads-up display from a body-worn computer programmed with a geo-positioning compass and a tunnel map made from imagery collected from space by ground-penetrating radar. An acoustic listening device helped him make his way without being ambushed or lost forever.

All of this gear was made from unmarked components to make it more difficult to identify the origin of its manufacture or his affiliation should he be apprehended. But in fact, if the enemy ever had a chance to go over this million-dollar-a-pound gear, they wouldn't have too hard a time guessing its national origin.

As of this moment, the ninja was still underground—awaiting the final act—armed with pepper spray and a stun gun to be used against any sentries or guard dogs and a killing knife of Czech manufacture for extreme emergencies. For hours he had been traversing the maze of tunnels and had carefully made his way deep below the streets of Moscow toward the Kremlin. He also had a poison-tipped needle concealed in the stem of his watch in case things went very badly. The ninja knew, as we all did, that the Soviets—given enough time—could get just about any information they wanted out of a prisoner. He had no intention of letting himself and his array of technical knowledge of intelligence operations become an open book to the KGB.

Besides his local master, the ninja was the only one who knew about ORB and his unique access to the Kremlin Communications Center.

As a KGB major from the Sixteenth Directorate, ORB was now a senior technical security officer for Gorbachev's worldwide communication network. His access to Soviet KAPELLE networks had proven vital to the United States' understanding of how Gorbachev was attempting to reform the Soviet Union, a country that seemed now to be in a perpetual tailspin. Just today, there had been four hundred thousand demonstrators filling Red Square, shouting "Down with the KGB." How much longer would the KGB wait before it came down with the fist of oppression, smashed this precipitous glasnost, and knocked perestroika back into the dark days of the Stalinist purges?

Although ORB's existence had been highly compartmented since he began working for the CIA in Indochina, I did wonder if his current predicament could be linked to the other string of arrests of our Soviet agents. Nevertheless, we knew that the KGB had not been able to read our communications on the ORB case, as no electronic communications had ever been used. At his insistence, and wisely so, everything had always been done by hand-carry.

From what I'd observed tonight of ORB's entrance, KGB surveillance was following him in force; so much so, it looked as if his arrest was imminent.

ORB and his wife were prepared to make a last sacrifice for the cause of freedom, and then, to cut off all ties to their homeland. If all went well, they would sail with their son, Dmitri, on the ferry out of one of the Baltic states to the West in a week's time.

If we failed, none of them would stand a chance, and some of us would surely be in a similar predicament.

THIRTEEN

THE PALACE
OF CONGRESSES

Jonna

Tony and I watched the first act of *Coppélia*—a love story about a
doll maker whose greatest desire is to create a beautiful doll with a
soul—oblivious of its grandeur. The Soviets spared none of their
scarce resources for their beloved national ballet company; the
scenery and costumes were breathtaking, and the depth of talent
in the cast was amazing—unmatched anywhere in modern times
for classical ballet.

But tonight, we were somewhat immune to the theatrical display on stage.

We were focused instead on another performance about to take
place in this hall, knowing that everything hinged on perfect timing and execution. Done right, it would be a classic demonstration of hiding the smaller motion within the larger motion—the
very mantra of magic, illusion, and misdirection.

We sat with our hands and fingers entwined and our minds
going over important details while we tried to breathe evenly and
will our bodies to stay loose. Only with great care and exquisite

planning had our fellow players made their way here to this country and this city in order now to be in position in this theater.

The houselights came up for the intermission. It was finally time.

Immediately, the audience leaped to their feet in typical Soviet style and began racing up the aisles to the lobby. There they pushed their way to the escalators and dashed up to the top floor of the great hall in an effort to be first in yet another Moscow queue. But this time the obligatory line was worth the trouble, for it led to the sumptuous spread of refreshments available at all Bolshoi performances. The most-sought-after items were the champagne and blinis with caviar, reasonably priced to accommodate the budget of the average Muscovite, but there were many other rich dishes to choose from.

Tony and I, working in concert to keep track of our players in the chaotic moment, were propelled by the crush up the aisle and toward the lobby. He held on to my arm for dear life—once separated, we could be swept dangerously apart.

We spotted Clint Bradley and Rose Cohen moving with the phalanx of babushkas who always led the charge. The standing Muscovite rule was, "If there is a line, get in it. You can always use whatever it is—for barter if nothing else." The great hips of the babushkas were perfect battering rams. Unsuspecting novices competing against them would find themselves sent reeling out of line at the refreshment table, only to turn around to find it was some old grandmother barging her way in with a hip like an ocean liner. I suppressed a smile, hoping that the slender Rose would be able to protect herself.

Then I spotted ORB—Petr Leonov and his wife, Lara, were making their way to the lobby by the parallel aisle, and arrived in the crowded lobby about the same time as Bradley and Cohen.

I picked out two of the KGB watchers assigned to the Soviet couple, elbowing their way toward the packed escalators and following their prey like two great white sharks cruising through the crowd and leaving a wake behind them.

The handsome Soviet couple made their way down the escalator to the next level, where the huge cloakroom and rest rooms were located; ORB in his well-tailored dark dress uniform, his blond hair in a closely cropped military brush cut, and his petite wife in her stylish gown. On closer inspection, her long dark hair was slightly tinted with the fashionable henna color preferred by Muscovite women of status. Her high cuff of a necklace glittered in the crowd. Clearly they were privileged members of the *apparat*.

It was time for my scene—time to enter stage left.

I took a deep breath, focused my thoughts, and turned to Tony. "I'm going to powder my nose," I said as nonchalantly as I could. "I'll see you upstairs. Be a dear and see if you can nab me a champagne."

Tony

Jonna looked terrific in her long gown, her newly long hair gently coaxed up into a twist. There were small wisps of hair that hadn't quite made it that I found very tender. That Japanese thing about the nape of a woman's neck—it never failed to move me.

Carrying her favorite fashion accessory, a large, black Gucci bag with a big double *G* for a clasp, she was about to commit herself to the riskiest part of the operation. Once it was put into motion, there was no going back for any of us, and no room for a miscue. While we had both taken risks with some frequency in our careers, this particular night we were playing for the highest stakes possible.

I looked into her eyes for an instant, trying to memorize her impassive face.

"I'll do my best to score some bubbly," I said softly. "Don't be long."

I gave her a peck on the cheek and then she moved away through the crowd.

I headed toward the escalator, planning to position myself far above the action to monitor the couples and their respective watchers, ready to sound the alarm and direct the players in the event of a change of plan. Mine was more the role of stage director than supporting actor. The women would not look up; the men would pause occasionally, scanning the height and breadth of the hall, seeming to admire its architecture and marveling at its soaring height and the enormous crystal light fixtures hanging four stories above them, thereby giving me an opportunity to signal them if there were problems only I could see.

Jonna

As I headed for the ladies' rest room, I tried not to move too quickly.

The last thing I wanted to do was to attract attention to myself.

Rose and Lara, independently, entered the enormous ladies' room on the cloakroom level shortly after I did. The room was completely lined in white marble, including the floor, and every noise was greatly magnified—a voice, the clicking of a hundred high heels, all together a cacophony of sound that was almost deafening.

Vicki arrived last.

I seemed to be scrutinizing my hair in the mirror when, in fact, I was counting heads. When all were present, I applied a small dab of powder and moved away from the mirror.

Although Rose and Lara each had their own KGB watchers, the surveillants were comfortable waiting for them outside the powder room, knowing that the attendants in the rest rooms would keep their eyes open and quickly report to authorities any strange goings-on, especially by foreigners.

I entered a stall toward the end of the huge room, setting my oversized black bag down just inside the door, where the attendants and anyone else could easily see it.

Shortly after that, the door to the stall next to me opened, and I spotted Vicki's Berioska bag being set down on the floor to my left.

Moments before Vicki's entrance, I had seen Lara enter the stall to Vicki's left.

Then, the stall door on my right closed, and I heard the latch slide into place.

Even the eagle-eyed attendants, however motivated they might be, could not possibly see the small, round cloakroom disks needed to claim one's outer garments being exchanged under the sides of adjoining rest room stalls, or a Berioska bag that slid from one cubicle to the other. The jeweled necklace collapsed into a handful of sparkling stones and old gold as it was handed off. Hairpins and rubber bands were put on and taken off, securing or freeing loose strands; other pins were flushed down the toilet.

Unadorned, Lara, Rose, and Vicki were three women who already looked quite similar, and of course, that was not by accident. Their height and hair were similar, and even their clothes were confusingly alike. Their faces, though, were different. But then, surveillance teams seldom had the opportunity to watch faces; they followed profiles and whatever other prominent and easy-to-spot handles they were given.

Tonight, two KGB teams were following two women with long, dark hair, both of whom were wearing long, dark gowns. It could be confusing in a crowd, couldn't it?

Another watcher was on me—the American woman with the large black purse. Unless I had tripped some wires upon my entry to the country, I wouldn't be of any particular interest to my watcher, other than as another routine assignment on a cold night.

With all the other persons of interest in tonight's crowd, these teams certainly wouldn't be the only KGB surveillance teams in the hall. None of the teams would communicate among themselves, however, but only with some central control.

Tony

The muscles in my shoulders grew tense as I waited, and I could feel the pulse in my carotid artery quicken its pace. All of my body's little emergency signals, like perspiration, seemed exaggerated in a tuxedo.

As I watched from above, one by one the ladies left the women's room and moved into the crowd on the lower level. The first one to emerge was a female champagne attendant, wearing the standard white uniform, followed closely by Lara, easily spotted because of that distinctive necklace and her dark hair pinned up in an elaborate bun. Next came Rose in her long black dress, her dark hair flowing down her back and over her shoulders.

A moment later, Jonna exited the rest room, shot me a look and a smile, and headed for the escalators to join me for champagne upstairs.

Clint and ORB were in close proximity near the cloakroom for an instant, but no one could pick this out in the crowd unless they knew exactly when it would happen.

Later, both couples were sighted separately on the escalator and by the champagne carts in the refreshment hall. It was a little dark at the end of the hall, back by the carts, where they kept the cases of backup champagne, linens, and the serving accessories.

Vicki and Johnny had already attended three other events at this theater in the past two weeks as part of their tour, and at each intermission they had noted that the setup and serving of the champagne was always the same, but the servers were a different crew each time. That observation had been useful information.

I could see Clint's and ORB's respective surveillance teams get a little tangled up once or twice in the various halls and on the escalators. Then, for a heart-stopping moment, Jonna and I both witnessed the confusion in the hall when the lights flickered to announce the end of the intermission. Somehow, ORB and his wife were missing in the confusion of the crowd, and their surveillance team panicked briefly. They quickly relocated them, however, and settled down as the crowd jostled them all down the escalators once more.

Lara's necklace was clearly visible, even from behind.

Jonna took the glass of champagne from my hand and held it out to me with a dip of her head. "Nice plan, Tony," she said.

I returned the gesture, and we stood there with both of our glasses raised. "Nice execution," I replied. "It's always in the details, isn't it?"

We sipped our champagne, scanning the crowd four stories below us with practiced eyes. They were gone.

No one noticed when two of the champagne attendants in their floor-length white aprons and white brimless hats drifted to the back of the hall and pushed the button for the service elevator. As the elevator doors closed, one of them looked vaguely as if he had a certain military bearing in spite of his disheveled appearance, and the other was a pretty, delicate-featured, flushed young woman.

Meanwhile, inside the theater, the switch had been made. Clint and Rose, wearing the same clothing and hairstyles that the Russian couple had arrived in, were in the seats that ORB and Lara had been in prior to intermission. Likewise, Vicki and Johnny, the only couple without surveillance, and whom we were counting on to not be missed until their tour bus left at the end of the performance, were equally prepared with attire and coiffure for the shift into Clint and Rose's seats.

No alarms had gone off. So far, so good.

The ninja heard the manhole cover up above him opening, then clanging shut.

It was too dark to see who came down the rust-covered iron ladder, so he remained hidden in the shadows until he could be certain who it was.

"Ready to rock and roll?" The heavily accented recognition signal came as a whisper in the dark.

The ninja turned on his IR helmet light, and through his goggles, saw that the source of the whisper was still wearing a white apron.

ORB quickly removed the prop.

The ninja handed over a spare pair of IR goggles. "Ready as I'll ever be," he said. "I have the jukebox right here."

They moved an ancient gate, and then ORB could see into the abyss beyond. A cloud of sewer gas enveloped them, sickening them with its stench. They entered the lower depths of an arched brick sewer; all they could see beyond the sweep of the IR beam was black everywhere.

ORB moved forward smartly as if he knew exactly where he was headed, then he stopped and drew back. He made a sign for silence. The ninja melted into the shadows, and ORB looked straight ahead into the unfathomable caverns. Then ORB made the signal to move forward.

They walked gingerly across the gleaming, stinking, slime-covered brick ledges that hung on the sides of the seemingly never-ending tunnel.

Traveling onward, they encountered a metal security door, which guarded a six-foot-wide brick tunnel. ORB put his shoulder to it, and the ninja joined in. First there was a groan and then a scraping noise as the door slid away from its pocket in the masonry. They pushed through sideways, and after several minutes were in a section of the now burgeoning cavern laden with telephone trunk lines and other mechanical conduits. They vaulted over bulkheads and shinnied down a brace of ductwork leading two or three stories down to a great hall of technical underpinning.

The ninja could tell they were deep under the Kremlin. His shoulders screamed under the load of the heavy device he had worn on his back for hours.

ORB pointed up at a bundle of the cables emerging from the roof of the tunnel.

The ninja unhooked a compact, titanium telescoping ladder from his web-gear.

After the final act of that night's stunning performance, the admiring crowd gathered and donned their wraps down in the cloakroom.

The roar of voices in the large hall was almost overpowering as the elated balletgoers praised the performance.

Clint Bradley and Rose Cohen were arranging their coats, hat, and shapka while immersed in the jostling crowds of people doing the same thing in front of the huge mirrors. He reached into an interior pocket of his suit and retrieved a small glass ampoule, which he broke quickly in his handkerchief. He then leaned down and wiped his and Rose's shoes with the dampened cloth as though removing dirt or mud.

As the crowd streamed over the long bridge through the Trinity Tower gate and across to Kutafia Tower before descending down onto Prospekt Marksa, two KGB Second Chief Directorate plainclothes officers moved out of the shadows, stepping in behind a couple strolling leisurely down the cobbled narrow street through the softly falling thick snow.

The man was wearing what appeared to be a military-style cap and a long camel coat. The woman was dressed in a floor-length green coat and wearing a particularly handsome gray shapka and carrying a gray muff. Both items were made of silver fox, a favorite fur in this part of the world, being both warm and beautiful.

The KGB officers moved forward quickly, coming parallel with the couple and each taking an elbow. Stopping suddenly, the KGB men spoke loudly to the couple and began leading them down the street toward a black Volga waiting at curbside, passing under a streetlight as they did so.

"To whom do we owe this honor, comrades?" asked Bradley in fluid Russian.

He removed his American diplomatic ID card from his coat pocket and handed it to the KGB officers.

The two KGB officers were startled. They scrutinized the pair under the streetlight, realizing these people were not the couple that they were after. The man's camel-colored topcoat had the same look as that worn by Comrade Leonov, but his beaked hat, similar to a KGB dress cap, had the dark braid of a black Greek fisherman's cap, now all the rage for gentlemen's formal winter wear. The woman's hat, muff, and green coat also matched those worn by Mrs. Leonov. But their hair was all wrong; she had removed her shapka, and her elaborately styled, upswept hairdo and the man's close-cropped blond cut were clearly western hairstyles. Their size was right, their gait matched, the clothes had seemed right, but the details were all wrong. The faces were wrong!

The men looked down at the couple's shoes and then at one another. They had strong reason to suspect that the soles of the couple's shoes carried the secret marking dust, but there was nothing more to do.

Lacking orders to arrest diplomatically accredited Americans, embarrassed and muttering apologies, the KGB officers released the couple. They quickly set off to retrace their steps. They had made a mistake. They must have missed them somehow on the dimly lit bridge. They headed back to the Palace of Congresses, lit up like a cruise ship in the cold dark night, and began to run as they approached the building. It was not healthy or wise to lose one's target. Bad things could happen.

Farther down the street, the Intourist bus was parked at the curb, its diesel engines idling noisily, the exhaust pipes belching a black and greasy plume, while the tour guide walked up and down the aisle of the bus, counting occupants. He turned on his heel and strode to the front again, exited the bus, and began sprinting back to the building. His count was two short, and he knew which two: the young American couple who seemed in love.

An hour later, when Bradley and Cohen entered Clint's apartment, they realized that they were not alone. There in the darkness of their living room awaited John Winslow and Victoria Sanderson, flushed with excitement. Their coats—actually Clint's and Rose's coats and hats and that Burberry scarf—were lying in a pile on a chair.

Without turning on the lights or speaking, Clint walked over to the couple and motioned them to the side of the room where the sofa was located. As their eyes grew used to the dark, Clint went into the kitchen and emerged with a tray holding a bottle of champagne and four glasses.

At the sound of the champagne cork popping, the Russians monitoring the audio devices at the command center gave each other quizzical looks. After they heard a whispered giggle and clinking glasses, they looked at each other again and smiled. Some universal behaviors needed no explanation.

Outside the window the snow began to come down more heavily again, almost obscuring the view of the street, which was swallowed up in the silence of the blizzard.

The next morning, Tony and I rose early and retrieved a copy of *Izvestia,* the newspaper that was promptly delivered to our doorway each morning—one of the few things that still seemed to be done on time in a country coming undone. It was placed there by the floor attendant, another of the controls found in every hotel in the city. There was no coming or going from hotel rooms that was not noticed and recorded by floor attendants.

Since we were traveling in alias as a couple, although not married, there was no problem with our sharing a room. Such was not an uncommon situation during operations, and sometimes it could be unpleasant and a real test of one's professionalism. Other times, like now, it was serendipitous.

We returned to bed with the paper, snuggling back in under the fine down comforter that had warmed us all night. In the paper there was a glowing review of the Bolshoi's production of *Coppélia.*

There was no other news of interest to us, a great relief.

We set the paper aside and called room service, ordering champagne, scrambled eggs, blinis, and caviar for breakfast.

For very good reason, we felt like celebrating.

The hyper–listening device—reverse-engineered with ORB's expertise based on the design of a particular KAPELLE that had gone missing two years earlier—had been placed on the trunk line, where ORB had identified a "bust-out," or a juncture where traffic from the Kremlin's communications center could be read in the clear, before encryption.

After their underground mission the previous night, the ninja and ORB had collected Lara, hiding inside a designated sewer entrance, and they had traversed through the tunnels to a place near the Moscow Zoo. The couple emerged in disguise, collected their son, waiting for them in the company of a trusted escort, and disappeared into the night.

Some days later, ORB, Lara, and young Dmitri were to pick up a dead drop package in a park in a Baltic capital. This would provide them with the wherewithal, travel documents, and details for their trip west; this Baltic state had already taken the brazen step and declared its sovereignty from the U.S.S.R. some months before.

Clint Bradley and Rose Cohen departed Moscow on a permanent change of assignment two weeks later, as had long been scheduled. Bradley returned to headquarters, where he was assigned as a deputy chief in the Internal Soviet Operations Group. His first tour overseas was regarded as highly successful, and he was considered to be on the fast track, a rising young star. Cohen was sent on a lateral assignment to Paris, where she would have a plum position chasing high-priority technology-transfer targets—individuals and firms attempting to siphon away classified American know-how.

Johnny Winslow and Victoria Sanderson departed Moscow with their tour group. When they had arrived back at their hotel after the ballet, they had been berated by their irate tour guide, who told them that he could have lost his job because of their violation of the rules. They apologized for their carelessness in missing the bus.

Upon their arrival home, Vicki and Johnny were both given one week of administrative leave. For her, it was enough time to recolor and restyle her hair to its original color. Because of the highly compartmented nature of the ORB operation, the majority of their peers never knew that the operation had taken place or even that they had been out of the country. Their SST colleagues were happy to have them back, however, and rumors soon began to spread that theirs was more than a friendship.

Tony and I knew how such things could happen.

FOURTEEN

MARYLAND

Summer 1991

Jonna

The great draft horse Chessie moved powerfully along the side of the road. Looming to the south was the first of the Blue Ridge Mountains, blue and green in the distance and cloaked in a humid haze. Ahead, down the long valley, the fields and forests of the countryside shimmered softly in the sun, which was pouring gloriously through the ever-changing cumulus clouds. The soft clip-clop sound of the horse's hooves made a staccato pattern, in high contrast to the sound of horns and congratulations offered by our guests as they passed by the carriage and went on ahead of us to our art studios and the waiting reception. Soon we were alone on the country road, hand in hand in the antique carriage that was taking us home from the church.

"Champagne, Mrs. Mendez?" asked Tony. He opened a door in the bulkhead of the carriage, revealing a silver ice bucket containing a bottle of Russian sparkling wine. He pulled two crystal stems from their compartment and poured each of us a glass.

"Looks like you got away with a whole bottle," I said. "This is the same champagne that they served at the Bolshoi, isn't it?"

"It is," Tony replied. "You know the importance of such details."

We silently tipped our glasses and sipped the ice-cold liquid.

The champagne that had been crisp and dry in Moscow now tasted a little vinegary, but we didn't care.

Our wedding had been small and elegant. We had chosen a cozy Episcopal church, St. Luke's, that dated back to the Civil War. It was only four miles from our house and studios, and was scenically perched on the edge of our valley, commanding a view both north and south.

The church would hold only a hundred guests, and we discovered that that was the perfect number. Exactly one hundred friends, family, and colleagues had filled the space while we exchanged our vows. The former pastor of the church, Father Grimm, had come out of retirement to conduct the service for his longtime neighbor, Tony.

The ceremony itself was simple; the only tailoring done to the standard service had been the omission of the verbiage relating to childbearing as the goal of the marriage.

"Don't want any giggling during the ceremony," Father Grimm had said.

Then in my mid-forties, I remained mum, holding the hand of the man I loved.

My mother stepped out of the crowd to join us, along with Tony's mother, who was in a turn-of-the-century satin-and-lace dress with a large matching hat, an outfit she had made herself for another family wedding earlier in the year that had had a Civil War motif. My mother was wearing a simple yellow linen sheath.

Clint Bradley moved forward from the garden, where he had been deep in conversation with Jacob Jordan, who had retired the previous year and was obviously enjoying reconnecting with so many old colleagues. As was often done with retired Agency personnel, Jordan had been brought back aboard on a part-time contract basis. At present, he was handling resettlement cases of foreign nationals who had provided loyal service overseas to U.S. intelligence.

"Good to see you again," Bradley exclaimed, "and congratulations!"

At that moment, Rose Cohen, who had flown in from France the night before, joined the group. We exchanged hugs and starting catching up with one another. The four of us looked up as Luke Swisher emerged from the crowd.

"Fabulous," Luke gushed. "What a beautiful wedding and a beautiful day!" He held up his glass of champagne, bowed to us, and swallowed the champagne in one long gulp, as if downing a shot of Russian vodka.

John Winslow, still the leader of the SST, strolled over, with Victoria Sanderson on his arm. "Congratulations, Mr. and Mrs. Mendez," he said.

"It was *so* lovely," Vicki said. "Like something out of a fairy tale."

Vicki, I had noted, had caught my bouquet of flowers, and wasn't letting go.

The crowd slowly moved from the gardens up the stairs to the show pavilion. The space had been hung with Tony's paintings, and his son Toby's sculptures were placed around on pedestals, just as they were for their twice-yearly art shows. It was like being in a museum. But now, the floor space was filled by tables and chairs set up for dinner.

Tony and I were aware of a presence behind us before we even turned around.

"Thank you for the invitation," said Miles Rhenquist. "I was rather surprised, and then pleased, to be included on your guest list."

"Thanks for coming, Miles" Tony said casually.

I was shocked at how worn-out Rhenquist looked. The last two years had obviously been difficult ones. Tony and I had heard some rumblings about what Rhenquist had been going through—after so many failures in Moscow, he had been pushed aside from access to further operations and assigned to a less prestigious job—but at that time we didn't know everything. We had no firm evidence, for instance, that Miles Rhenquist was high on the CIA/FBI Mole Hunting Team's shortlist of possible traitors. In fact, he was only cleared when the finger eventually pointed to Aldrich Ames.

We had heard also that Rhenquist, no doubt realizing that his career was all but over, had turned into a bitter man. We were about to see evidence of that for ourselves.

"I don't want to cast a shadow over your day," said Miles, looking around at the crowd. "Perhaps this isn't the best time. But I did want the two of you to know that, as it turned out, ORB was just another dangle."

I caught my breath, and looked at Tony. His eyes had turned steely hard.

"We never got a bit of information out of that fancy device that he put in that night," Rhenquist went on, seeming to enjoy dispensing the bad news. "I'm not sure that ORB didn't sabotage the whole operation from the beginning. Anyway, wanted to let you know before you heard it elsewhere. The operation was a dud. Zero."

"What happened to ORB?" Tony asked. "The exfiltration plan was good to go."

"Didn't work out. Things are never what they seem to be, you know?"

My mind was doing backflips. I didn't know what to think. Could we believe what Rhenquist was saying? Did he have the correct information, or was he spoofing us? Or had he himself been spoofed into believing the operation had gone badly when, in fact, it had simply been put in another compartment and he was no longer privy to the information?

One thing was clear to me, however: Rhenquist gave all indications of being filled with a kind of malicious glee at telling us about the loss of an agent we had taken great risks to rescue.

Had he turned *that* bitter at how badly his career was ending?

Rhenquist turned, moved across the pavilion, then went down the stairs and out into the dusk of the evening. He would not be staying for dinner, and it was just as well.

As the servers began to bring fresh glasses of champagne to our guests, a pair of them headed over to our table. One was a well-built man, the other a shapely female; they were both dressed in formal tuxedos, as were all the waiters. These two were also wearing long white aprons and carrying silver trays with a number of filled glasses.

I looked at the couple closely. The man looked vaguely familiar, with a muscular build and short, dark brown hair. He had a mustache trimmed with almost military precision and a small goatee. He wore wire-rimmed glasses, slightly tinted, as they do in Europe. The young woman was beautiful, with shoulder-length blonde hair, and she wore tortoiseshell glasses.

The male server smiled at us and made a small bow. Moving around the circle, the woman offered everyone a glass of champagne, including Luke, Johnny, Vicki, Clint, and Rose. When we each had a glass in our hands, they, too, picked up champagne flutes.

"Let's rock and roll," the waiter said with a heavy East European accent.

The circle broke into a group grin; now we knew who they were and why they had looked familiar.

And in that instant Tony and I knew that ORB and his family *had* made it out!

But how had they found us? How had they made it to our wedding? What had happened to them after Moscow? We had so many questions, none of which we got around to asking Petr and Lara. We were just happy to see them, and relieved—*very* relieved after Miles Rhenquist's tawdry little performance—that they were all right.

Unable to contain his curiosity, Luke asked, "How did the jukebox do?"

"I understand it played wonderful music for some time," ORB said, grinning broadly. "Favoring Russian waltzes, of course."

Tony raised his glass. *"Nostrovia,"* he said. "To your health, and to your life."

We all drained our glasses.

The handsome Russian couple who had a new life somewhere in America moved away from our group, out of our circle on the deck, and down the steps into the courtyard.

We saw Jacob Jordan's black BMW sedan pull up, and ORB open the back door.

Unbeknownst to us until that very moment, Jordan had for some time been handling the resettlement in the United States of Petr, Lara, and eleven-year-old Dmitri, who, we would later learn, had become quite a soccer star.

Once the two special passengers were inside, the car pulled slowly away.

TEXAS

Seven years later

Tony

On a cold, wintry day in 1999, Jonna and I traveled to the home of Texas A & M University and the site of the George Bush Presidential Library and Center for Presidential Studies to attend a conference being hosted by the CIA's Center for the Study of Intelligence and the George Bush School of Government and Public Service.

Both now retired, we looked forward to a reunion with many of our former colleagues and a chance to revisit our Cold War history with the perspective of time.

From Washington, D.C., we had flown into Dallas, leaving our seven-year-old son with relatives, and driven the rest of the way. Our curly-haired boy, Jesse, was a package that had arrived unexpectedly but with great fanfare, as Jonna and I had had neither the hope nor the expectation of starting a family together.

The conference was attended by six former Directors of Central Intelligence—former president Bush, current DCI George Tenet, Richard Helms, William Webster, Robert Gates, and R. James Woolsey. Also present were former senior intelligence officers from both sides in the Cold War, former senior U.S.

policymakers, academic specialists on the Cold War, members of the media, and other interested citizens. Altogether the event drew some four hundred attendees.

. During the welcoming luncheon, President Bush spoke about the value of intelligence to his administration as the Cold War was ending. Looking back at the turbulent and far-reaching changes in the world order that occurred during his presidency, he said, "There can be no substitute for the president's having the best possible intelligence in the world, which means we must rely on the CIA and the entire intelligence community."

Jonna and I exchanged glances, and I knew that we were thinking the same thoughts, as we do so often. We knew that the information provided to President Bush had come from a variety of sources—not the least of these were many of the agent operations we worked on and the multitude of technical collection systems deployed by the intelligence services, such as the communications package that ORB had placed that night in the Moscow sewers.

These kinds of successes had yielded the reports that were the lead items in the president's daily brief (PDB), the paper that the CIA produced for the president and a handful of his top aides. Through a succession of these briefs, Bush had been able to keep track of his Soviet opposite number's progress as the Soviet Union slowly crumbled, and this led to a truly remarkable Cold War moment during the attempted coup against Gorbachev by the hardliners, led by KGB head Vladimir Kryuchkov, in August 1991.

On August 17, Bush's PDB warned that the coup was about to happen. Sitting on the deck of his retreat overlooking the Atlantic in Kennebunkport, Maine, the president was briefed by DCI Gates on the seriousness of the situation. The next morning, as predicted in the PDB, Chairman Gorbachev was being detained by the KGB, and Russian President Boris Yeltsin was barricaded inside his headquarters in the Moscow White House, surrounded by tanks. At that moment, Yeltsin's phone rang—it was President Bush.

Yeltsin is said to have listened in amazement to Bush, wondering how the U.S. president was able to keep so up to date on the Soviet Union's internal affairs. The words of President Bush reassured and fortified him, Yeltsin later attested, and from there he went outside and stood atop the tank to make his famous address to the cheering crowds. The world had changed that suddenly.

The rest of the conference was composed of panels that examined various elements of the intelligence community's performance during the Cold War. At one panel, there was a particularly remarkable exchange between two old foes.

In the red corner was General Oleg Kalugin, who had become the youngest general in the history of the KGB after his successful intelligence exploits in the United States. He eventually rose to be head of foreign counterintelligence before being fired for speaking out against KGB excesses.

In the blue corner was former CIA officer Paul Redmond, who had been a case officer and chief of station before becoming deputy chief of SE Division. For many years he had been devoted almost exclusively to espionage and counterintelligence operations against the Soviet Union. His last assignment had been as associate deputy of operations for counterintelligence, and as such he had led the hunt for the KGB mole in the CIA that had sidelined more than one career and resulted in the capture of Aldrich Ames in 1994. Only then had Jonna and I realized that one of our principal adversaries for the final five years of the Cold War in Moscow had been a high-placed CIA turncoat.

These two old warriors, Kalugin and Redmond, offered to provide an historical perspective on CIA and KGB operations, and finally, to issue an informal verdict on who won the *human intelligence* war. Information derived from this type of intelligence, known in the CIA as HUMINT, comes usually from foreign nationals.

General Kalugin spoke first. He had the look of a wolf, with his high forehead and a prominent widow's peak of graying salt-and-pepper hair, which was combed straight back in an East European pompadour. This was accentuated by his sharp features, high Slavic cheekbones, and piercing gray eyes.

"The great collection of information provided by Soviet intelligence was subordinated to a single cause," Kalugin said, "to weaken, deceive, confuse, injure, damage, and destroy the other side. We managed with the help of Aldrich Ames to expose a whole ring of CIA spies in the U.S.S.R."

"And they shot them all, didn't they?" whispered Jonna, leaning toward me while glaring at the general onstage as he continued his remarks.

"Not all," I whispered back. "Ames caused as many as ten to die, but think of the hundreds that we got out of there over the years before they were discovered."

"In the final analysis, the score would be five to one in favor of the United States on counterintelligence issues," Kalugin said, surprising the audience with his candor.

I thought about the numbers that the former Soviet general had used. He was saying that for every five successful penetrations into our intelligence services, we had infiltrated or turned twenty-five of theirs. Was that possible? Was he to be believed? Or did he want to downplay—considering the outcome of the war in which he had fought—the damage inflicted by his side?

Paul Redmond was well known inside the Agency. Shorter and heavier than Kalugin, he had a dry wit and commanding delivery.

"Tradecraft developed in Eastern Europe was elegant," Redmond said. "It enabled us to do operational acts when we had surveillance twenty-four hours a day, seven days a week, three hundred sixty-five days a year. There's a man in this room who was exfiltrated from an Eastern European country by the CIA in spite of such surveillance. Still, we could pull that off."

I found Jonna's hand and gave it a squeeze.

I knew the man Redmond spoke of; I had been involved in his exfiltration. With luck, I would be able to introduce Jonna to him later today. Our tradecraft—including our disguise techniques and the exhaustive work of the SST—had kept people like him and ORB alive, and in place, for years in spite of the treacherous acts of American traitors.

"We also evolved," Redmond continued. "If we got caught and the tradecraft we were using was exposed, we'd make new trade-craft so we could continue to run people in Moscow successfully."

The silver bullets. The Moscow rules. They *had* made a differ-ence.

"By the time 1985 came along—what became known as 'The Year of the Spy'—we had into double digits good penetrations of the Soviet government, most of them being run out of Moscow."

I looked at Jonna to check her reaction, then back to the stage. Yes, some of them had been given away, betrayed by Edward Lee Howard, Aldrich Ames, and, we learned a few years later, FBI counterintelligence agent Robert Hanssen. *But not all of them.* The CIA had been able to continue to run some incredibly productive assets against overwhelming odds. We knew who had won the Cold War, and how, and why.

Redmond then asked about the KGB's reputed plan to kidnap some of our intelligence officers. "What was that all about?"

Kalugin explained that so many of their officers had gone miss-ing during the final years of the Cold War that the KGB was sure that *we* were kidnapping *them*.

In part, he was correct about so many of his people going "missing." He was no doubt referring to the scores of important defectors that we had exfiltrated and who had disappeared from their homeland without a trace, ORB included.

The conference culminated in a memorial service, "In Mem-ory of Those Who Died That Others Might Be Free," which honored foreign agents who had lost their lives in the Cold War's silent intelligence war. To my knowledge this was the only official ceremony ever devoted solely to honoring the CIA's foreign agents who had fallen.

Jonna and I held hands while the current DCI, George Tenet, delivered the eulogy to those foreign agents who had died in the cause of freedom. The service was organized and conducted by the Texas A & M University Corps of Cadets, Band, and Singing Cadets.

As the ceremony ended, I saw tears running down Jonna's cheeks, and I was doing what I could to keep my own emotions in check. We were both going over the lists in our heads of those agents we knew who had died during our tenure—a group who had been working with U.S. intelligence in an effort to make a better world.

Then, she squeezed my hand hard, and somehow I knew that we were both remembering ORB and Lara—and the others like them whom the CIA had been able to run for the benefit of freedom-loving people everywhere and who, in the end, we had been able to protect. The ones who had *not* been handed over, who had *not* been caught and killed. The ones who, along with their loved ones, were delivered to safety. We can only hope that this type of honor in service can be preserved in future conflicts against tomorrow's villains.

ACKNOWLEDGMENTS

This book would never have been begun but for the gentle prodding of our former editor, Betty Kelly, at HarperCollins. Having elicited the story of how we worked together for many years, finally coming together for one long, final duel with the "evil empire" at the end of the Cold War, she encouraged us to write that story. She has our thanks to this day.

The writing of the book began as a string of solitary undertakings. Jonna would begin one of her sections upstairs in our library, on her computer. Tony was normally ensconced in the third-floor tower of our exhibition pavilion, working on his laptop. Eventually our friend and colleague Bruce Henderson would polish our prose on his own computer. It could have dissolved into confusion and disarray at any moment. But it did not. We do think, however, that three people writing one book is quite enough.

We would like to thank the team that worked with us on this book and actually made it happen. Christy Fletcher, our literary agent at Carlisle & Company, has performed with warmth and enthusiasm on this project, stepping beyond the responsibilities normally expected of an agent to actively participate in every stage of the book's preparation. Our editor at Atria Books,

George Lucas, has likewise been an involved and supportive colleague. George's eye for detail and keen understanding of his craft have helped us greatly. Bruce Henderson undertook what may have looked to be a dangerous mission in serving as the glue that would hold all of the many pieces—and viewpoints—together. He became something of a mind reader, anticipating where we needed to go and making altogether useful suggestions along the way. Judi Farkas, our manager at AMG, provided encouragement and creative thinking as our story developed. We could not have done it without them.

A great many readers, advisors, and friends in the intelligence community have helped us with material, offering us corrections and clarification, to the extent possible. Writing a memoir such as this is not unlike walking through a no-man's-land, never being sure where the mines are, or when the bombs are going to go off. To all who helped—and they know who they are—we reaffirm our appreciation.

We would like especially to acknowledge the members of the CIA's Special Surveillance Team. They actually changed our lives, and we believe they changed the lives of the CIA case officers whom they helped train. A diverse and uniquely skilled pool of people formed themselves into a precise and priceless training tool, doing it as volunteers and dedicated intelligence officers. We learned many life lessons from them and changed some of the ways that the CIA operates. Thanks to all of you.

We would also like to thank the CIA's Publication Review Board for helping us navigate the maze of classified information that we skirted. We appreciate their professional approach to the job and understand their frustrations. It is a tough job.

Tony and Jonna Mendez

action officer The case officer designated to perform an operational act during a clandestine operation, especially in hostile territory.

agent A person, usually a foreign national, who has been recruited by a staff case officer from an intelligence service to perform clandestine missions.

agent-in-place An agent serving as a penetration into an intelligence target who has been recruited or has volunteered to stay in place.

ambush The surprise capture and arrest of a case officer in an act of espionage by an opposing counterintelligence or security service.

(the) Appendix The tower in Lubyanka that houses the KGB's most sensitive departments. It is a nine-story tower that connects the old and new wings of the building and overlooks an inner courtyard.

asset A clandestine source or method, usually an agent.

bailout point The point, during a vehicular run under surveillance, at which the action officer riding as a passenger is planning to bail out of the car in order to elude surveillance.

bang and burn Demolition and sabotage operations.

BIGOT list A list of the names of all persons who are privy to the plans for a sensitive intelligence operation; it dates back to World War II when Allied orders for officers were stamped TO GIB for those being sent to Gibraltar for preparations for the invasion of North Africa; later their orders were stamped BIG OT (TO GIB backwards) when they were sent back to begin planning Operation Overlord, the invasion of Normandy.

black bag job A surreptitious entry operation usually conducted by the FBI against a domestically located foreign intelligence target.

black operations Clandestine or covert operations not attributable to the organization carrying them out.

bona fides An operative's true identity, affiliation, or intentions.

bridge agent An agent who acts as a courier or go-between from a case officer to an agent in a denied area.

brief encounter Any brief physical contact between a case officer and an agent under threat of surveillance.

brush pass A brief encounter where something is passed between a case officer and an agent.

bumper-lock A harassing move in which vehicular surveillance follows the target officer so closely that the surveilling car's front bumper is almost locked to the rear bumper of the target car.

burned When a case officer or agent is **compromised,** or a surveillant has been made by a target, usually because they make eye contact.

bust-out A leak of electronic communications from a secure enclosure before they are encrypted by the code machine.

cam-car A vehicle equipped with a concealed camera used for clandestine casing and surveillance operations.

(the) Camp (also Camp Swampy) A nickname for the CIA's secret domestic training base.

case officer An operations officer serving as an official staffer of an intelligence service.

casuals Casual observers to a surveillance exercise; nonparticipants visible in the area.

(the) cellar The room in the cellar of Lubyanka Prison where Russian intelligence executed traitors prior to WWII.

(the) Center Russian intelligence headquarters in Moscow.

Cheka Russian secret police founded in 1917 to serve the Bolshevik Party; one of the many forerunners of the KGB.

chokadar A gatekeeper commonly used in the Asian Subcontinent for guarding the entrances to walled compounds.

chokepoint A narrow passage—such as a bridge, tunnel, or Metro station—used as a surveillance or countersurveillance tool for channeling the opposing force or monitoring their passage.

CIA The Central Intelligence Agency of the United States, formed in 1947 to conduct foreign intelligence collection, covert action, and counterintelligence operations abroad. Also responsible for providing finished intelligence to U.S. policymakers.

CID The Clandestine Imaging Division of the Office of Technical Service of the CIA. Responsible for providing technical support to clandestine agent operations in the form of photography, secret writing, and video surveillance.

(the) Citadel A supersecret department in U.S. intelligence responsible for collecting foreign signals and communications intelligence.

clandestine operation An intelligence operation designed to remain secret as long as possible.

Clandestine Service The operational arm of the CIA responsible for classic espionage operations, usually with human assets. Also known as the Directorate of Operations (DO) and formerly the Directorate of Plans (DP).

CLOAK A sensitive disguise and deception illusionary technique first deployed by the CIA in Moscow during the mid-1970s.

code A system used to obscure a message by use of a cipher, mark, symbol, sound, innocuous verse, or piece of music. ("Two lanterns in the church tower . . .")

COMINT Communications intelligence, usually gathered by technical interception and code breaking, but also by use of human agents and surreptitious entry.

commo, communications The various forms of secure electronic and nonelectronic communications used in clandestine operations.

commo plan The various secret communications methods employed with a particular agent.

compartmenting: vertical; lateral; double The various ways that information is held to only those who "have-a-need-to-know" in an organization. *Vertical* denies information up or down the chain of command, and *lateral* denies information from peer groups. *Double* is **spoofing** the original group who held the information into believing the operation has ended when it has simply moved to a new compartment.

compromised When an operation, asset, or agent is uncovered and cannot remain secret.

concealment device Any one of a variety of innocuous devices used to secretly store and transport materials relating to an operation.

control In a surveillance exercise, the one directing the team remotely, usually by electronic communications.

controller Often used interchangeably with *handler,* but usually means a hostile force is involved—that is, the agent has come under control of the opposition.

cover stop A stop made while under surveillance that provides an ostensibly innocent reason for a trip.

covert action operation (CA) An operation kept secret for only a finite period of time, or an operation whose real source remains secret because the operation is attributed to another source.

cryptonym   Code name; *crypt* or *crypto* for short, always capitalized. GT and CK prefixes to code names are used to identify the nature of the clandestine source. These two prefixes were both "diagraph" identifiers for the Soviet and East European program during this period. The diagraph is used in front of the cryptonym of the source as a more formal way of referring to the subject, not unlike putting "Mr." in front of "Smallwood."

cutout   A mechanism or person that acts as a compartment between the members of an operation but which allows them to pass material or messages securely.

DAGGER   A sophisticated disguise first used in the Soviet Union in the 1970s.

dangle operation   An operation in which an enticing intelligence target is dangled in front of an opposition service in hopes they will think him or her a bona fide recruit. The dangle is really a double agent.

DCI   The Director of Central Intelligence.

DDO   The Deputy Director of Operations of the CIA, and head of all **HUMINT** operations; formerly the **DDP.**

DDP   The Deputy Director of Plans *(see* **DDO).**

dead drop   A secret location where materials can be left in concealment for another party to retrieve. This eliminates the need for direct contact in hostile situations.

dead telephone   A signal or code passed with the telephone without speaking.

defector   A person who has intelligence value who volunteers to work for another intelligence service. He may be requesting asylum or can remain in place.

DGI   Dirección General de Inteligencia; the Cuban intelligence service.

DIRECTOR   The cable address of CIA Headquarters.

DIRTECH The headquarters cable address of the Office of Technical Service.

DO and DODO The Directorate of Operations of the CIA and the Directorate of Operations Duty Office, where all espionage communications worldwide are managed from CIA Headquarters.

double agent An agent who has come under the control of another intelligence service and is being used against his original handlers.

Dzerzhinsky Square Historic site in Moscow of Lubyanka Prison, longtime headquarters of the Soviet security organs, including **Cheka, NKVD,** and **KGB.** Now the headquarters of the **FSB,** the internal security service that replaced the Second Chief Directorate of the KGB.

EEI Essential elements of information; an outline to be used for collecting intelligence on a particular topic.

EEO complaint A complaint leveled at a supervisor or peer regarding unlawful discrimination under the Equal Opportunity Amendment.

ELINT Electronic intelligence, usually collected by technical interception, such as telemetry from a rocket launch collected by receivers at a distance.

(the) Emerald City The code name the Special Surveillance Team used for the CIA Headquarters Building during their exercises.

escort officer The operations officer assigned to lead a defector along an exfiltration route.

EXCOM The Executive Committee of the CIA, made up of the deputy directors and chaired by the executive director (EXDIR).

exfiltration operation A clandestine rescue operation designed to get a defector, refugee, or operative and his or her family out of harm's way.

(the) eye   The person on the surveillance team who has the target under visual observation at any given moment.

film loop   A loop of film used to project or record a sequence of images on a continuous basis.

FINESSE   Sensitive disguises developed by the CIA using a Hollywood consultant and contractors.

First Chief Directorate (First CD)   The foreign intelligence arm of the **KGB,** now known as the **SVR.**

FLASH   The highest precedence for CIA cable communications.

FLIR   Forward-looking infrared device.

foots (feet)   Members of a surveillance team who are working on foot and riding as passengers in a surveillance car.

(the) Forest   New location of KGB headquarters outside of the Moscow Ring Road.

FSB   Internal security service in Russia, successor to the KGB's **Second Chief Directorate** (internal counterintelligence).

GAD   The Graphics and Authentication Division of the Office of Technical Service, responsible for operational disguise and false documentation capabilities for the CIA.

GAMBIT   A highly sensitive disguise developed for the CIA with the help of their Hollywood consultant. It was first used in Indochina in 1971.

ghost surveillance   Extremely discreet and seemingly omnipresent surveillance, working mostly out of the view of the target.

GRU   The Soviet military intelligence organization.

(the) Hole   The special security enclosure where the KGB's **KAPELLE device** was kept.

hostile service, surveillance, etc.   Terms used to describe the organizations and activities of the "opposition services," aka "the enemy."

HUMINT   Human intelligence, collected by human sources, such as agents.

HVA   East German foreign intelligence service.

illegal   A KGB operative infiltrated into a target country and operating without the protection of diplomatic immunity.

IMINT   Image intelligence, usually collected by high-altitude planes or space vehicles.

IMMEDIATE   The second-highest precedence for CIA cable communications.

impersonal communications   Secret communication techniques used between a case officer and a human intelligence asset when no physical contact is possible or desired.

infiltration operation   The covert moving of an operative into a target area with the idea that his presence or true affiliation will go undetected for the appropriate amount of time.

Internal Operations   CIA operations inside the Soviet Bloc during the Cold War.

in the black   Surveillance-free for a time span greater than a few seconds.

in the gap   Surveillance-free for a few seconds but not as long as a minute.

in the wind   When a target of surveillance has escaped and left for parts unknown.

IOC, Internal Operations Course   A special training course devised for those being assigned to the Soviet Bloc.

KAPELLE device   A supersecret communications security device used by the KGB.

KGB   The all-powerful intelligence and security service of the U.S.S.R. during the Cold War. Ultimate successor to **Cheka.** Disbanded into the **SVR** and the **FSB** in 1991.

> **First CD**   First Chief Directorate of the KGB; foreign intelligence.
>
> **Second CD**   Second Chief Directorate of the KGB; internal security.

Seventh Directorate of the KGB Surveillance.

Sixteenth Directorate of the KGB Science and technology.

legend (cover) The complete cover story developed for an operative.

local agent An agent recruited in a particular target area to do a local task.

lockstep When a surveillance team is following so close on foot they seem to be moving in lockstep with the target.

"L" pill A lethal cyanide capsule issued to intelligence operatives who would prefer to take their own life rather than be caught and tortured.

Lubyanka The prison on Dzerzhinsky Square in Moscow that is the traditional headquarters of the Soviet intelligence services. Now occupied by the **FSB.**

METKA A KGB umbrella program that encompassed research on all their various tagging and marking substances, like **spy dust.**

microdot A photographic reduction of a secret message so small it can be hidden in plain sight under the period at the end of this sentence.

MI5 The British domestic and foreign counterintelligence service responsible for national internal security.

mili-man A militia man; a member of the national police force under the Soviet Ministry of Justice.

MI6 The British foreign intelligence service.

mole A human penetration into an intelligence service or other highly sensitive organization. Quite often a mole is a defector who agrees to work in place.

Moscow rules The ultimate **tradecraft** methods for use in the most hostile of the operational environments. During the Cold War, Moscow was considered the most difficult of operating environments.

Mossad Israel's foreign intelligence service.

NE Division The Near East Division of the CIA's Directorate of Operations.

NIACT The CIA cable slug that indicates that "night action" is necessary.

NKVD The Soviet security and intelligence service from 1934 to 1946.

NOC A CIA case officer operating under nonofficial cover, similar to the KGB **illegal.**

OC, Operations Course The eighteen-week course that all CIA case officers take at the beginning of their careers.

OGPU The Soviet intelligence and security service from 1923 to 1934.

Okhrana The secret police under the Russian czars, 1881–1917.

one-time pad (OTP) Sheets of paper or silk printed with random five-number group ciphers to be used to encode and decode enciphered messages.

OP An observation post manned by a static surveillant.

operative An intelligence officer or agent operating in the field.

opposition The enemy service; any hostile operational force.

Ops Fam Course The Operations Familiarization Course; a six-week course for CIA staffers who work with case officers in the field.

optical system A tracking system that uses optical marks and sensors.

OSS The Office of Strategic Services; forerunner of the CIA, 1942–1945.

OTS The Office of Technical Service, formerly the Technical Services Division, the CIA's technical arm of the **Clandestine Service.** Develops and deploys technical **tradecraft** needed for clandestine and covert operations.

overhead platform A technical platform, aboard an airplane or satellite, used for technical surveillance and reconnaissance.

OWVL One-way voice link; shortwave radio link used to transmit prerecorded enciphered messages to an operative, who is usually working in place in a hostile area.

passive probe Someone sent on an intelligence mission just to passively observe and record details about the target location or organization.

pattern The overt behavior and daily routine of an operative that makes his identity unique.

PDB The president's daily brief, the CIA briefing document delivered to the president of the United States first thing each day. It is always accompanied by a senior CIA officer.

personal meeting A clandestine meeting between two operatives, always the most desirable but a more risky form of communication.

PHOTINT Photographic intelligence; renamed **IMINT,** image intelligence. Usually involves high-altitude reconnaissance using spy satellites or aircraft.

pianist A **KAPELLE** operator. Also used to describe a clandestine radio operator.

PLASMA A secret technique or device used to defeat a lock.

point The member of the surveillance team who is following the target from the closest position, the point position.

prober An operative assigned to test border controls before an exfiltration is mounted. Usually a specialist in false documents.

profile All the aspects of an operative's or a target's overt physical or behavioral persona.

provocateur An operative sent to incite a target group to action for purposes of entrapping or embarrassing them.

provocative A harassing act or procedure designed to flush out surveillance.

put up a signal To clandestinely signal another operative or secret source, as in putting up a signal like a chalk mark on a light pole.

Q Branch   The fictional part of the British intelligence service (MI6) that provides spy gadgetry to James Bond. **OTS** is the real "Q."

rabbit   The target in a surveillance operation

remote viewing   The paranormal ability of a subject to have an out-of-body view of a facility or person from an extremely remote position.

repro   Making a false document.

rezident   A KGB chief of station in a foreign location, usually under diplomatic cover.

rezidentura   A KGB station, usually located in their embassy in a foreign capital.

rolled up   When an operation goes bad and the agent is arrested.

rolling car pickup   A clandestine car pickup executed so smoothly that the car hardly stops at all and seems to have kept moving forward.

RYBAT   A code word meaning that the subject matter is extremely sensitive.

safe house   An apartment, hotel room, or other similar site considered safe for use by operatives as a base of operations or for a personal meeting.

Sanctum   The secure location of a **KAPELLE** device in a Soviet stronghold abroad.

SB   Special Branch; usually the national internal security and domestic counterintelligence service.

SDR   Surveillance detection run; a route designed to erode or flush out surveillance without alerting them to an operative's purpose.

Second Chief Directorate (Second CD)   The counterintelligence arm of the KGB responsible for domestic counterintelligence. Currently known as the **FSB.**

secret writing   Any **tradecraft** technique employing invisible messages hidden in or on innocuous materials. This includes invisible inks and **microdots,** among many other variations.

security service Usually a country's internal counterintelligence service.

SE Division The Soviet and East European Division of the CIA's Directorate of Operations **(DO)** during the latter part of the Cold War.

sensing device A technical sensor designed to react to a concealed mark, chemical compound, or passive element.

Seventh Directorate The internal surveillance arm of the KGB. These are the watchers that include the mobile surveillance teams and the technical eavesdroppers.

SIGINT Signals intelligence; the amalgamation of **COMINT** and **ELINT** into one unit of intelligence gathering dealing with all electronic emanations and transmissions.

signals Any form of clandestine **tradecraft** using a system of marks, signs, or codes for signaling between operatives.

silver bullet The special disguise and deception **tradecraft** techniques developed under **Moscow rules** to help the CIA penetrate the KGB's security perimeter in Moscow.

SIS Senior Intelligence Service of the CIA, which assigns the executive ranks equivalent to a general in the military. So an SIS-1 is equal to a one-star general.

SITREP Situation report, sent to CIA headquarters during an operation or crisis.

Sixteenth Directorate The science and technology directorate of the KGB.

smoking-bolt operation A covert snatch operation in which a special entry team breaks into an enemy installation and steals a high-security device, like a code machine, leaving nothing but the "smoking bolts."

SPO Security Protective Officer at CIA headquarters responsible for providing physical security.

spoofing A ploy designed to deceive the observer into believing that an operation has gone bad when, in fact, it has been put into another compartment.

spy dust A chemical marking compound developed by the KGB to keep tabs on the activities of a target officer. Also called **METKA**. The compound is made of nitrophenyl pentadien (NPPD) and luminol.

SST Special Surveillance Team, formed at **OTS** to simulate hostile surveillance tactics in training simulations.

staff agent A CIA staff officer without access to CIA secure facilities or classified communications.

stage management Managing the operational stage in a deception operation, so that all conditions and contingencies are considered: point of view of the hostile forces and the casual observers, physical and cultural environments, etc.

star-burst maneuver A countersurveillance ploy in which more than one target car or target officer is being followed and they suddenly go in different directions, forcing the surveillance team to make instant choices about whom to follow.

Stasi East German State Security; included internal security, counterintelligence, and foreign intelligence collection.

stronghold A foreign-based Soviet mission.

Sun Tzu The Chinese general who wrote *The Art of War* in about 400 B.C.

Surreptitious Entry Unit Unit in OTS whose specialty was opening locks and gaining access to enemy installations for the purpose of supporting bugging operations.

SVR The Russian foreign intelligence service that succeeded the KGB's **First Chief Directorate**.

swallow A female operative who uses sex as a tool.

TDY Temporary duty assignment.

technical operations officer An OTS officer responsible for working with the case officers in the field and providing all manner of **tradecraft** techniques.

techs   The technical officers from OTS.

timed drop   A **dead drop** that will be retrieved if it is not picked up by the intended recipient after a set time.

tosses (hand, vehicular)   **Tradecraft** techniques for placing drops by tossing them while on the move.

tradecraft   The methods developed by intelligence operatives to conduct their operations.

trunk line   A major electronic communications line, usually made up of a bundle of cables.

TSD   See **OTS.**

tunnel sniffers   Technical air sampler sensors designed to sniff for hostile substances or parties in a dark tunnel system.

201 file   The file at CIA that contains all the personal information on a staff officer or an agent, including any training and operational details unique to the person.

volunteer   See **walk-in.**

walk-in   A defector who declares his intentions by walking into an official installation, or otherwise making contact with an opposition government, and asking for political asylum or volunteering to work in place. Also known as a **volunteer.**

warming room   A location out of the weather where a surveillance team can go to keep warm and wait for the target.

watcher team   A surveillance team usually assigned to a specific target.

window dressing   Ancillary materials that are included in a cover story or deception operation to help convince the opposition or casual observers that what they are observing is genuine.

Wizards   An ad hoc collection of top U.S. scientists, researchers, and other technical experts assembled from time to time by OTS to consult on a one-of-a-kind problem.

(The) Year of the Spy   The year 1985 was labeled "The Year of the Spy" by the media because of the number of espionage-related incidents that came to light that year. Unbeknownst to the media and the CIA at the time, several other significant spying ventures started during this same year and would not come to light until years later.

ZEPHYRs A cadre of CIA case officers who were specially trained to operate in hostile areas like Moscow during the Cold War.

(the) zone The area set aside in Washington, D.C., by the Special Surveillance Team **(SST)** to run simulations against the **ZEPHYRs.**

INDEX